ALSO BY MARY ANNE WEAVER

A Portrait of Egypt: A Journey Through the World of Militant Islam

PAKISTAN

PAKISTAN

*In the Shadow of Jihad
and Afghanistan*

MARY ANNE WEAVER

Farrar, Straus and Giroux

New York

Farrar, Straus and Giroux
19 Union Square West, New York 10003

Copyright © 2002 by Mary Anne Weaver
All rights reserved
Distributed in Canada by Douglas & McIntyre Ltd.
Printed in the United States of America
First edition, 2002

Some of the material in chapters 2, 3, 4, and 5 first appeared, in different form,
in The New Yorker.

Library of Congress Cataloging-in-Publication Data
Weaver, Mary Anne.
Pakistan : in the shadow of jihad and Afghanistan / Mary Anne Weaver.— 1st ed.
p.   cm.
Includes index.
ISBN 0-374-22894-9 (hc. : alk. paper)
1. Pakistan—Politics and government—1971–1988.   2. Pakistan—Politics and
government—1988–   *3. Pakistan—Description and travel.   I. Title.*

DS384 . W43 2002
954.9105—dc21

2002026388

Designed by Abby Kagan
Map designed by Jeffrey L. Ward

www.fsgbooks.com

1   3   5   7   9   10   8   6   4   2

For all friends in Pakistan who,

over the years,

shared their hopes

and their stories with me

CONTENTS

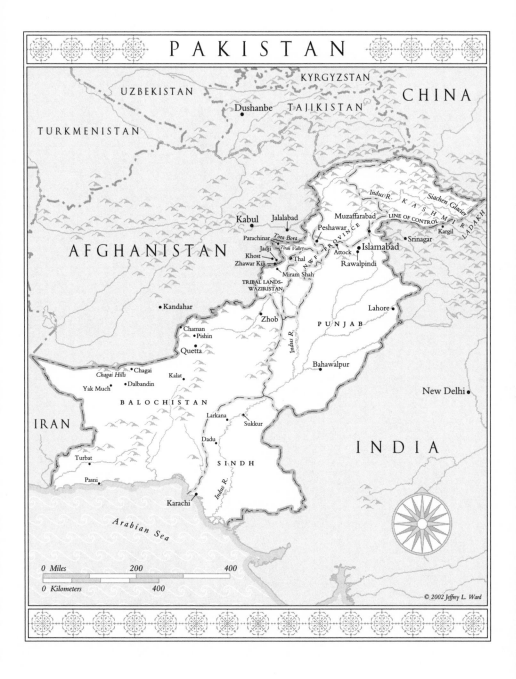

PAKISTAN

PRELUDE

ON SEPTEMBER 11, 2001, I was watching CNN when I learned of the unprecedented terror that visited the United States when nineteen militant Islamists hijacked and crashed four commercial flights into the World Trade Center towers, the Pentagon, and a Pennsylvania field. Like everyone, I was stunned by the news, and my mind traveled back to Pakistan and to the U.S.-financed jihad of the 1980s against the Soviet occupation of Afghanistan. Pakistan had been the key staging area for that war: a war of unintended consequence, as all of us who covered it and followed its aftermath knew. With the Soviet defeat in 1989, the CIA closed down its arms pipeline to the Afghan mujahideen. Left behind were tens of thousands of well-trained and well-armed Arab, Asian, and Afghan fighters available for new jihads.

Mohammed Atta, a thirty-three-year-old Egyptian, was one of those men: polite and well educated, everyone now recalls, an unobtrusive man leading an unobtrusive life. A skilled pilot and engineer, he passed quietly—a man in the shadows—in and out of Pakistan and Afghanistan during the jihad years. On August 28, 2001, he booked a one-way ticket, business class, on an American Airlines flight from Boston to Los Angeles. At 7:45 on the morning of September 11, flight number 11 took off. One hour and three minutes later, Mohammed Atta, who was at the controls, crashed it into the World Trade Center's north tower, leaving behind a letter of instruction and encouragement to his fellow hijackers, which was interpreted by many as a suicide note.

Where did the United States go wrong? How do we deal with an invisible enemy? What do we do now?

Sketching the outline of a new and aggressive American foreign policy, the Bush Administration gave the nations of the world a stark choice: stand with us against terrorism and deny safe havens to terrorists, or face the certain prospect of destruction and death. The corridors of power in Washington resounded with the talk of war. And not unlike the earlier jihad in Afghanistan, no nation was more critical in the U.S. equation than Pakistan.

For Pakistan had long supported—indeed, it was the major lifeline to—the Taliban, Afghanistan's ruling student militia, which had long embraced not only the terrorists who lived in the shadows but also their mentors and financiers, including the United States' prime terrorist suspect, Osama bin Laden. Pakistan's support of U.S. military objectives was crucial to their success. At the time, there were simply no other bases on Afghanistan's borders that the United States could use. And access to Afghanistan—which is mountainous and landlocked—would have been exceedingly difficult, if not impossible, from anywhere else.

But when Washington requested—then demanded—that its former ally permit the United States to use its country as a launching pad for military strikes against bin Laden and a network of terrorist training camps inside Afghanistan, the ruling generals of Pakistan responded, initially, with equivocation at best. Although they pledged their "full support" in the hunt for those responsible for September's outrage, they carefully avoided committing themselves to any active military role, and then, to the fury of the United States, they pledged their continuing support to the Taliban. It was only after intense pressure from Washington—including the implied threat of an embargo on all financial aid and the ostracism of Pakistan as a pariah state—that the generals reluctantly agreed to provide the Pentagon with overflight rights, access to their ports and their bases, and, as important as anything else, access to their intelligence on bin Laden's network and his whereabouts. But the generals insisted that any U.S. military presence on the ground be restricted to the most remote corners of Pakistan: the mountainous corridors of the North-West Frontier Province and the deserts of Balochistan. Once among the loneliest outposts of the British Empire, these tribal lands have beguiled and fascinated, bewitched and repelled potential conquerors for thousands of years.

I had first come to these Pakistani border regions nearly twenty years earlier to cover the jihad, a war that was never fully resolved. There had been no peace conference, no imperial carving of the spoils. And the war had thus continued in increasingly lethal form. It was a war of contradictions and confusions; a war fought in Kipling's world, between independent peoples and independent tribes whose ancient codes of honor and animosities have coalesced to make this one of the most volatile, dangerous, yet fascinating places on earth. And the war's contradictions were, in every sense, mirrored here, in the jihad's staging area: Pakistan.

Looking back on those early years, which for me began in 1982, I find it nearly impossible to recall anything about Pakistan that was predictable. I began to wonder whether anomalies weren't the rule. I visited immaculately groomed cricket fields where smart young men, dressed in immaculate whites, knelt on the ground, facing Mecca, for midday prayers. Then I drove, only a few blocks away, to a dun-colored soccer field, where men in turbans and flowing pantaloons practiced the ancient art of *buzkashi*, which is perhaps best described as American football—on horseback—with few rules. The ball, so to speak, is a headless calf.

This is Peshawar, the dusty border town near the Khyber Pass, which served as the key staging area for the jihad of the 1980s in Afghanistan. Exquisite Islamic architecture exists side by side with teeming Afghan refugee camps and nomadic Pakistani tent societies. In the tony neighborhood of University Town, well-appointed villas—including a number owned by Osama bin Laden—nestle concealed behind towering, whitewashed walls. Every man seems to carry a weapon, and bandoliers festoon their chests, a testament, perhaps, to the world of the undefeated Pathans. The few women in evidence are shrouded in burkas, covered from head to toe. Anonymous forms, they glide in and out of storefront shops. I always found a constant stream of visiting clerics and mullahs, freedom fighters and spies roaming Peshawar's narrow lanes and calling, one by one, at the offices of the seven major Afghan resistance groups, which—though they had been fighting one another for years—were still, in a manner of speaking, coordinating the war effort inside Afghanistan. Then, they fashioned themselves under the banner of the Central Alliance but have since changed their name to the Northern Alliance. Twenty years later, they—like Pakistan itself—were once again fighting America's Afghanistan war.

There had been discernible changes, however, over the years, as the initial ambivalence of Pakistan's generals showed. The generals' constraint in the face of Washington's demands had been based, in large part, on their growing fear of a violent backlash either among the burgeoning number of Islamic hard-liners within their own Army officer corps or from the dozen or so private Islamist armies based in Pakistan—armies that grew out of the first jihad in Afghanistan—and whose numbers have proliferated over recent years. Too close an association with the United States could lead to insurrection by either of these groups, or insurrection by a combination of the two. Yet Pakistan desperately needed Washington's support and, as a result, acted as its emissary in the weeks before the U.S. bombing of Afghanistan began in October of 2001. It dispatched a high-level delegation to the Taliban with a blunt ultimatum from the American government: hand over Osama bin Laden or suffer massive military retaliation by the United States. Pakistan's generals from the start sought to cleave to a tenuous middle ground.

Washington's longtime, most valued ally in South Asia appears to have lost its way. Always a gateway or crossroads, since the days of the ancient Silk Route, Pakistan had served U.S. foreign policy interests well. It was instrumental in our opening to China, and in conduiting CIA-supplied arms to the Afghan mujahideen—Washington's largest covert operation since Vietnam, on the last battlefield of the Cold War. Its early efforts to act as a bridge to the Muslim republics of the former Soviet Union were of immense importance to Washington. Now it feels betrayed.

With the Cold War over, Pakistan's basic instincts are that it is in deadly danger from India, with whom, in May of 2002, it had nearly gone to war—a war that could have led to a nuclear exchange between the two longtime foes, who had already fought three conventional wars (all of which Pakistan lost). There was also concern in Islamabad that the long-held assumptions that had guided its foreign policy no longer held; that its alliance with Washington was not permanent. Therefore, its generals had detonated a nuclear bomb.

And the accumulation of disorder in Pakistan is such that it could well be the next Yugoslavia.

The man who will determine Pakistan's future course is the little-known, enigmatic General Pervez Musharraf, the last in a line of military dictators who have ruled Pakistan for nearly twenty-eight of its fifty-five independent years. It was September 2000 when I first met the general, in his hotel suite in New York, and I wasn't at all certain what to expect. He had been described to me as "a chameleon: a man who can be anything."

Musharraf stood surrounded by aides, a man of medium height and stocky build who carried himself like a battle-hardened commando, which for a number of years he was. He wore an open-necked shirt and khaki trousers—a new look for him, I was told, and a sartorial experiment by his staff. He was too stiff in his military uniform; its starched creases gave him a ramrod look. He was uncomfortable in a business suit. So the question was would the man who has absolute control over some 156 million people and thirty to fifty nuclear bombs be more comfortable in an open-necked dress shirt or a polo shirt?

I puzzled over who the general was.

A "soldiers' soldier" is the way Musharraf is often described, and he told me that he would like to be seen as a genuine patriot in the mold of Ataturk. But is he? Or is he rather more one of the "Children of Zia," who came of age during the jihad when Pakistan's last military ruler, Mohammed Zia ul-Haq, orchestrated the battle against the Soviets and, as a result, transformed Pakistan into the hub of U.S. policy on the Indian subcontinent? He also, as a consequence of both, launched Pakistan on its present militant Islamist course.

What legacy did Zia bequeath to Pakistan?

Afghanistan, increasingly shambolic, was being governed, as it were, by the Pakistani-spawned, black-turbaned, extremist militia, the Taliban, and Pakistanis felt increasingly betrayed by the United States, now that their country was no longer a frontline state. Anti-Americanism was on the rise. And the relative stability that Zia brought to Pakistan in the first years of his rule was being grimly tested. (As early as 1987, of 777 terrorist incidents recorded worldwide, 90 percent took place in Pakistan.) The country continued to suffer bomb explosions or acts of terrorism at an alarming rate. A drugs culture and an arms culture, which were products of the Afghan war, were rife in the North-West Frontier Province bordering Afghanistan. Dacoits, or bandits, armed with CIA-supplied AK-47s, which were meant for the mujahideen but were sold on the black market, roamed with impunity through tribal Balochistan and feudal Sindh. From the bazaars of Peshawar to the Rawalpindi headquarters of Pakistan's military command, the country was reminded daily that it had paid an enormous price for the jihad in Afghanistan.

In the months preceding September 11, 2001, when I traveled through Pakistan, the country's economic decline was unmistakable. There was also a tangible fear, which I had never perceived before, that Pakistan was drifting, perhaps inexorably, toward chaos. One of my most vivid impressions was of decay: of overcrowded cities and crumbling buildings, seen through a patina of dust; of bands of children, with dirty faces and outstretched hands, enveloping me wherever I walked; of the breakdown of law and order, as dark-haired, dark-eyed men moved through villages with AK-47s slung from their shoulders, swaying gently against their hips. Men with full-length Islamic beards now seemed common, and there were far more turbans of militant Islamic green. Madrasahs, or Islamic religious schools, were everywhere now, or so it seemed to me—an estimated forty thousand of them, dotting the country in various shapes and forms—some with vast acreage and dormitories, others tiny makeshift rooms in mosques in poor neighborhoods.

But perhaps what struck me most was that in every city and town there are monuments to Pakistan's nuclear bomb. In Quetta, Peshawar, Karachi, and Lahore towering replicas rise from central squares of the Chagai Hills, the site in the desert of Balochistan where Pakistan's scientists—and its generals—tested their bomb in 1998, two weeks after India exploded its own. And in the capital of Islamabad a futuristic granite structure soars by day and is illuminated by night in fiery hues of orange. As I stood before it one evening and puzzled over what it meant, a Pakistani friend explained that the interior lighting was meant to impart the glow of the nuclear weapon that had exploded in the Chagai Hills.

This book grew out of my own personal journey through Pakistan and my curiosity about the paradoxical forces that shape Pakistani life. I was determined in the mid-1980s, when I was based in India, as I was in later years, to try to see the Pakistanis as they see themselves, to tell their stories in their own voices and through their own eyes, both the rulers and the ruled, whom I met on this journey of mine: the Generals Musharraf and Zia; the first woman prime minister in the Islamic world, the phlegmatic Benazir Bhutto; Islamic militants and intellectuals; mullahs, Marxists, and sheikhs; gun-runners and drug dealers; anarchists, feudal landlords, and tribal chiefs. This book also grew out of a distant Friday evening, twenty years ago, when I first traveled to Peshawar and met the leaders of the jihad. I then had the first of many meetings with General Zia ul-Haq and began another journey, through his world of militant Islam.

I continued watching Pakistan over the years and kept returning, most intensely over the last ten years, in order to understand the dynamics of a movement to which I was introduced during the first American Afghan war but which had, since then, assumed so many different faces and forms. Was it possible, I wondered, that Pakistan—the second largest country in the Islamic world—could lose its struggle against militant Islam? And, in the event that that occurred, what would it mean for U.S. foreign policy?

We all had a tendency—journalists, diplomats, government officials, Pakistanis, Afghans, and Americans alike—to paint the 1980s in Pakistan (and in Afghanistan) upon a monumental tapestry of bold color and design. There were grand battles fought and grand illusions shattered during the jihad. There was monumental confusion, contentiousness, and change, as generals grappled with generals; secularists battled Islamists; terrorists, nihilists, anarchists, rogues, and mystics came and went, accommodated by the season, as whimsical as the sandstorms blown by the desert winds. By the time it was over, Pakistan had been transformed into one of the most frightening places on earth. Yet at the same time it remained, at least for me, one of the world's most fascinating countries: a place where geopolitical choices fused with a vivid land; with its people, mysteries, and clans; with the turmoil of a nation that was the setting not only for *Kim* but, three times in recent history, for the "Great Game" in Afghanistan.

What are the increasingly dangerous scenarios facing Pakistan if General Pervez Musharraf fails in his attempts to reform his ancient land? The country's true military hard-liners will take over; the religious hard-liners will take over, and Pakistan will become a theocracy like Iran; or the country will be faced with complete chaos and fall apart.

Pakistan could well become the world's newest failed state—a failed state with nuclear weapons. And September's day of terror in the United States could be repeated again, not only by the men in the shadows in Afghanistan but by their compatriots across the border in Pakistan.

CHAPTER 1

GENERAL ON A TIGHTROPE

O N OCTOBER 12, 1999, at precisely twelve o'clock, General
Pervez Musharraf, Pakistan's powerful Chief of the Army
Staff, settled into the first seat of the first row of a Pakistan
International Airlines plane for the six-hour flight from the Sri
Lankan capital, Colombo, to Karachi, Pakistan. He was a man of ex-
actitude, having spent his entire adult life in the Armed Forces,
where little was left to chance. He was a brilliant tactician, if not an
overarching strategist. He was in an ebullient mood that afternoon,
he later recalled to me, having just performed better than he had expected in a golf game. He was traveling with only a small entourage
(which he liked): his wife, Sehba; his military secretary, Brigadier
Nadeem Taj; and an aide-de-camp. A thunderstorm had just passed
over, but as the plane, an Airbus 300, began its climb in a light driz-
zle, everything about PK 805 seemed normal, at least at first.

There was a bit more confusion than usual in tourist class, as
some fifty children from Karachi's American School dashed up and
down the aisles. The general smiled, thinking of his newly born first
grandchild. The following morning, he was to meet the Pakistani

Prime Minister Nawaz Sharif. The relationship between the two men had grown tense over recent months, following Sharif's agreement to withdraw Pakistani troops from India's side of the Line of Control in the former princely state of Kashmir—a state that both India and Pakistan claimed in a dispute born with their independence, and that had been divided between them for more than half a century. The retreat had humiliated General Musharraf and the Army command, which had considered their infiltration across the Line of Control to be a major tactical coup. It had also provoked history's first direct combat between two nuclear states and brought them to the brink of all-out war.

In the cockpit, Captain Sarwat Hussein, a senior pilot and twenty-six-year veteran of PIA, checked his instruments, gauges, and fuel. His estimated time of arrival in Karachi was 6:55 p.m. He knew that General Musharraf was on board. The two men had never met; only later would they discover how much they shared. Both were in their mid-fifties, both had spent considerable time abroad, and both had chosen their career paths—from which neither had ever deviated—more than a quarter of a century earlier. General Musharraf had entered the Army in 1964 and had just celebrated his first anniversary as the Chief of the Army Staff. His appointment had surprised many in Washington and many more in Pakistan, for unlike most Pakistani generals, Musharraf has no ethnic or tribal base. He is a *mohajir* (as those who migrated from India are called), an outsider among the Army's traditional general-officer corps: the Pathans and the Punjabis who, since the days of British rule, have comprised the country's martial class.

Now as the general sifted through his files and began taking notes, pondering his meeting with the prime minister, the pilot made his routine walk through the cabin and welcomed General Musharraf aboard. Then he continued on to tourist class, where he was mobbed by the schoolchildren, whom he had flown to Sri Lanka a few days before to participate in a sports competition among South Asia's American Schools. The children from Karachi had done well. "The sky had now cleared and it was a beautiful day, with a magnificent view of the sea, so I invited the kids to the cockpit in groups of three and four," Captain Sarwat told me afterward. "They were coming and going through first class for an hour or so. The general didn't seem to mind. He appeared deep in thought."

The flight passed uneventfully, until two or three minutes before Captain Sarwat was scheduled to begin his descent, then he noticed that the tone of the air-traffic controller at Karachi Airport had become tense. "He began to ask me questions," Captain Sarwat said. " 'What is your fuel position? What endurance do you have? What is your alternate airfield?' " He paused for a moment, and then he said, "You don't ask these questions when a plane is about to land!"

Over the next twenty minutes or so, Sarwat realized that something was very wrong on the ground. He was told, without explanation, that Karachi Airport had been closed. The runways had been blocked and the lights at the international airfield had been switched off. But three other aircraft had already been permitted to land at nearby fields; he knew this from monitoring their radio contact. None of them had a VVIP aboard, and he would ordinarily have received priority clearance to land. Yet he remained in a holding pattern at ten thousand feet.

"How many people do you have on board?" the control tower asked.

"One hundred and ninety-eight," the captain responded, "including the Chief of the Army Staff."

"And your endurance?"

"One hour and twenty minutes of fuel."

"And your alternate airfield?"

"Nawabshah," Captain Sarwat replied, referring to a tiny desert airstrip in the interior of the Pakistani province of Sindh. It had never accommodated an Airbus 300 before. But, according to air-traffic controllers, it had the capability.

Unknown to the captain or the general, a series of conversations were taking place on the ground between the offices of the director-general of the Civil Aviation Authority, PIA, and the prime minister's residence. Transcripts of these conversations later revealed the increasingly urgent directives of Director-General Aminullah Chaudhry shouting to the tower on the line: "Divert that plane! Get it out of Pakistan! Close all the airports! Block the runways! Turn out all the landing lights!"

"PK 805, what is your remaining fuel?" Captain Sarwat was asked again. It was now 6:40 p.m.

"One hour," he replied.

The air-traffic controller went on. "If your alternate is Nawabshah, then Nawabshah airfield is also closed."

Captain Sarwat now grasped what was happening on the ground. The tower wasn't interested in safely bringing the plane down. It also occurred to him that whatever was happening had something to do with the general.

"Okay, sir," he told the tower. "We understand the situation very, very clearly now."

"I was totally unaware of what was happening in the cockpit or on the ground," General Musharraf told me later, as we sat in his drawing room at Army House in the Rawalpindi cantonment, a colonial legacy of the British Raj. "We were very close to Karachi, perhaps thirty minutes or so away, and the plane had begun to descend when Brigadier Nadeem, who had been in the cockpit, came to me and said that the pilot wanted to have a word with me. When I entered the cockpit, he told me that we were not permitted to land anywhere in Pakistan."

The general asked the pilot what their options were.

"An Airbus 300 is not a car that you can park on the roadside," Captain Sarwat said to me later. "This is a three-hundred-mile-an-hour machine hurtling through the air. Time was literally flying. I looked to my right and could see the lights of the Indian city of Ahmadabad. To my left was the Iranian base of Bandar Abbas. I told the general that if we moved immediately, with no delay, we could make it to Ahmadabad."

I asked General Musharraf what his response had been.

"We're not going to India! Over my dead body will we land there!"

The control tower came on the line. "PK 805, can you proceed to Muscat?"

Captain Sarwat answered, with growing irritation, that he could not. His fuel situation by that time would permit him to land only somewhere in Pakistan.

Then, as the general looked on, the pilot pulled up the nose of his plane and began climbing to twenty thousand feet.

"What are you doing?" a voice shrieked on his radio line.

"I'm trying to save fuel!"

"It was as though I was in the cinema," General Musharraf said to me. "The pilot was shouting his head off: 'You stupid idiots! We can't go anywhere! If we don't land immediately, we're going to crash!' " (The pilot and the general had already agreed that if it became necessary, Captain Sarwat would declare an emergency and crash-land the Airbus at the Karachi field.)

As the pilot continued to gain altitude, Musharraf and Brigadier Nadeem asked if they could use their mobile phones. Captain Sarwat nodded his head. "Please, use any means you have. Just find me an airport in Pakistan!"

The general and the brigadier tried over and over again to reach their people on the ground with their mobile phones, but they could not get a connection: not with Army headquarters in Rawalpindi, not with the Karachi corps, not with the elite commando units, in which General Musharraf had served for a long time. Captain Sarwat then turned over his internal PIA channel to the two Army men, in an attempt to arrange a telephone patch. General Musharraf gave the operator the numbers of General Headquarters and of the Karachi corps. He was never connected. The chairman of PIA blocked the channel. The PIA operator hung up on the general.

Captain Sarwat checked his fuel again. It was 7:07 p.m., and he had forty-five minutes left.

At about the same time, Lieutenant General Muzafar Osmani, the corps commander of Karachi, was checking his watch and pacing back and forth in the VIP lounge of Karachi Airport. He had been there for nearly half an hour waiting to receive the Chief of the Army Staff and had made numerous inquiries about his flight. Each time he was told, perfunctorily, that PK 805 had been delayed. His irritation was considerably greater than his concern, and he dispatched one of his Karachi commanders, Major General Iftikhar, to the control tower, which was in a state of turmoil. Orders were being given, then withdrawn, then countermanded by the various voices crackling over wireless and mobile phones. (A year later, it was still unclear whether it was the director-general of Civil Aviation, or the chairman of PIA, or one of Prime Minister Nawaz Sharif's military aides who realized the folly of their plan. The reality was that PK 805 could soon crash.)

"Go to Nawabshah! Go to Nawabshah!" an air-traffic controller finally shouted across the line. "Can you make it?"

"Just," Captain Sarwat replied.

"Take on maximum fuel there. No one is to leave the plane," the air-traffic controller continued, as Captain Sarwat began his climb.

"We were about halfway to Nawabshah when General Iftikhar came on the line," General Musharraf said. "At that point, I still had no idea what was happening on the ground. I hadn't been able to make contact with anyone. But, obviously by now, I certainly could guess that whatever was happening had to do with me. Iftikhar told the pilot: 'Tell the chief to come back to Karachi immediately. Everything is under control.' Control? I mused over Iftikhar's message a bit, and I didn't accept it immediately. So, I went on the line."

The line was crackling. General Iftikhar's voice was unclear. And General Musharraf did not immediately recognize it.

Only Brigadier Nadeem knew the name of Iftikhar's pet dog. Iftikhar was asked the question. He passed the test.

"It was only then that Iftikhar told me that a few hours earlier I had been relieved of my command," General Musharraf said. The nation had been startled, but the generals had been prepared.

The Army moved swiftly to support its chief—the second Chief of the Army Staff to be fired in only a year by an increasingly un-popular civilian prime minister, who had amassed near dictatorial powers in his hands. As General Musharraf and Captain Sarwat cir-cled Karachi at twenty thousand feet, armored personnel carriers and truckloads of commandos had careered through the streets be-low, taking control of key installations in and around the capital of Islamabad, including the prime minister's official residence. Now Karachi Airport was also under its command. It was Pakistan's fourth military coup in its fifty-two-year history.

"Can we make it back to Karachi?" the general asked his pilot now.

"We can go either way, but you've got to make an immediate decision."

General Musharraf answered, "Turn around."

"PK 805. This is the control tower in Karachi. Surface wind is variable and light. You are cleared to land on runway twenty-five."

Captain Sarwat began his final approach, but he still wasn't sure. "I didn't know General Iftikhar. I didn't know the situation on the ground—which side the Karachi corps commander was on. I looked down at the runway, and I thought: Musharraf is a dead man if I'm wrong."

As PK 805 came in to land, all of the Airbus 300's warning lights flashed on. Captain Sarwat maneuvered what he called his three-hundred-mile-an-hour machine to the VIP area of the airport and switched its engines off. He was still uncertain. General Musharraf returned to the cockpit and gave him a broad smile.

"I hope I've not put you in a difficult situation . . ." Captain Sar-wat began.

"Don't worry, Captain. They're my men."

The doors were opened, and General Musharraf left the aircraft, one hour and forty minutes after his pilot's ordeal began. He was fol-lowed by the children from the American School and the other one hundred and forty-five passengers aboard. None of them had any idea what had occurred.

Captain Sarwat put on his jacket and collected his briefcase. Before getting off the plane, he glanced at the gauges on his flight deck. He had about ten minutes of fuel left.

When I arrived in Pakistan late the following year, Nawaz Sharif had been convicted of hijacking by a special antiterrorist court and sentenced to life imprisonment. He was now residing in a sixteenth-century Moghul prison fort. General Musharraf had just completed his first year at the helm of his country's newest military dynasty, but he had failed to resolve in any significant way the four most troublesome difficulties Pakistan faced: a deteriorating economy, tension with India, violence among warring Muslim sects, and the increasing power of Pakistan's Islamists. As for the man who, in a sense, changed the history of Pakistan, Captain Sarwat Hussein, his life was the only one that was little changed. He continued to fly his Airbus across South Asia and into the Middle East. But each time he approached Karachi, he could not help but remember that October night.

It had been a year since I was last in Pakistan, and the country's economic decline was unmistakable. Pakistan was also clearly drifting toward chaos. I was struck, more than ever before, by the impression of a country that was angry and out of control. People seemed to be living on the edge, as much of the nation's infrastructure, like its ancient monuments, was being reduced to dust—as deteriorating as the city built by Alexander the Great in memorial to his favorite horse, Bucephalus, who died in battle here, on the plains of the Punjab in 326 B.C. Corruption flourished and political stagnation ossified. Pakistan now suffered a bomb explosion or act of terrorism nearly every other day. The drugs and the arms dealers continued to be rife in the North-West Frontier Province bordering Afghanistan, products of the ongoing warfare there, now between that country's Pakistani-spawned, black-turbaned student rulers, the Taliban, and their surviving mujahideen opponents.

When Musharraf and his generals seized control, tensions between Pakistan and India, particularly over the disputed Himalayan
territory of Kashmir, were also at a high point. The dispute over
who will control the Muslim-majority state—nearly two thirds of
which has been ruled by India since Partition's aftermath, and the
rest, excluding a small bit in China, by Pakistan—had already provoked two wars (in 1947–48, and then in 1965). And these were before Pakistan and India became the world's two newest nuclear
powers. Their fractured and bloody history, encapsulated by Kashmir's low-level proxy war—which has raged for more than a dozen
years and has claimed some forty thousand lives—is a large part of
why their border is often seen as the world's most dangerous place.

The generals' problems—and their sense of isolation—had been
compounded by a new rapprochement between India and the
United States, which Zia ul-Haq and *his* generals had presumed
would be Pakistan's long-term, non-censorious ally. With the Cold
War over, however, Washington had felt free to join New Delhi in
insisting that Pakistan end its dangerous obsession with Kashmir.
The United States was also frustrated by Pakistan's refusal to assist in
the extradition for trial to the United States of the Saudi multimillionaire Osama bin Laden—who had been indicted for allegedly
masterminding the 1998 bombings of two U.S. embassies in Africa.
Based in Afghanistan since 1996, bin Laden was America's most
wanted terrorist. And if the United States ever hoped to bring him
to trial, it would need the support of Pakistan to lure him out
of his mountain lair and apprehend him. The United States, like
all other nations in the world except for three, did not recognize
the Taliban, and, except for Saudi Arabia, Pakistan, whose powerful military intelligence organization—Inter-Services Intelligence,
or ISI—had assisted the Taliban in its rise, was the only benefactor
of it.

As I traveled around Musharraf's Pakistan in November of 2000,
it seemed to me that the general's choices over the coming critical
year—on, among other things, his country's growing fragility, its

support of bin Laden, and its escalating insurgency in Indian-controlled Kashmir—and the way in which Washington would respond, could well determine Pakistan's future course.

"My worry is that Musharraf may be the last hope for Pakistan," Marine Corps General Anthony C. Zinni, the Bush Administration's peace envoy to the Middle East and the retired head of the U.S. Central Command—who is also one of Musharraf's closest American friends—told me in the spring of 2001. "The pressures he faces are extreme: the economic conditions in Pakistan, the tensions with India, the country's relationship with the United States. If he fails in carrying out his reforms and putting Pakistan back on track, I can foresee three worst-case scenarios: the true military hard-liners will take over; the religious hard-liners will take over, and we'll see a theocracy like Iran; or Pakistan will be faced with complete chaos and fall apart. Then we'll have another failed state in the region, like Afghanistan. And any of these scenarios will be extremely dangerous for the United States."

General Pervez Musharraf had been little known outside military circles before the autumn of 1998, when Nawaz Sharif promoted him over two other generals to become Chief of the Army Staff. Sharif had considered Musharraf a pliable, self-effacing choice, but only a year had passed when Musharraf overthrew him.

It had been a long journey for the general from his native India, where he was born in New Delhi, in August of 1943, into a family of civil servants and socialists. His father was a diplomat in the colonial foreign office, when India lay undivided, still ruled by the British Raj. Its violent Partition in 1947—in which at least a million people died as Hindus moved east out of the new Pakistan, and Muslims moved west into it—was an event that affected Musharraf's thinking for the rest of his life.

"He was only four," his mother, Zarin, told me, "but it was a nightmare for all of us. It was early August, and the communal riots had already begun. We fled for our lives. We took the last train out of Delhi for Karachi. Millions of people were coming and going at the time, by road, by train, by foot. The train passed through entire neighborhoods that had been set to the torch. Bodies were lying along the rail tracks. There was so much blood. Blood and chaos were everywhere. The train journey took us three days, and we used to halt at night. We were terrified of the Hindus and the Sikhs, who were massacring people in the trains moving west. We had no water, no food. It was summer and it was terribly hot. I had three small children. We could take nothing with us. We had to leave every-thing behind—our house, my father's house, my mother's house. We had to start over from scratch. My mother refused to flee with us. She was determined that she was not going to leave her home. She was old and quite ill. But she was a proud woman and, for those times, had considerable property. Pervez adored her. When she was finally forced to flee, and we found her in a refugee camp, her clothes were threadbare and filthy. She wasn't even wearing shoes."

When I asked Musharraf what he remembered most about that train journey fifty-three years ago, he didn't answer immediately, and then he said, "A lot of tension. A lot of worry. A lot of fear. I also remember my father. He was carrying a small metal box, about this size." He measured it out with his hands. "It was full of money— six hundred to seven hundred thousand rupees, which was an im-mense amount of money at that time. It was Pakistan's share of the foreign ministry's funds. He was guarding this little box with his life. He used to sleep with his head on it. And when he was awake, he'd sit on it."

When I first met Musharraf in the early days of September 2000 in New York, I had not known what to expect. He had requested the appointment—curious, I thought, that the newest military ruler of Pakistan whose most visible threat was the growing Islamic mili-tancy in his country and, more important, within his Army officer corps, had specifically asked to see only two journalists during his trip. Both of us were women and American. We met in his suite at the modest Roosevelt Hotel, which is owned by PIA. His staying there was part of a conscious attempt, I was told, to set a personal example of austerity at home, a country where elected leaders traditionally have lived apart in sprawling mansions and maintained foreign bank accounts; they had also been convicted by Pakistani courts of having skimmed off billions of dollars from the exchequers of various governments. General Musharraf was in the city to attend the United Nations Millennium Summit, and, as part of it, to improve the image of his military regime. His key priority was to garner international support for Pakistan's position on Kashmir, but things had not gone well. At every turn, the general found himself upstaged by Prime Minister Atal Behari Vajpayee of India.

General Musharraf is a difficult man to describe, for each time I saw him he looked astonishingly different, depending upon whom he was seeing, where he was, and the mood in which he had dressed that day. "He's a cipher," one of his former commanding officers told me. "He can be anything." His demeanor is modest, his manner pensive, his voice calm. His grin is triumphant, especially when he believes he has outwitted India. "He's a modern, Westernized man, yet on some subjects he becomes a Doctor Jekyll and Mr. Hyde," a Western diplomat says. "Like others of his generation, who have been branded by the humiliation of Pakistan's defeat in the 1971 war, when India and Kashmir come up, he's transformed into a hard-line, table thumper. He's a terrible dichotomy."

Nearly everyone to whom I spoke about Musharraf proffered two adjectives without considerable thought: the general was described as "voluble and impetuous," an impetuous soldier who took risks too bold, too ill-considered. Yet the government over which he presides—a government that was welcomed by most in Pakistan—was now more often than not described as laconic, indecisive, and weak: a government that was not taking any risks, a government that was not upsetting the cart.

In a sense, Pervez Musharraf is as anomalous as his country.

His father was a leftist; he is not. The elder Musharraf was also nearly a *hafiz*—one who has memorized the Koran by heart. His son describes himself as a moderate Muslim and, before dinner, he occasionally enjoys a Scotch. He is a product of Christian missionary schools, an avowed secularist. Yet each time he was challenged by Pakistan's militant mullahs, he backed down. Even after his coup against Nawaz Sharif, he claimed to have no political aspirations and pledged to step down once he'd completed his program of political and economic reform. Yet as I watched him one evening in Islamabad, as he inaugurated a secondary school and the children chanted on cue—"Long live Musharraf!" "Long live Pakistan!"—the general responded with clenched fists, rhythmically swaying his arms. He reminded me a bit of Argentina's military strongman Juan Perón in the early scenes in *Evita*.

Musharraf often speaks the language of a populist: of devolving power, of taxing the rich and arresting the corrupt. And during his first year in office, he had done just that. Bands of tax collectors had swept into the offices of businessmen and collected nearly a billion dollars thus far. Sleuths from the improbably named National Accountability Bureau, or NAB, had lived up to their acronym as they pursued, perhaps on occasion too zealously, allegedly corrupt officials, mostly politicians—for they had assiduously shied away from investigating either the Army or the judiciary—and loan defaulters, who owed the country's banks nearly $4 billion. And, on New Year's Eve of 2000, Pakistan took its first tentative step toward a return to democracy, in the first phase (the last was held in July 2001) of scattered local elections in rural constituencies; the polls were held on a nonparty basis and candidates were carefully vetted, but it was a start.

So one morning as we sat in Army House, I asked the general what the key priority was for him.

He responded without hesitation. "The economy. Only with a viable economy will the security of Pakistan be guaranteed. Economic revival is the key to everything. Out of a nation of 150 million people, only 1 percent—*1 percent*—pays income tax! Our debt burden is $38 *billion*, and we have got to prioritize reducing it. My program, simply put, is to concentrate on reducing our fiscal deficit, improving our trade balance, and broadening our tax base. We also have to privatize our assets, which are being mismanaged, and revive our moribund industries." The general's plan had been convincing enough that, in November, the International Monetary Fund approved a nearly $600 million loan that helped Pakistan avoid defaulting to its foreign creditors. But attracting foreign investment remains a key priority, and that will be in danger if the regime adopts a controversial law, which was meant to go into effect on June 30, 2002, that bans the use of interest in all financial transactions in accordance with the mullahs' interpretation of Islamic law. Six days before the deadline, on June 24, the government was given a reprieve, when the Supreme Court—after a number of foreign banks threatened to leave Pakistan—reversed itself, and referred the law back to the Federal Shariah Court for new deliberations.

A bearer entered the drawing room with coffee and cakes, and as we ate and drank, I asked General Musharraf when his government would be ready to face the voters. The Supreme Court had ruled that parliamentary elections must be held by October 2002, but the generals had yet to set a date. He deflected the question. It was one of the things about him that had always been most vexing to governments in the West.

For the moment, Musharraf relied on the continuing support of the generals.

Thirty-six years had passed since he began his rise in the Pakistani Army, often against the odds. It was the general's mother, Zarin, who made the choice for him. "From the very beginning, when we were children, she said I would go to the Army, my elder brother would become a civil servant, and my younger brother, a doctor," Musharraf told me one afternoon. "And that's exactly what we are." Of Zarin Musharraf's three sons, who journeyed by train across a burning India then spent their early years in Turkey, where their father was posted as a diplomat, only Pervez has remained in Pakistan.

He graduated from the Military Academy in 1964 and, the following year, at the age of twenty-two, he was awarded his first medal for gallantry after he refused to leave his post, even though it had been ignited by shellfire, during the second Indo-Pakistani war. Musharraf advanced steadily through the Army's ranks: commanding artillery brigades; distinguishing himself at Britain's Royal College of Defence Studies, which he attended twice; then entering the Army's policy-making elite—to which he was first exposed during the early 1980s as a staff officer in the martial law regime of General Zia ul-Haq. But Musharraf played no role in the jihad in Afghanistan, over which General Zia would preside, and he spent most of the war years at the Command and Staff College and the National Defence College, where he both studied and taught, and, according to one of his former commanding officers, with a Pakistani military contingent in Saudi Arabia.

By the mid-1990s, the Soviets had been gone from Afghanistan for over five years, and the government that eventually came to power there—which consisted of Burhanuddin Rabbani, Gulbadin Hekmatyar, and the other leaders of the jihad—was ruling Afghanistan so disastrously that it, in turn, had triggered the revulsion that gave rise to the Taliban, an odd assortment of moralistic students who came of age in Pakistan, in the madrasahs and the refugee camps of the North-West Frontier Province and Balochistan. They were all ethnic Pashtuns drawn largely from Afghanistan's south, and they were inspired by a vision not only of extremist Islam but also of Pashtun supremacy. They had first come to prominence in the spring of 1994—during Prime Minister Benazir Bhutto's second term—in the southern Afghan city of Kandahar when they rescued a number of teenage boys and girls who had been abducted and raped by government commanders, who most often fought among themselves and generally extorted everyone else. Then, in quick succession, the fundamentalist student militia began to disarm the competing and most often corrupt tribal leaders and warlords, opened roads and bridges, and attempted (but failed) to force open a crucial trade route—crucial especially to Pakistan if it was to be a bridge to the Muslim republics of the former Soviet Union. And all of this happened despite the fact that the Taliban appeared to spring from nowhere.

Bhutto's delight was overshadowed only by that of General Nasirullah Babar, her powerful Minister of the Interior. They, like the ISI and the Army itself, had grown weary of Pakistan's shoring up the protagonists in Afghanistan's fratricidal civil war. A grateful Bhutto abandoned the mujahideen and rewarded the Taliban with her support. She was assisted in her efforts by her little-known Director-General of Military Operations—Pervez Musharraf.

He, and General Babar, and the ISI—as Zia ul-Haq and his generals had done over a decade before—crafted yet another Afghan policy that would insure a Pakistani presence in a compliant Afghan state. Their rationale was known in military parlance as "strategic depth": to secure a friendly northern and western border as a bulwark against India.

At the beginning, their reasons were economic as well: the trade route that would connect Pakistan to the new Muslim republics of Central Asia, and which, in turn, would open the way for a much coveted natural gas pipeline, a pipeline that would connect Pakistan and Turkmenistan. The Pakistani Army—working through the ISI and supported by rich Pashtun merchants on both sides of the frontier—believed that the arms and training it freely gave to the Taliban was an investment for the future. And although the Bhutto government—as the governments of Nawaz Sharif and Pervez Musharraf would later do—routinely denied that it was shoring up the Taliban, the fact remained that the planes, tanks, and armaments that the black-turbaned Talibs frequently showed off were clearly not all captured in battles with their remaining mujahideen opponents.

Few governments were as shrouded in secrecy as the Taliban was from the day that the mysterious bearded clerics emerged from obscurity. Most of them were orphans of the jihad, with scant knowledge of Afghanistan. They were, in a sense, far more part of Pakistan. For they were raised, or even born, radicalized, and schooled, here in the madrasahs and the refugee camps, largely under the tutelage of barely literate mullahs, whose loyalties lie with the mercurial leaders of Pakistan's major fundamentalist parties, the

Jamaat-e-Islami and the Jamiat-i-Ulema-i-Islam, along with their Wahhabi backers in Saudi Arabia.

Yet it was not only Pakistan that embraced the Taliban with its covert military and financial support but, in the militia's early days, the Clinton Administration considered the twenty-thousand-strong seminarist soldiers to be a potential asset as well. Despite its public— and often vehement—denials, officials in Washington told me that the U.S. administration viewed the Taliban as a useful force in preventing the spread of Islamic revolution from neighboring Iran, as a potential ally in the international war against drugs, and, most important, as a possible lifeline to the vast oil and gas riches of the landlocked republics of Central Asia—areas that held the last untapped reserves of energy in the world. As a result, by the spring of 1996 the U.S. administration was working quietly, but forcefully, behind the scenes in support of the American company Unocal, the lead company in a consortium to build an estimated $2.5 billion natural gas pipeline from Turkmenistan to Pakistan, across Taliban-controlled Afghanistan. (After three years of protracted frustration working with the Taliban, Unocal, in December of 1998, pulled out of the deal.)

Looking back now on those early years of Taliban rule, a strange confluence of bedfellows had been born: Benazir Bhutto, the secular—but ambitious and flawed—first woman prime minister of the Islamic world; Pervez Musharraf, the secular general—who was her Director-General of Military Operations from 1993 to 1995—whom few people knew, and even fewer understood; and Osama bin Laden, who fortuitously, perhaps, had reemerged on the scene in Afghanistan. For he returned at precisely the time, in May of 1996, when the warlord government that grew out of the jihad was being besieged by the Taliban. The student militia's leader was Mullah Mohammed Omar, who like bin Laden had fought in the jihad. The two men had a similar ideology and complementary needs: bin Laden needed refuge and the fledgling Taliban needed cash. Bin Laden gave the mullah an initial payment of $3 million for the cause, and the Taliban was able to capture the key center of Jalalabad in September of 1996. Ten days later, the capital, Kabul, fell. And sometime after that, according to U.S. officials, bin Laden, through the marriage of one of his daughters, became Mullah Omar's father-in-law. They remain very close. And as bin Laden moved between a farm outside the eastern city of Jalalabad, and from camp to camp near the Pakistani-Afghan frontier, Mullah Omar's protection enabled him to continue to wage the struggle that was most important to him: for the past decade, Osama bin Laden's primary battle had been with the House of Saud—which, paradoxically, was the key financial backer of the Taliban. In bin Laden's eyes, the United States was, for the moment, of secondary concern.

Pakistan's entanglement with the Taliban—which had consumed Pervez Musharraf for six years—was an undertaking that some in power, including the general, regretted now.

Yet it was Musharraf's two tours as a commando, in the late 1960s and early 1970s, that most shaped him. He was young and impressionable, his Army friends say, in 1966, when he joined the elite Special Services Group, or SSG. The commando unit had only recently been raised, in a joint undertaking of the Pakistani Army and the Special Forces of the United States. At this point, still early in his career, Musharraf began forming a bond with the United States. As a major and company commander, Musharraf proved himself—he was tough, eager, and fearless—and, over the years, he was dispatched to some of his country's most crucial battlefields: to the Siachen Glacier, where he had his first direct encounter with Indian-controlled Kashmir; to East Pakistan, which during the 1971 Indo-Pakistani war became Bangladesh. Known as a brilliant field tactician—although he is not, according to one of his Army friends, a great strategic thinker— Pervez Musharraf has spent his entire adult life battling India.

One senses in talking to Musharraf that the role of chief executive— a misleadingly modest title created specifically for him—was not an easy one for him to adopt, and that he is often uncertain how to project himself: Should he be the secularist, the bridge-playing sketch artist with two pet dogs? (Dogs are considered impure in Islam, and Musharraf's appearance for photographers with his Pekinese provoked a collective howl from the mullahs.) One of the last British-style, aristocratic generals trained in the West? An ideological protégé of the founder of modern, secular Turkey, Kemal Ataturk? Or should he be the impetuous commando and architect of a 1999 campaign to infiltrate Indian-controlled Kashmir, a covert operation in and around the mountain peaks of Kargil, which nearly led to a fourth Indo-Pakistani war?

Whether that operation was a tactical masterstroke is still being debated among Pakistani generals. No one, however, disputed its outcome: the Pakistani Army, as the world watched, was forced into an ignominious withdrawal. Musharraf and two of his closest Army friends—Lieutenant Generals Mohammed Aziz Khan, his chief of the General Staff; and Mahmud Ahmed, the corps commander of Rawalpindi—had gambled heavily when, over a period of three months during the spring, just as the snows began to melt, they succeeded in infiltrating what eventually became some 1,500 men, along with snowmobiles, mountaineering equipment, and supplies, across the precipitous peaks. They had two military objectives and one diplomatic one: to cut India's key communications network and its road and supply links to the Siachen Glacier and to Ladakh; to present India with a fait accompli on the ground; and, as a result, to force it to negotiate and resolve the Kashmir problem, once and for all. What Musharraf, Aziz, and Mahmud did not anticipate was the ferocity of India's response. In six weeks of warfare, according to U.S. intelligence estimates, nearly seven hundred Pakistanis died.

Musharraf's friend, General Zinni, who was then the head of the U.S. Central Command, was hastily dispatched to Islamabad by the Clinton Administration in an effort to arrange a cease-fire. I asked him how close Pakistan and India had come to all-out war.

"Very," he responded. "Both sides were on automatic pilot; both sides were escalating without much control. The danger of the situation was not fully appreciated, even in Washington. But it certainly was on the ground. I think one of the reasons that Musharraf and Nawaz Sharif were glad to see me come was that they had really scared themselves to death."*

On the weekend of July 4, Nawaz Sharif flew to Washington for hastily arranged talks with the American President, who acted as broker with the Indian government and arranged a withdrawal of General Musharraf's troops. The general, however—to the fury of his Army commanders—was not consulted on the terms.

"We hadn't even decided on a cease-fire at that point!" General Musharraf said to me. "We had debated this at a meeting of the Defense Committee of the Cabinet, which lasted all day Friday, and no agreement was reached. We decided to meet again on Monday morning. On Saturday, I went off to [the hill station of] Murrai for the weekend. At about eleven o'clock that night, I was contacted by the prime minister, who told me to come to the airport immediately to see him off. He had decided to go to Washington. He took this sudden decision without consulting anyone! And, I might add, the decisions taken in Washington were totally his."

The ensuing battle of wills between the Chief of the Army Staff and his prime minister grew bitter and intense. The die had been cast for Musharraf's dismissal, and for an Army coup. The only remaining question was, which would come first.

The shadow of Kargil continues to loom over relations between India and Pakistan. After their near war, New Delhi expects Islamabad to make the first move toward improving relations between the two. Hard-liners within Pakistan's Army and the religious right appear to have blocked General Musharraf from doing so. For although Kash-

---

*According to a report by President Clinton's chief adviser on South Asia, Bruce Riedel, published by the University of Pennsylvania in May 2002, Musharraf and his Army high command may have prepared their nuclear weapons for deployment then.

mir is a battle that neither India nor Pakistan can win militarily, it is a battle that neither can lose politically.

As a result, what began as an indigenous, secular movement for Kashmiri independence more than a decade ago has increasingly become an Islamist crusade to bring all of Kashmir under Pakistani control. According to a State Department official, 40 percent of the militants fighting Indian troops in Kashmir are not Kashmiris: they are Pakistanis and Afghans. Virtually all of them belong to the dozen or so private Islamist armies, based in Pakistan, which are offshoots of earlier groups launched during the 1980s by American and Pakistani intelligence during the jihad. At least 128 military training camps now dot the valleys and mountains of Pakistan. More than a thousand eager young men pass through them each year, joining the ranks of some sixty to a hundred thousand Islamic militants who have fought or trained in Afghanistan and then, well armed, returned home to Pakistan. They were once proxies of various Pakistan governments that, since the days of Zia ul-Haq, have used and nurtured Islamic militancy for reasons of state. Thus far, Musharraf's military regime had been unable, or unwilling, to rein them in.

The Clinton (and later the second Bush) Administration had demanded that Musharraf do this. But Musharraf is beholden to his fellow generals, who carried out the October coup in his name. And the men on the ground—including two of the three architects of Kargil, the powerful Generals Aziz and Mahmud—who secured the capital and Karachi Airport as Captain Sarwat circled overhead are generally more religious, and even more hawkish toward India, than he is. Some are Islamic hard-liners, and the line dividing them from the radical Islamists—whose ranks include a significant number of retired Army officers—who trek across the mountains into Indian-controlled Kashmir, is a line that is becoming increasingly blurred.

For years, Musharraf was known in the Army as "the Cowboy" because of his Westernized ways. The irony is that the Cowboy was brought to power by an Army that has become increasingly anti-American and fundamentalist.

Both supporters and detractors of General Musharraf say that much of the responsibility for this lies with the United States. In October 1990, only nineteen months after the U.S.-sponsored jihad in Afghanistan came to an end, the first Bush Administration cut off all military and most economic aid to Pakistan because of its program to develop a nuclear weapon—something that had been largely overlooked since 1974, when the program began, after India had conducted a "peaceful" underground nuclear test. Eight years later, in May 1998, when India and Pakistan, in quick succession, tested nuclear weapons, U.S. sanctions were imposed on both. But in October of the following year, the economic sanctions on India were waived. Those on Pakistan remained in place.

The aid cutoff fueled the Islamist flame in the Pakistani Army, which General Zia had sparked, and the Army became increasingly vulnerable to it, as the tradition of better-educated men joining the forces began to fade. When General Zinni asked Musharraf, shortly after he became Chief of the Army Staff, what his greatest concern was, Musharraf had responded, "Seventy-five percent of my officers have never been out of Pakistan."

What Musharraf didn't mention at the time was a military operation that had occurred only a month and a half before his elevation to the Army's top post: an operation that had been debated heatedly among the nine corps commanders—including himself—with whom much of the power in the Pakistani military rests. And it was not a Pakistani operation, but an American one.

Things had begun innocently enough, on August 20, 1998, when Musharraf's predecessor as Chief of the Army Staff, General Jehangir Karamat, was playing host in Islamabad to his American counterpart, General Joseph Ralston, the vice chairman of the Joint Chiefs of Staff. Around ten o'clock in the evening, as the two men were having dinner, Ralston looked up from his chicken tikka, checked his watch, and informed his host that in ten minutes some sixty Tomahawk cruise missiles would be entering Pakistan's airspace. Their destination, he said, was Afghanistan, where Osama bin Laden was believed to be operating four training camps. General Karamat was stunned and appalled.

"It was a 'This is happening as we speak' kind of conversation," an American intelligence official said to me. "Ralston was there, on the ground, to make absolutely certain that when the missiles flew across Pakistan's radar screen they would not be misconstrued as coming from India and, as a consequence, be shot down." The intelligence official paused for a moment and then said, "This is one hell of a way to treat our friends."

By the following day, General Karamat's anger—and that of his corps commanders and the Nawaz Sharif government—had turned to rage. A number of the Tomahawks either had been poorly targeted or had not fallen where they were aimed. Two of the four training camps that were hit and destroyed, in the Zhawar Kili area of Afghanistan's Paktia Province, were facilities of the ISI. Five ISI officers and some twenty trainees were killed. The government of Pakistan was not only furious but embarrassed because it had not been taken into Washington's confidence. Why had there been only ten minutes' notice? And why had General Karamat been notified, instead of the prime minister?

The United States had reason to be embarrassed as well. For, despite President Clinton's claim in a televised address a few hours after the missile strikes that a "gathering of key terrorist leaders" had been expected to take place at one of the target sites, bin Laden and his top lieutenants were more than a hundred miles away when the missiles struck. The meeting that Clinton referred to had occurred a month earlier, in Jalalabad.

The United States had expended $79 million on satellite-guided cruise missiles to destroy just thousands of dollars' worth of obstacle courses, field barracks, and tents. Only one of the six facilities struck was a bin Laden training camp. "It was all rather biblical," a former intelligence official told me at the time. "The President was very specific: he wanted two targets, for the two American embassies in Africa that were bombed." (The second target was the al-Shifa pharmaceutical plant, in the Sudan, which the administration claimed was used by bin Laden in either the manufacture or the distribution of chemical weapons. The administration retreated from that theory in May of 1999, when, in refusing to answer a lawsuit, it released the frozen assets of the owner of the plant.) Of the missile attacks, the former intelligence official asked, "Was it an intelligence failure or a policy failure? Or both?"

Talks between the United States and Pakistan on bin Laden had been intense and often acrimonious, both before and after the missile attacks. Shortly before Musharraf overthrew Nawaz Sharif, one of the prime minister's key officials had said to me, "I think what the Americans are really trying to say to us is 'Why don't you do our dirty work—get bin Laden and deliver him or, preferably, eliminate him?' " He thought for a moment and then he said, "Quite honestly, what would Pakistan gain by going into Afghanistan and snatching bin Laden for you? We are the most heavily sanctioned United States ally. We helped you capture Ramzi Yousef"—who was sentenced to life in prison as the mastermind of the first bombing of the World Trade Center in New York. "We helped you capture Mir Aimal Kansi"—who was sentenced to death for the murder of two CIA employees outside the agency's headquarters in 1993— "and all we got were thank-you notes. You lobbed missiles across our territory with no advance warning! You humiliated our government! You killed Pakistani intelligence officers! And then you come to us and say, 'It's your problem. You've got to get Osama bin Laden for us.' "

The bitterness in Pakistan—and in its Army—toward the United States grew even more pronounced in March of 2000, when President Clinton made an awkward six-hour visit to Islamabad. He arrived in an unmarked jet, preceded by a decoy one, and was swept through the capital's empty streets. (His motorcade even traveled on the wrong side of the road to outwit potential terrorists.) After lecturing Musharraf—and then the nation, on TV—on Islamic extremism, terrorism, and democracy, the American President was gone. Few failed to grasp the humiliation of the trip: the President had spent five days in India.

"Through our sanctions, through our attitudes toward them, we're *forcing* the Pakistani Army to turn inward," General Zinni said. "Our training courses had been an enormous plus for them. But now we're seeing a lot of beards in the Army, a lot of grumbling in the junior ranks, and growing frustration with the United States. It's because of us that they've fallen way behind India in conventional arms. And, as a result, their weapons of mass destruction are the only kind of deterrence they have."

Peshawar—only thirteen miles southeast of the Khyber Pass, with Afghanistan beyond—is a rugged, lawless sort of place, riven by religious fervor and violence, and rich in political intrigue. The capital of Pakistan's North-West Frontier Province, it retains the feel of a sprawling town of pastel-colored villas and Afghan refugee camps; militant training centers and madrasahs, the religious schools where jihad more often than not is preached; arms, drugs, and a booming black market economy. The key staging area for the jihad in Afghanistan, it is, in a sense, a metaphor for Pervez Musharraf's inheritance: an official economy nearly bankrupt, with a $38 billion foreign debt; a black market economy that flourishes, and now exceeds nearly half of Pakistan's official GDP; a gun-loving culture, in which a weapon is considered a badge. Here, in the North-West Frontier Province and its surrounding tribal agencies alone, there are thought to be roughly seven million Kalashnikovs, or one for every grown man.

When Musharraf came to power, he pledged to reverse all of this: to crack down on endemic corruption, to jump-start the economy, to "de-weaponize" the country, and to rein in its growing band of Islamic militants, who are schooled in the madrasahs, trained in Afghanistan, and go on to fight in Kashmir. It is a vicious cycle, and one that the general had been unable, or unwilling, to reverse.

His supporters insisted that if Musharraf had not fulfilled his promises it was too soon to conclude that he had broken them. Yet over the previous year, as he acquiesced consistently to the demands of the religious right—retreating from his pledges to document the madrasahs and bring them under state control, to liberalize the country's draconian blasphemy laws (which were first instituted in 1981 by Zia ul-Haq), to consider (under the strong urging of the United States) the feasibility of signing the Comprehensive Test Ban Treaty—it had become difficult to differentiate between Musharraf's surrenders and his tactical retreats, which, in turn, made it difficult to say which direction Pakistan would take.

I had come to Peshawar to meet Maulana Sami ul-Haq, one of the most powerful and anti-American of Pakistan's religious militants. He is the chancellor of the al-Haqqania madrasah, which his father founded, and which is the largest in the Frontier and, like its leader, one of the most militant in Pakistan.

As we sped along the highway, we passed brightly painted trucks, designed in a style that originated in the North-West Frontier, whose cargoes more often than not contained smuggled electronic goods, a lucrative business controlled in large part by the Afghan Mafia. We weaved our way in and out of a procession of cars festooned with religious banners and flags, whose occupants were on their way to a fundamentalist rally outside Islamabad, which would attract thousands of people, both Pakistanis and Afghans. (Political parties and political activities were banned in Musharraf's Pakistan, but the religious right continued to organize, rally, and recruit, having convinced the government, or so it appeared, that their organizations were more Islamic than they were political—all of which had led the Human Rights Commission of Pakistan to accuse the general of being a "silent spectator" in the rise of the orthodox clergy and militant Islam.)

I looked out the window and watched clusters of Afghan refugees tending their tiny shops. Afghanistan had been at war for more than twenty years, and the refugees continued to spill across the frontier, now fleeing the more oppressive aspects of the Taliban, whose Islamic strictures were extreme and brutal, and often bizarre: women were not permitted to work; girls could not attend school; television, cinema, and music were banned—so was kite flying— and women were not permitted to wear noisy shoes or white socks. Both of the latter were considered to be sexually provocative. Indeed, the only public entertainment that the puritanical Taliban would permit were weekend public executions in football or soccer fields.

Afghan refugees now dominated Pakistan's northern towns and, as we continued toward the madrasah, it became apparent that for all practical purposes Afghanistan had effectively moved fifty miles south.

A friend had come with me to act as an interpreter, and when we entered al-Haqqania's gates, we were struck by how vast the madrasah is: spread over seven acres, on the Grand Trunk Road, an hour or so east of Peshawar, it has scores of classrooms, administrative buildings, mosques, and dorms, and, also, a computer room. Much of its funding comes from the wealthy kingdoms and sheikdoms of the Persian Gulf, particularly Saudi Arabia. No armed men were visible early that afternoon, but a few weeks after our visit scores of gunmen in camouflage fatigues, their faces covered by black ski masks, stood guard across the campus as some three hundred of Pakistan's leading Muslim clerics met to pledge their support to Osama bin Laden.

We were ushered to an outdoor veranda abutting the maulana's drawing room. There, a dozen young men lounged about, including the maulana's second son, Rashid, who was in the middle of a three-day marriage ceremony. His father was supervising the final arrangements for the festivities, so Rashid and his friends had been asked to entertain us until the maulana arrived. They proceeded to brief us on Peshawar's events of the day. The previous evening a dozen or so armed militants had met with great success in smashing satellite dishes and TV sets. The papers that morning had reported that the

United States was about to bomb Afghanistan again (as it had done in August of 1998, after accusing Osama bin Laden of bombing its African embassies).

"What will happen here if that occurs?" I asked.

"Holy war," one of the young men politely said.

Maulana Sami ul-Haq rushed onto the veranda, followed by servants ferrying trays of tea and coffee, fruits and sweets. A weathered man of sixty-five with a heavily lined face, small brown eyes, and a straggly beard, dyed orange with henna (which is quite fashionable among clerics here), the maulana is also a politician, a former senator, and a leader of one of Pakistan's more radical Islamist parties, the Jamiat-i-Ulema-i-Islam, which seeks the immediate imposition of the more punitive aspects of Shariah law. He told me immediately that al-Haqqania had 2,500 students, had issued nearly a million *fatwas* over the years (not mentioning the fact that a number of them had endorsed the *fatwas* issued by bin Laden in Afghanistan), and that 95 percent of the leadership of the Taliban had studied here.*

Pakistan's commitment to that leadership had been reinforced since General Musharraf seized control. Everyone appeared intent on imposing Pakistan's own solution on Afghanistan. As a result, the ISI had accelerated its military training of the Taliban, and its recruitment of volunteer soldiers from madrasahs such as this. And, since the previous spring, it had also planned pivotal military operations for the fundamentalist regime in its attempt to wrest control of the 10 percent of the country in the north that remained in the hands of the remnants of an opposition force—that was led by a legendary mujahideen commander, Ahmed Shah Massoud, and sup-

---

*In the vast majority of Pakistan's madrasahs, Saudi Arabia's austere school of Wahhabi Islam merged, as it did nowhere else, with the Deobandism of the subcontinent—an Islamic movement born in India during the days of the Raj but which has, since then, evolved into one of the most absolutist schools of Islamic thought. Radicalized by Abdul Ala el-Mawdudi, the late leader of the Jamaat-e-Islami, Pakistan's largest fundamentalist political party, the school of Deoband is heavily subsidized by the rulers of Saudi Arabia.

ported by the region's powers: India, Russia, and Iran. I asked the maulana to tell me about the Taliban's mysterious ruler, Mullah Mohammed Omar. For despite the fact that Pakistan had gambled heavily on him, except for a handful of officers from the ISI, few in successive governments of Pakistan, including General Musharraf, had ever met the man.

"He's a very good friend of mine," Sami ul-Haq began. "He considers me as a teacher, and your country should give him a medal for saving Afghanistan! Mullah Omar and the Taliban didn't just fall out of the sky. They're the children of the mujahideen, the children of the jihad, which your CIA trained. Mullah Omar was an ordinary soldier who fought in that war and he lost an eye in it. He was an unnamed, unknown Talib who came from nowhere. We think that God must be behind him. When I last visited him in Kandahar, I found him in a garage outside his house. He was sitting on the floor, with a wireless, ruling Afghanistan. He has no need for pomp and ceremony, for television or air conditioners. He didn't even have a fan!"

"What do you think of Osama bin Laden?" I asked.

"What do you think of Abraham Lincoln?" he said.

Earlier in the week, I had asked General Musharraf if he was not concerned about the Talibanization of Pakistan. For many of the madrasahs—although they had begun as religious schools that had educated, among others, the Taliban—had by now, in a role reversal of sorts, begun preaching the Taliban's ideology of militancy and jihad.

"Okay, okay," the general had responded, slightly irritably. "I've never been to a madrasah, but I do know that all this talk about their teaching militancy is just hearsay. I've met with some of their leaders"—including Sami ul-Haq—"and they've said to me: 'Who comes to the madrasahs? Has anyone from the Ministry of Education ever come? No. Only people from the police, from the intelligence agencies. We're being treated as though we are dacoits!'"

So I now asked Sami ul-Haq what he and his fellow maulanas thought of General Musharraf. "We had lots of hopes, but the poor chap has been caught up in a lot of problems," he said. "He's been very firm on Kashmir and, of course, that's very good. But I wish he'd use the stick and clean up corruption and the politicians' mess."

"What would happen if he brought the madrasahs under government control or closed them down?" I asked.

"Impossible!" the maulana said. "I asked him that question directly, and he replied: 'Do you think I'm mad! The madrasahs are doing so much for the poor; you're giving poor children free education, free lodging, free food. Why should I close them down?'"

Wedding guests had begun to arrive, so my interpreter and I said our good-byes. Before leaving, I asked the maulana if I could meet some of his students, but Ramadan was about to begin and, as a result, al-Haqqania was now closed for the coming month. As he walked with us to our car, one of the young men from the veranda explained that all of the students had left. Most had gone off to join some ten thousand other Pakistani volunteers who were training or fighting in Afghanistan.

By mid-January of 2001, the United Nations Security Council—at the behest of Russia and the United States—had imposed harsh new sanctions on the Taliban for its refusal to close Afghanistan's terrorist training camps, or to extradite Osama bin Laden. General Musharraf, unexpectedly—and to the anger of most Pakistanis—had pardoned Nawaz Sharif from his life prison term and sent him off to Saudi Arabia after the former prime minister agreed to pay nearly $8.5 million in settlement of charges of corruption. And Prime Minister Atal Behari Vajpayee of India had extended a unilateral cease-fire in Kashmir for a second time since it began, at the end of November to coincide with Ramadan. Hours later, Pakistan announced a partial withdrawal of its forces from the Line of Control. Both of these developments, which were quickly followed by the first meeting between General Musharraf and the Indian high commissioner in Islamabad, led diplomatic officials to hope that they might comprise the first, tentative steps toward a summit between the leaders of India and Pakistan.

When I asked General Musharraf if such a summit seemed probable, he replied, "I have said over and over again that I would meet the prime minister of India anytime, anyplace. Kashmir is the oldest unresolved dispute in the world, and it needs to be solved. It's been before the United Nations since 1948, and there it remains. Let the United Nations or the United States come aboard and mediate. For I want to make it very clear that peace through the status quo is *not* the answer. The issue should not be allowed to be hijacked by one party, even if that party is a large country, with an arrogant power base." He paused for a moment, and then he said, "There can be no real improvement in our relations with India until New Delhi openly acknowledges that the Kashmir conflict exists. This is what we've killed each other for. I know it. I fought in two of the wars."

Some months after our conversation, in July of 2001, Pervez Musharraf traveled to India for a crucial summit meeting with Atal Behari Vajpayee, his most obvious nemesis, yet a man whom he had never met. It was the first time in fifty-three years that the Pakistani general had set foot in the nation of his birth. Some three weeks earlier, on June 20, in anticipation of it—and in what he termed a "personal embarrassment"—Musharraf declared himself Pakistan's president. According to his critics, including the former Prime Ministers Benazir Bhutto and Nawaz Sharif, he had stripped away Pakistan's last façade of constitutional rule and there were howls of protest from the West, particularly from Washington. But as the West grumbled, one of the stranger twists surrounding the general's assumption of unbridled power was a congratulatory phone call from the prime minister of India. Musharraf was quietly pleased, for even though it seemed inevitable that one day he would elevate himself to the presidency, his timing, to a great extent, reflected his desire to walk tall at the summit in the Moghul city of Agra. He wanted to silence any questions about his legitimacy, or about his long-term viability as a negotiating partner with India on Kashmir. He had also been displeased, one of his advisers said to me, by the minimal protocol he was to receive as Chief of the Army Staff.

Musharraf was confident and determined, sincere yet tough, during the three days he spent in India. Kashmir was *the* issue, he said repeatedly, describing all other bilateral problems between India and Pakistan—including nuclear risk reduction and troop levels along the Line of Control—as merely "minor irritants." No breakthrough was achieved during the talks, which ultimately collapsed based in large part on Pakistan's insistence on the centrality of Kashmir, and India's equal insistence that the dispute not be internationalized— something that Islamabad has demanded, and New Delhi has rejected, for more than half a century. For India has always claimed Kashmir to be an integral part of it, while Pakistan has insisted all along that it is disputed ground and that its inhabitants must be permitted to vote in a plebiscite, based on United Nations resolutions passed shortly after the two independent nations were born. Another divisive issue was Vajpayee's demand that the infiltration into the Indian part of Kashmir by Pakistani-based Islamic militants cease immediately. It was a concession that the hawkish Muslim general certainly would not grant to a man who rose to power as a strident Hindu nationalist.

In one of my conversations with General Musharraf, I had asked him what he expected from the United States. He didn't answer immediately, and then he said, bitterness entering his voice, "The United States must help clean up the mess that you created during the days of the Soviet occupation of Afghanistan. Pakistan served your interests very prominently as a frontline state. But when the Soviets withdrew, the U.S. government also pulled out, leaving us high and dry."

"Are you disappointed?" I asked.

"Of course, I'm disappointed," he replied. "And this is not just my personal view. The people of Pakistan certainly expected much, much more from your government. For fifty years—*half a century*— we supported your policies. And then you walked away."

A Western diplomat had told me earlier, "Musharraf is a man occasionally short of patience, and you'll know immediately when you've gone too far." I decided to move to more prudent ground.

"Will your government assist Washington in bringing Osama bin Laden to trial?"

The question seemed to relax the general a bit. He ran his hand across his forehead and settled himself more comfortably on the sofa, reflecting, perhaps, that bin Laden appeared to be the most important leverage that Pakistan retained in its relationship with the United States.

"The United States used to think very strongly that we could deliver bin Laden," he said. "But I have been telling everyone, 'We can assist, not assure,' and I think we have been successful in driving that point home. Where we can help, we will, but the United States needs to tackle this with the Taliban directly. Your government must understand the reality—I will go even further, the bitter reality—on the ground. The Taliban controls 90 percent of Afghanistan and, irrespective of their views, they must be engaged. This is the only way that we can moderate them. The answer is not for the international community to increasingly put Afghanistan up against the wall, to keep imposing sanctions. For, if it does, the Taliban will simply become more obstinate."

A bearer, wearing a golden turban with green cockscombs, entered the drawing room with coffee and tea. I asked General Musharraf how he would compare himself to his country's last military ruler, General Zia ul-Haq, who had launched Pakistan on its present Islamist course.

He smiled. "The biggest difference is that Zia wanted to be there forever. I have a time frame, a specific agenda that I want to fulfill. Zia was also not at all involved in institutional change: in reform and restructuring." He paused and then said, "He was also much more religious than I am. Zia was a manipulator; he used religion to insure his own power, and I strongly believe that religion should not be manipulated for political gains. Also, the people of Pakistan, perhaps, were not really with Zia, but they certainly are supportive of my government and me."

On the most fundamental questions that the West had about

Musharraf—the question of whether he would be able to curb the rise of Islamist extremism in his country's affairs—he was unforthcoming, and even misleading at times. I mentioned to him that a number of Pakistanis and Western diplomats had expressed their concern to me that what they perceived to be his tilting at windmills in Kashmir had made him increasingly vulnerable at home. For if he moved against the Islamic militants, who were his greatest threat, he was moving against the foot soldiers who fight in Kashmir and against the Taliban, which his intelligence service continued to train and arm. I asked General Musharraf if he wasn't playing a dangerous game of Russian roulette.

He looked at me across the table and, all testimony from foreign observers about the flow of men and arms to the contrary—and despite the fact that he was under increasing pressure from the United States, Russia, India, and Iran to disengage from Afghanistan—he denied that Pakistan was militarily involved in Afghanistan at all.

"This is a total misperception," he said, and his voice began to rise. "We do not have the resources! We're already short of arms, weapons, and equipment for ourselves. The world is giving us *nothing*! We are already threatened from the east, and we cannot divert any resources anywhere else. We'd be *mad* to give them anything! Everyone is against the Taliban! So what do we do? Go in and throw them out? Then what is the scenario? Is the problem of Afghanistan settled? No, it is not. I am 100 percent certain that Afghanistan would return to the anarchy of 1989 [after the Soviet withdrawal] when the country fell apart into small fiefdoms controlled by feudal lords fighting among themselves. So if the world expects me to go in and throw the Taliban out, *I will not!* I cannot and will not compromise the national interests of Pakistan. I do not want a second front! We are already facing a threat from the east, and I will not permit a second front from the west."

The general leaned back on the sofa, looking suddenly beleaguered and tired. Then he said, seemingly to no one in particular, "Have I made myself clear?"

CHAPTER 2

"THIS WAS PAKISTAN"

WITH HIS DOMESTIC AND FOREIGN POLICIES largely buried in the wreckage of the World Trade Center and the Pentagon, General Pervez Musharraf faced a stark choice: to align his country solidly behind the United States in its war against terrorism, or to be ostracized as the leader of a pariah state. After much equivocation, the general made his choice. In a hesitant, even apologetic, address to the nation on September 19, 2001, he explained that he faced an American ultimatum—join us or fight us—and that he believed Pakistan's very survival was at stake. In quick succession, he abandoned his government's sponsorship of the Taliban and confronted tens of thousands of angry demonstrators on his streets, whose loyalties were not so much with him as they were with Osama bin Laden, Pakistan's militant Islamists, and the Taliban. Then to the collective astonishment of even his general-officer corps, he consolidated his power by retiring or moving aside any potential rivals, including the men most responsible for staging his coup only two years before—the powerful Generals Osmani, Aziz, and Mahmud. Any lingering doubts that Musharraf was, in fact, merely the nominee of a cabal of fellow generals were laid to rest.

But no sooner had Musharraf committed himself to the United States than strains in the relationship began to appear—strains that were accompanied by growing restiveness among Islamist sympathizers in his Army officer corps—over the length of Washington's bombing of Afghanistan, the composition of a broad-based government there, and whether U.S. troops would be permitted to operate inside Pakistan. Indeed, only twenty-four hours after the U.S. bombing campaign was launched, the public airing of differences had begun. Musharraf made it clear that the Taliban should not be displaced until a successor government, friendly to Pakistan, had been agreed upon, and that the U.S. bombing must be brief—no longer than a week or ten days. He then went on to tell the press that he had received "definite assurances" from the United States that the war would be short. When President Bush was asked about this, he did little to mask his irritation with the general, telling reporters, "I don't know who told the Pakistani president that."

The standoff between the two leaders at such an early stage hinted at how delicate and potentially fragile their partnership could be if rapid success was not achieved. The internal pressures against Musharraf began to mount, for Pakistan was the most prominent Islamic ally in America's war. Thus, as the months passed and the air war went on, the question being asked, in both Islamabad and Washington, was: How long would their new relationship last?

Yet at the same time, by the spring of 2002, there was also a sense of déjà vu. For not only was the United States back in Pakistan—and, also, still in Afghanistan—but the mujahideen armies, which Washington had armed and trained twenty years earlier, had largely been returned to power in Afghanistan—by the United States.

For his part, Pervez Musharraf, now with the blessing of Washington, appeared to be emulating Zia ul-Haq, the general who had presided over the jihad against the Soviets and, as a result, became indispensable to the United States—precisely as Musharraf was indispensable now. (Washington had richly rewarded Musharraf for his participation in its war with a promised aid package worth more than a billion dollars. The economic sanctions imposed on Pakistan were lifted as well, but the far more politically sensitive military ones largely remained in place, and U.S. officials continued to refuse to release twenty-eight F-16 fighter planes that Zia ul-Haq had purchased during the jihad years, but which were subsequently withheld as part of the sanctions against Islamabad's program to become a nuclear power.)

Musharraf and Zia. Both products of British India. Both military rulers who suspended the constitution and banned political activity; both of whose armies remained their primary constituencies; both shunned by the Western world; neither of whose governments was doing well. Their economies were stagnant; international aid and investment ground to a halt; their governments were expelled from the Commonwealth. Then, as the phoenix rose from the ashes, both were reborn: now, Musharraf; then, Zia, twenty years before, during Washington's first Afghan war.

One of the legacies of that earlier war had been the "Children of the Jihad," who came of age on the Afghan battlefields. Zia and the CIA and Saudi Arabia had created them. Musharraf, in later years, had inherited and embraced them. Like Zia, Musharraf disdained Pakistan's politicians, whom he regularly denounced; he flirted with the Islamists; and, under the cover of a provisional constitutional order, had declared himself president. Now, just as U.S. Special Forces began to arrive in Pakistan in the spring of 2002, he announced that, on April 30, he would legitimize his self-appointed post through a controversial referendum, just as Zia ul-Haq had done eighteen years earlier.

"I do not believe in power sharing . . . I believe in unity of command. There has to be only one authority for good government," Musharraf told the press.

It was a surreal spectacle: General Musharraf barnstorming the country, campaigning unopposed, in a one-man contest in which voters could vote only "yes" or "no" to a question that was framed in such a way that "no" seemed not only unpatriotic but unthink-able. The referendum question asked Pakistanis to endorse a five-year term for the general in order to permit economic recovery, the restoration of democracy, the end to extremism, and "the achieve-ment of the vision" of Pakistan's founder, Mohammed Ali Jinnah.

Pakistani newspapers ran varying accounts of how much govern-ment money was spent on organizing rallies, busing in crowds, and festooning the country with pictures of Musharraf, which were everywhere now—in full face and in profile; smiling and brooding; as a stern leader of the nation, in full military dress; as the benevolent father of the country, in a dark business suit; as a son of the soil, in a *shalwar kameez* and any number of flamboyant regional turbans, sometimes slightly askew on his head. The political establishment was aghast. Benazir Bhutto and Nawaz Sharif—the only two demo-cratically elected leaders in unrestricted polls in the last quarter of a century—called for a boycott of the referendum; so did the leaders of the religious parties, and the major associations of students and lawyers. But Musharraf continued apace.

For time was running out for the general. National elections, mandated by the Supreme Court, were scheduled for October, and he had no guarantee that the new parliament—which, together with the four provincial assemblies is constitutionally charged with elect-ing the president—would give its vote to him.

Many Pakistanis and Western diplomats had already begun to suggest that the way in which the referendum balloting was con-ducted could portend whether the October polls would be free and fair or whether they would be fashioned on the elections held sev-enteen years earlier by Zia ul-Haq.

No one man has dominated all aspects of Pakistani life as did Gen-eral Mohammed Zia ul-Haq, who died in a mysterious, still unex-plained August 1988 crash of his military transport plane. Zia seized control of the government in a military coup in July of 1977, prom-ising to restore democracy in ninety days. He never did. Instead, he consolidated his power by deft maneuvering, and after the Soviet invasion of Afghanistan in 1979, he embarked on policies that transformed Pakistan into the hub of American policy in South Asia for the next decade. From the beginning, Pakistani officials insisted that the crash that killed President Zia and twenty-nine others, including Arnold L. Raphel, the American ambassador to Pakistan, was an act of sabotage—an assassination—but they have never provided any conclusive, public evidence to establish its cause. Conversely, White House and State Department officials at the time believed that a malfunction in the plane was most likely to blame.

A few weeks after Zia's death, a high-ranking Pakistani Army officer I spoke to in Islamabad told me that the investigation was proving far more difficult than had originally been expected. "Whoever did it had extraordinary precision and extraordinary intelligence," the officer said. At the time of our conversation, there were five "working theories" on the cause of the crash, but one of them— a missile attack—had already been discounted, even by Pakistan. There had been no midair explosion, and investigators who spent three weeks combing the desert area where the plane had crashed turned up no evidence that a missile had been deployed. The four other theories, the officer told me, were "mechanical failure, pilot error, sabotage of the plane, and instantaneous crew incapacitation"—the last presumably from poison gas.

In addition to General Zia and Ambassador Raphel, those killed when the plane crashed included Brigadier General Herbert M. Wassom, an American military attaché; ten Pakistani generals, among them General Akhtar Abdul Rehman, the former director of ISI and then-chairman of Pakistan's Joint Chiefs of Staff; and Lieutenant General Mian Mohammed Afzaal, the Chief of the General Staff. The plane crashed just after taking off from Bahawalpur Airport, 330 miles south of Islamabad, on a return trip to the capital. The presidential party had flown to the Bahawalpur area earlier that day to watch a demonstration of an American tank that Pakistan was interested in purchasing.

The tiny civilian airport, set in a dusty patch of desert in eastern

Pakistan, from which the presidential party had flown, was relatively new. And although it had grown accustomed to the whirl of military helicopters from a nearby cantonment and to receiving commercial flights from southern Karachi, the flights arrived only twice a week. Then, on the day of Zia's visit, the sleepy airstrip was jolted alive. There was a constant din of C-130s arriving and departing, DC-3s, an assortment of military helicopters and transport planes. Mayors and provincial government officials, the Army's High Command, and corps commanders from the vitally important province of Punjab overwhelmed its facilities; their sleek limousines blocked the roads, spilling out from the airstrip's tiny parking lot. And, although commandos had ringed the airfield and sharpshooters crouched on the terminal's roof, remote Bahawalpur, with all of its comings and goings, was a security man's nightmare.

Zia was in a particularly jovial mood as he reboarded the plane. As soon as he was seated, in its midsection, the last of his smartly dressed commandos hopped aboard, then fanned out between the cockpit and the rear of the plane, where four crates of mangos had been brought aboard at the last minute. The mangos may or may not have been screened. Two were gifts from the mayor of Bahawalpur, who knew that Zia had a particular passion for the fruit and the season was at its end. Bahawalpur was the only area where they were still available in Pakistan. Even today, no one knows for certain who gifted the two other crates.

If General Zia was in fact assassinated, who was responsible? The list of candidates was long. Some government officials were quick to blame Pakistan's old enemy, India, or its newer enemies, the Soviet Union and Afghanistan. All three countries had, of course, denied the allegations, and Western diplomats I had spoken to gave little credence to the idea of either Indian or Soviet involvement. Two of the diplomats did concede, however, that the Afghan security service, KHAD,* which was trained and directed by the KGB, could

---

*In Dari, KHAD stands for Khedamat-i-Ettela'at-i-Daulati, which roughly translates as State Information Service and is uniformly known as "security service."

conceivably have brought down the plane without the KGB's knowledge or consent. In recent years, KHAD had been held responsible for hundreds of terrorist bombings in Pakistan—bombings carried out in retaliation for Pakistan's aiding and arming the Afghan resistance forces fighting the jihad. "KHAD doesn't play by the rules," one Western official told me at the time. "If they were responsible for the sabotage of the plane, it could have been a maverick operation. The Kabul regime is so riddled with rivalries and splits that it is impossible for President Najibullah or the ruling party to say that it controls every act of the Afghan government."

In any event, those seeking to explain the crash as an assassination did not necessarily have to look beyond Pakistan's borders, for Zia ul-Haq had a great many enemies at home: field-grade Army officers, discontented with the military's continuing political role and Pakistan's growing involvement in the Afghanistan war; restive potential secessionists from the provinces of Balochistan and Sindh; Pakistani drug barons; and militants from the minority Shiite sect. There were also some five hundred well-trained and well-armed members of the former underground organization Al-Zulfikar. This group, founded in 1980 by the sons of Zulfikar Ali Bhutto, the democratically elected prime minister whom General Zia overthrew in 1977—and hanged two years later—stopped functioning in 1985, but according to one Pakistani intelligence official, "the ranks are still here, and are potential assassins for hire."

The most unsettling aspect of Zia ul-Haq's death—if, indeed, it wasn't an accident—was the suspicion that disaffected members of the Army or the Air Force might have been involved. Bahawalpur Airport was under military security on the day that Zia died, but the security was lax. A Pentagon official told me at the time that the presidential plane, an American-built Lockheed C-130, "wasn't checked out that thoroughly" for explosives or bad maintenance. But even if the ground security forces were negligent, how would an assassin have known that Zia would be in Bahawalpur the afternoon of August 17 and aboard that particular plane? The decision to fly the C-130 had been made only the previous night—thirteen hours

before Zia boarded the plane. When he left his official Army residence in Rawalpindi that morning, Zia told his wife—as all the
other officers making the trip told their families—that he was going
not to Bahawalpur but to the city of Muzaffarabad, in northern
Kashmir.

In the first official report on the crash, issued on October 16,
Pakistani technical investigators raised more questions than they answered and were far more conclusive on what did not happen than
on what did. The investigators ruled out a high-intensity explosion,
a missile attack, pilot error, and crew fatigue. According to Air
Commodore Abbas Mirza, who headed the technical investigating
team, the investigators had reached the conclusion that sabotage or
"another criminal act" was "most probably" involved because they
were unable to substantiate a mechanical failure or a technical fault.
(When asked at a press conference why "another criminal act" had
been included along with sabotage, Mirza said that it was possible
that one of the four members of the presidential crew could have
intentionally disrupted the controls.) An Air Force general, who
briefed me later on the still unreleased, 365-page report, told me that
a flight lieutenant, who had been hastily added to the manifest, was
under investigation. It was later discovered that he was a member of
a militant underground Shiite group, whose leader had been assassinated only a few months earlier.

The general went on to tell me that for him two of the more in-
triguing questions the report raised were the possibility that a low-
intensity explosion may have brought down the presidential plane.
Abnormal amounts of chemicals often used in explosives were found
throughout the aircraft, from the supporting rod of the cockpit to
the aft cargo doors. They were also found on the charred remains of
the four crates of mangos that, at the last minute, were brought
aboard. The report also raised the "distinct possibility," the general
continued, that the crew could have been incapacitated by a poison
gas such as carbon monoxide, large amounts of which were also discovered at the scene of the crash. But neither this report, nor two

subsequent ones, answered the crucial question of who was responsible for bringing the plane down.

In the early months of 1989, without explanation, the investigation into Zia's death was abruptly stopped.

One of the most baffling mysteries surrounding the crash, which none of the reports explained, was the absence of radio transmissions or distress signals from the stricken plane. According to officials at Bahawalpur Airport, the C-130 lifted off routinely. For the first four minutes, nothing was amiss. Air speed was normal, and the plane had reached five thousand feet. Until then, conversations with Wing Commander Mashhood Hasan, who for five years had been Zia ul-Haq's pilot, had been routine. But just as Mashhood was saying, "Doors will next be opened at . . ." he was interrupted by an unidentified voice. Air-traffic controllers heard someone shouting in the cockpit, "Mashhood, Mashhood, Mashhood." Then silence. All contact was lost. Within two minutes, Zia ul-Haq's aircraft exploded as it hit the ground.

The Islamic Republic of Pakistan—a name meaning Land of the Pure—was carved out of British India to provide a homeland for the subcontinent's Muslims. The idea of a Muslim homeland has never fully worked. No leader since independence has been able to bind the people together in the name of Islam, because in Pakistan you must ask, "Whose Islam?" There are three major Sunni Muslim sects and also Shiites, Ahmadis, Sufis, Ismailis, and many subsects. Beyond these divisions, the country still labors under a de facto system of caste. Several years ago, Adil Mufti, a Karachi businessman, told me, "Regardless of what we say, Pakistan is as caste-conscious as India. Perhaps our castes are more subtle—structurally less defined—but we are casted according to province, according to education and wealth. And beneath the Brahmans is the Army. It is our second caste."

Personalities have always loomed larger than institutions in Paki-

stan, except for the 550,000-man Army, whose leaders are the arbiters of power here, and have been for fifty-five years. At the time
of Zia's death, the Army had ruled Pakistan for twenty-four of its
forty-one independent years, and there had been only three general
elections in four decades. Zulfikar Ali Bhutto, who was elected in
December of 1970, was the only popularly elected leader ever to
govern the country. Pakistanis had thus turned to violent agitation
as a means of political change. Street mobs brought about the removal of General Mohammed Ayub Khan, an elegant soldier of the
old British school, who ruled the country from October of 1958 to
March of 1969, and street mobs brought about the removal of
Bhutto, by provoking Zia's 1977 coup. A military defeat by India in
1971 removed yet another military leader, General Yahya Khan.

(In the years following Zia's death, four general elections would
be held, and power would ricochet between Benazir Bhutto and
Nawaz Sharif: she, the heir of the Bhutto dynasty; he, the inheritor
of Zia's legacy. After an eleven-year tussle between the two, Pervez
Musharraf staged his military coup.)

Islamabad, the capital from which Zia ruled, is an artificial city
that was carved out of the Margala Hills in the 1960s by a Greek architect at the behest of another military ruler, General Ayub Khan.
When I returned to it in the days after Zia died, I was startled anew
by what an abrupt contrast the capital is to the rest of Pakistan; it
seems somehow detached from it.

As I waited for my luggage at the nearby airport in Rawalpindi,
enveloped by a jostling crowd, my mind wandered back to the first
time I had come to Pakistan, in November of 1982. Then, I had
arrived in Karachi in the middle of the night, and the airport
was swarming with people, clamorous with shouts and noise. Families sat by great heaps of baggage. Pilgrims waited patiently for the
next flight to the holy city of Mecca, shuffling through the departure lounge, dressed in white, crocheted prayer caps and long, flowing white robes. Here and there, wandering about, were almsgivers
and alms seekers, all with outstretched hands. Outside the terminal
there was a persistent din: car horns tooting, vendors hawking their

wares, and muezzins, their voices shrilly amplified, calling the faithful to prayers.

Looking back on those early years, which lasted until the end of 1985, some of my most vivid memories were of dinner in the desert, just as the sun was beginning to set; of the only sustained rebellion against Zia's rule, in the interior of the province of Sindh, when a friend and I, in the midst of the confusion that prevailed, were permitted to tour a tiny jail in a place called Dadu, in the middle of nowhere. To our astonishment, we found many of Sindh's major politicians incarcerated there. I also remember the afternoon that I accompanied a tribal chief from Balochistan to an arms bazaar, where he was intent on buying a Stinger antiaircraft missile—which the CIA had "lost"—as the centerpiece for his garden, which was already bursting with marble statuary and relics of the Raj. I remember the mountain passes of the North-West Frontier, where men still rode on horseback; the Moghul gardens of Lahore. And then, almost as an afterthought, I also remembered Islamabad.

As I sped along its wide boulevards from the airport to my hotel, I passed featureless developments of concrete buildings and numbered zones. Addressees have an Orwellian ring: House Number 10, Street Number 20, Zone F/2. Islamabad's institutional architecture is barren and bleak—a sprawl of gray, white, and ochre concrete office buildings, shopping centers, and government ministries. It is peopled by diplomats, by generals, and by bureaucrats, who career through its tree-lined streets in chauffeur-driven limousines. From the old British military cantonment of Rawalpindi, a dozen miles away, clerks and servants commute each day to the new capital on the hill—clogging its boulevards with four-wheel-drive vehicles, bicycles, and motorbikes.

One former American ambassador described Islamabad as "rather like a New York cemetery: half the size, but twice as dead."

With a population of less than eight hundred thousand, the capital is spread over an area of 351 square miles; its sister city, Rawalpindi, the seat of military power, has a population of 1.4 million in an area of fifty-five square miles. To the west and southwest of

Islamabad lie Afghanistan and Iran; to its east, India; and the Arabian Sea to its south. The Indus is the great river of Pakistan: it irrigates the country and cleaves it in half. Four disparate provinces are divided by language, by ethnicity, by feudal and tribal clans, which continue to wield enormous power even now. The country's illiteracy rate of 54 percent is among the highest in Asia; its annual population growth rate of 2.4 percent is among the highest in the world. Pakistan is a brooding, changeless place, seemingly caught between the twenty-first and the nineteenth centuries. It is also a country with a fierce appetite for change.

It was just before sunset, the prettiest time of the day, when I arrived at my hotel. The surrounding buildings were bathed in a luminous glow. As I entered the lobby, a friend rushed toward me to tell me the latest news. Rumors in Pakistan, a country with a strong tradition of storytelling, have assumed a reality of their own. Conspiracy theories, like in much of former British India, are woven into the fabric of the nation's political cloth. As we continued talking, I glanced around. Young men dressed in dark business suits filled the lobby café, sifting through briefcases or chattering into mobile phones; old men dressed in tribal robes sat at a nearby table, seeming to glower at the world. In a far corner, stout men wearing sparkling rings spoke in whispers to a bedraggled group of Afghan mujahideen. Zia, the general who had never commanded his Army in the field, had found his war in Afghanistan.

Mohammed Zia ul-Haq was born in 1924, twenty-three years before his country, into the family of a civil servant—who was also a *maulvi*, or devout religious man—in Jullundur, now part of the Indian Punjab, when India was still ruled by the British Raj. Its violent Partition in 1947, which created Pakistan, was an event that affected his thinking—as it affected Pervez Musharraf's—for the rest of his life. At the time of Partition, Zia, who had been trained in the British Indian Army, was an Army captain; his family was in a refugee camp. (His mother, he told me later, walked ninety miles to

arrive in Pakistan.) Zia himself was an escort officer for the last Pakistani train to leave Babina, a military training center in India's
Uttar Pradesh, for West Pakistan.

I spoke with Zia in January of 1983, when he had been in power
more than five years, and he told me about the trip from Babina
thirty-six years earlier. "It was ghastly," he said. "It should have been
a journey of sixteen or eighteen hours. It took me seven days. I had
consignments of military equipment and some fifty refugees. We
were under constant fire. The country was burning until we reached
Lahore. Life had become so cheap between Hindu and Muslim. It
was a civil war. I saw very little greenery, little evidence of life—
only the mutilated bodies of men and women lying along the rail
line. You can't imagine my feelings when I finally reached Lahore. I
felt, for the first time, that I could smell free air. I then realized that
we were bathed in blood, but at last we were free citizens. This was
Pakistan."

Zia ul-Haq rose from obscurity in the Army in March of 1976,
when Zulfikar Ali Bhutto promoted him over ten other generals to
become Chief of the Army Staff. Bhutto had considered Zia—
as Nawaz Sharif would later consider Musharraf—a pliant, unimag-
inative choice, but sixteen months later Zia overthrew him. From
the time Zia seized power, he began catering to the country's four
strongest groups—the Army, the Muslim clergy, the financial and
industrial barons, and the feudal landlords. He embarked on a
sweeping Islamization program to make Pakistani laws conform with
the teachings of the Koran. And although much of his Islamization
was cosmetic—no thieves had had their hands cut off, no adulterers
had been stoned—Zia nonetheless put the laws on the books. He
also gave priority to Pakistan's program to develop a nuclear
weapon—a program started by Bhutto in 1974 after India's "peaceful" underground nuclear explosion. But because of Pakistan's vital
strategic importance and Zia's pro-American views, both the Carter
and the Reagan Administrations tended to overlook Pakistan's nuclear program—and also Zia's patchy record on human rights.

President Carter did cut off aid briefly in 1979, but in December of that year, just as some Pakistanis began predicting that Zia would fall because of rising prices, an idle economy, and the overthrow of the Shah of Iran, Soviet troops crossed the border into Afghanistan and thus bestowed a new legitimacy on his regime. In January of 1980, Carter reversed the ban. No longer treated as a pariah by the Western world, Zia grew from a "simple soldier"—as he often described himself—into a surefooted leader who enjoyed the company of presidents and kings.

Although he ruled as a military man, he retained a common touch that was bred of a middle-class background in British India. He startled visitors by nearly always escorting them to their cars, then waiting, in what were sometimes temperatures of a hundred degrees, to wave them off. When he returned to New Delhi's prestigious Saint Stephen's College for a reunion in 1982, he astonished his former classmates when he addressed his old English master as "Sir." "By jingo" and "old chaps" peppered Zia's speech, but he disdained other traditions of the English officers' mess—attributing his country's successive military defeats by India to "too much tippling" by Pakistan's military command. He was wily and adroit, a master manipulator of power, yet he could be disarmingly candid at times. I can't help but remember a dinner I attended at his official residence on Thanksgiving of 1982, when he told me, "I've discovered that gaining power is much easier than giving it up."

Like most military men, Zia lived surrounded by trophies, photographs, regimental badges, and other emblems of a military career. But in his private library there were some surprising things: a pair of ivory elephant tusks, a Japanese doll, a framed print of the Mona Lisa. He never moved into the presidential residence in Islamabad, but continued to live in Army House, the official residence of the Chief of the Army Staff. One sensed that the man who would rule Pakistan longer than any other leader in its independent years was far more comfortable there, amid daily reminders of a soldier's life.

Zia had two passions—Islam and Afghanistan—and the actions they moved him to take had powerful effects; he divided his country by the imposition of the harsher aspects of Islamic law and by his agreement to provide the Afghan mujahideen with ever-increasing shipments of arms supplied by the CIA. The United States had an enormous stake in Zia's Pakistan. From 1981 until Zia ul-Haq died, Washington committed more than $7 billion in military and economic aid to Pakistan, and at least $2 billion in covert assistance to the Afghan mujahideen, all of it channeled through Pakistan's powerful ISI. From the day of the Soviet invasion, Afghanistan dominated Zia's domestic and foreign policies. In a sense, everything else sprang from it: Pakistan's close relationship with Washington, and its role as a frontline state; the strain on its social and economic structure caused by the influx of three million Afghan refugees; a new "Kalashnikov culture," bred from the profligate slippage of arms from the CIA's pipeline; and the continuing dominance of the military in Pakistan's political life.

Zia basically distrusted politicians. "If I turn things over to the politicians, they will simply mess things up," he once told me. Yet in February of 1985 he did permit restricted, nonparty elections for parliament, and the following month he appointed Mohammed Khan Junejo, a wealthy landlord from the province of Sindh, to serve as Pakistan's prime minister. But Junejo began to act as though he really were the head of government, and in May of 1988, Zia dismissed him. The two men disagreed profoundly on two issues—the role of the Army, which remained Zia's primary constituency, and Afghanistan.

Zia, for his part, had crafted his Afghan strategy to a large extent on a line drawn upon the map in 1893 by an exhausted British Raj. After it expanded its empire into northwest India, Britain had attempted to push farther on. Twice it invaded the kingdom of Afghanistan, in 1839 and 1878. Both incursions ended in disastrous defeats. And so it was that Sir Mortimer Durand, the foreign secretary in the colonial government of India, met with the Amir of Afghanistan in Kabul and, with a green felt-tip pen, demarcated one of the wildest and least governable terrains on earth. This side of the line, he said, shall belong to you and the tribes; the other side to us. The British thus gained a buffer between the Raj and the Russian Empire, having concluded that, in any case, the Afghans were impossible to tame: given their history of isolation and their culture of insurrection, the better part of reason was to subsidize the tribal chiefs rather than to attempt to battle them. What became known as the Durand Line meandered for 1,200 miles across mountains then dropped into deserts, where Pakistan, Afghanistan, and Iran meet. It cleaved into the North-West Frontier and into Balochistan, returning or awarding large swaths of these tribal lands to the Amir of Afghanistan. In the process, it split in half the land known as Pashtunistan.

On this side of the line, the Pashtuns—whose total number is at least twenty million—are known as the Pathans, a garbled Hindustani rendering of their native tongues: Pakhtu for those who live in or north of Peshawar; Pashtu for the tribes across Afghanistan or scattered to the south. But whatever their dialect, they bonded as one, and they disdained the artificial lines that swept across the map, continuing to come and go as they always had, between what became Pakistan's North-West Frontier Province and Balochistan, and their larger homeland in Afghanistan.

Zia ul-Haq, like Zulfikar Ali Bhutto before him—and, indeed, like every leader of Pakistan who followed him—lived in dread of the resurrection of the call for a united Pashtunistan. Thus, in 1973, when the Pashtun leader Sardar Mohammad Daoud took over the government in Kabul and called on the Pathans of Pakistan to secede and join their brothers under the Afghan flag, Bhutto struck back. He invited Afghan Pashtuns to Pakistan, and some five thousand came: students and mullahs, warlords and tribal chiefs. To a greater or lesser extent, all of them were viscerally antisecular and champions of a fundamentalist state in Afghanistan. None embraced Pashtunistan. Bhutto organized them into a guerrilla force to harass Daoud's regime. Six years before the Soviets invaded Afghanistan, the mujahideen had been born.

Zia had overthrown Bhutto, of course, but, nevertheless, he continued—and accelerated—Bhutto's policies in Afghanistan. Pakistan needed a client state there to, among other things, protect itself against Pashtunistan.

Though Zia was an intensely religious Muslim, he was neither fanatical nor doctrinaire, but he was committed to an Islamic Pakistan. "Other than Israel, Pakistan is the only state created on religious grounds," he once told me. "We were *created* on the basis of Islam. Look at Israel: its religion and its ideology are the main sources of its strength. We in Pakistan have lost sight of the importance of these things. And without them you're like a straw being thrown about in the ocean. You're a Sindhi, a Baloch, a Punjabi, a Pathan. Pakistan's binding force has always been Islam. Without it, Pakistan would fall."

But Zia's vision of Islam was often confusing, as were his Islamic laws. When he died at the age of sixty-four, nobody really knew for certain where he stood. He was preparing for general elections that he did not believe in and that many people doubted he would hold. He was also pushing his Army and the Afghan resistance into a more aggressive role, hoping to secure a military victory as the Soviets began withdrawing from Afghanistan. It was increasingly emerging that the Pakistani Armed Forces, the United States, and the less fundamentalist wing of the Afghan resistance were unhappy with that role. In their view, after the Soviet withdrawal only a broadly based government in Kabul could prevent a bloodbath between the Marxist government of President Najibullah and the mujahideen, especially the Hizb-i-Islami, the most radical of the resistance groups. Nevertheless, Pakistan's Army was ordered to give the resistance forces maximum support, and some two dozen majors and captains from the ISI were sent to Afghanistan in the spring of 1988 to direct operations and determine strategy. A hundred others came and went, according to the need. But their help failed to prove decisive in capturing major towns. Nine members of the Pakistani Army died in a battle that July, and three were arrested—with much fanfare—by the Soviets.

Pakistan was undergoing a particularly delicate transition when

Zia ul-Haq died. With the Soviet withdrawal from Afghanistan—
which would be completed in February of 1989—many Pakistanis
were already wondering how Washington would view their country
once it was no longer a frontline state.

Nine years had passed since the CIA began providing weapons and
funds—eventually totaling more than $3 billion—to a fratricidal al-
liance of seven Afghan resistance groups, none of whose leaders
were by nature democratic, and all of whom to a greater or lesser
extent were fundamentalist in religion, autocratic in politics, and
venomously anti-American in both respects.

When the Soviet Union invaded Afghanistan to prop up its pro-
Communist regime in the last days of December 1979, the same year
that the Ayatollah Khomeini was swept into power in Iran, startled
American policy makers were ill prepared for either event, and they
responded in ways that would have powerful and lasting conse-
quences. For the Reagan Administration, the jihad was a battle to
"bleed the Soviets," and it was curiously popular on Capitol Hill.
With bipartisan support, a zealous Congress doubled, and even
tripled, the administration's requests for assistance to Afghanistan.
Tons of Soviet and Chinese weapons bought from friendly governments, including those of Egypt, China, Israel, and South Africa,
were sent to the battlefield. The provision of weapons from Communist countries was meant to camouflage Washington's direct links
to the war, a policy referred to—somewhat implausibly—as "plausible deniability." The American effort to punish the Soviet Union at
a time when it was perceived to be overextended and potentially
vulnerable was complemented by a Pan-Islamic effort to establish
the "perfect Islamic state"—a return to the ideals and dreams of the
seventh-century caliphate. The two agendas were mutually reinforcing for more than a decade.

Washington's policy of "fighting to the last Afghan" seemed
shortsighted even then, for it allowed the generals of Pakistan to de-

cide the allocation of the CIA's weapons and supplies. And the attitude of Zia and the ISI—both of whom had long embraced the most fundamentalist of the resistance groups—was that the more militant the jihadi fighters, the more ferociously they would battle the Soviets. As a result, the United States, intentionally or not, launched Pan-Islam's first holy war in eight centuries.

For during the years of the jihad, and up through 1992—three years after the Soviets had left Afghanistan and its Communist government finally fell—not only did thousands of Pakistani militants fight in Afghanistan but some twenty-five thousand others, from nearly thirty countries around the world, streamed through Peshawar on their way to the jihad. Known as the "Afghan Arabs," they came without passports and without names, from Egypt's Gama'a al-Islamiya and al-Jihad; from the Palestinian organization Hamas; from Saudi Arabia's Islamic Movement for Change; from Algeria's Islamic Salvation Front; and from the Philippines' Moro Islamic Liberation Front. Among those who came and went over the years was Sheikh Omar Abdel-Rahman, the blind Egyptian cleric who was sentenced in New York in January of 1996 to life imprisonment for seditious conspiracy to wage a "war of urban terrorism against the United States." The man known as Ramzi Ahmed Yousef also came and he, too, was later convicted by an American court as the architect of the 1993 terrorist attack against the Twin Towers in New York. Mir Aimal Kansi, like Yousef a Pakistani from the tribal area of Balochistan, had followed a curiously similar route to Yousef's, in and out of the United States, to wreak carnage at the headquarters of the CIA. Then, like Yousef, Kansi flew back to Pakistan and crossed the mountainous border, returning to Afghanistan. Nearly all of the defendants in Sheikh Omar's conspiracy trial had fought in the jihad; and so had Osama bin Laden.

(The post-jihad generation—including the majority of the nineteen young men who visited terror on the United States in September of 2001—would later train in bin Laden's Afghanistan camps.)

By the early months of 1996, seven years after the jihad formally came to an end, a thousand or so Afghan Arabs remained in Pakistan. Some were in Peshawar, while others were encamped in the mountain passes of the ungovernable tribal areas on both sides of the border with Afghanistan. Then, that May, under pressure from the United States and Saudi Arabia, the government of the Sudan asked bin Laden (who lived in exile there) to leave, and he returned to Afghanistan permanently—accompanied by two military transport planes carrying some of his wealth, more than a hundred of his Afghan Arab fighters, and his four wives. Of the fighters who had stayed on in Pakistan, they now moved with ease between Peshawar and bin Laden's bases in Afghanistan, planning and executing what U.S. officials today believe were terrorist acts that have reached from Pakistan to Saudi Arabia, from Yemen to the Philippines, Cairo to Nairobi and Dar es Salaam—and, most prominently, on September 11, 2001, to the streets of New York.

There was an intoxication among Zia's inner circle, among Pakistan's clerics and mullahs and fighters during the years of the jihad. For by the early 1980s armies in Pakistan, Afghanistan, and Iran were all ruling—or fighting—in the name of Islam.

But even before Zia died, there were those—including members of his Army establishment—who had begun to question his high-risk gamble in Afghanistan. One such man was Lieutenant General Mirza Aslam Beg. In late 1986, as corps commander of Peshawar, he had delivered an address at the Army Staff College in Quetta, Balochistan, in which he took exception to Zia's policies on Afghanistan. It was a bold and unusual step, but little was predictable about General Beg. "The ideology of standing up to the Soviets was not what he differed with," a military expert who attended the address told me afterward. "His basic argument was that Pakistan cannot afford a two-front situation. We're being squeezed by Afghanistan on our western border and India on our eastern one. Beg's argument was that we have got to defuse the Afghan situation rather than fuel it, so that we can better protect our eastern front." This was a view that a number of officers shared.

After the crash of Zia's plane, Mirza Aslam Beg was the only surviving member of Pakistan's High Command. In three major wars, the country had lost only one general. Now, two full generals, one lieutenant general, three major generals, and five brigadiers were dead. On the evening of August 17, 1988, General Beg succeeded Zia as Chief of the Army Staff, and thus became the most powerful man in Pakistan. Unlike his predecessors—and, indeed, most Pakistani generals—Beg was not a Punjabi or a Pathan, but a *mohajir*, as Pervez Musharraf was. Nor was he a product of the British Indian Army, as those predecessors were. He was in a sense, as one junior officer told me, the Pakistani Army's "first homegrown son." A softspoken man of fifty-seven, General Beg was a professional soldier but was not unsophisticated politically.

In November of 1971, Beg, who was a colonel at the time and stationed in what was then East Pakistan, submitted a report to his commanding officer, a general, on how badly the political situation had deteriorated there. The general rewrote the report. Colonel Beg protested and was disciplined by being immediately transferred out of East Pakistan. The transfer, ironically, may have saved him from becoming a prisoner of war. A few weeks later, the Indian Army moved into East Pakistan, and the third Indo-Pakistani war in twenty-three years began. In December, East Pakistan, backed by a victorious India, became the independent nation of Bangladesh.

Beg continued his military career, and, in March of 1987, as Vice-Chief of the Army Staff, he became Zia's deputy. Yet he never belonged to Zia's inner circle as other generals had. After the crash in which Zia ul-Haq died, some American officials expressed concern to me that if General Beg decided to seize power he could not be counted on to continue close military cooperation with the United States. I remarked to a Western diplomat in Islamabad at the time that General Beg had the reputation of being an apolitical soldier. He laughed and said, "If he was, he isn't now."

Beg moved deftly in the hours following Zia's death, and with the support of the Air Force and Navy chiefs, followed the constitution. He met with Ghulam Ishaq Khan, a seventy-three-year-old economist who, as the head of the Senate, was next in line to the presidency, and assured him of the Army's support. Later that evening, Khan was sworn in as Pakistan's president. Initially viewed as a transitional figurehead, he immediately pledged that the parliamentary elections that Zia had called would be held, as scheduled, on November 16.

Much of the power in the Pakistani Army rests with its nine corps commanders, and if any of them had thought about trying to seize power and fill the formidable vacuum left by Zia ul-Haq's death, such ambitions were thus checked, at least temporarily.

Like the other senior generals, Beg was aware that a growing number of field-grade officers disliked the Army's continuing political role—an attitude not shared by many of the generals. There had been so many intelligence reports about discontent in the field-grade ranks because officers wanted to return to soldiering and let the politicians do the governing, that in May, when Zia dismissed his civilian prime minister, he dispatched one of his generals to Army units around the country to pacify angry colonels and brigadiers. The general he sent to do the job was Aslam Beg.

Two weeks after Zia's death, I went to the Ministry of Defense to try to find out what might happen next in Pakistan. Politically, there were only two choices: elections or another coup. Would the generals permit Benazir Bhutto, the daughter and political heir of the executed Zulfikar Ali Bhutto, to come to power if she was elected? Many people in Pakistan were skeptical. The assumption was that Ms. Bhutto, the head of the Pakistan People's Party, who was regarded as the front-runner in the electoral race, would want to avenge the death of her father, whom Zia and his generals—despite international appeals for clemency—permitted to hang. The other key question following Zia's death was whether there would be a change in his high-risk policy toward Afghanistan—a change that could prove troublesome in Pakistan's relations with the United States.

The defense ministry, a sprawling complex of red-, pink-, and white-brick buildings, is in the old British cantonment of Rawalpindi, where spacious villas are protected by lofty brick walls. Sweeping, arched ceilings and sprawling verandas evoke memories of the Raj.

On the mantel of a fireplace in the office of the Minister of Defense, there were condolence cards. An oil painting of Zia, framed by a black border, hung on one of the walls.

Mahmood Haroon, the defense minister, had been in Zia's cabinets since 1978. A man in his late sixties, he was a veteran politician, a wealthy Karachi businessman, and an owner of *Dawn*, one of Pakistan's most respected English-language newspapers. Dressed in a light-blue *shalwar kameez*, the long shirt and bloused trousers that are Pakistan's national dress, topped by a black silk vest, he offered me sandwiches, cakes, and tea. A bearer, wearing a white waistcoat and a black wool Jinnah cap, the cap favored by Mohammed Ali Jinnah, the founder of Pakistan, served them.

I asked the minister about the likelihood of a coup.

"We have a well-disciplined Army, and it obeys the orders of the Chief of the Army Staff," he replied. "After the plane crash, before anything could happen, General Beg said, 'We will go according to the constitution,' and I haven't heard a peep from the Army since."

"Had ISI warned of an attempt on Zia's life, only days before the crash?"

The minister did not respond directly and merely remarked that assassination attempts against Zia were "nothing new." (Seven junior officers were then in prison, having been convicted in 1984 by a military court of such an attempt.)

When Haroon excused himself to take a telephone call, I reflected on how lax the security in the defense ministry was. My driver had dropped me at the wrong entrance, and I had wandered down long, empty, carpeted halls until I found a bearer who, in turn, escorted me to the private office of the defense minister.

When Haroon finished talking on the phone, he assured me that the elections would take place, but when I asked him how he would respond to the country's political leaders, who were urging the president to dismiss Zia's cabinet and appoint an all-party interim government to conduct the polls, to ensure that they were free and fair, he responded less as a politician than as one of Zia ul-Haq's heirs.

"I just cannot understand why they are now shouting for an interim government," he said, referring to the politicians. "When Parliament is dissolved in Britain, doesn't Mrs. Thatcher stay on? Did Ronald Reagan step down before your elections? What is the issue here? They are simply working up emotions. And have you ever seen the People's Party praise the Army, as it's doing now?" He refused to say whether Benazir Bhutto had any support within the Army, especially at the level of colonel and brigadier, but one of his aides told me later that she had "no discernible support."

Toward the end of our conversation, Haroon talked of Zulfikar Ali Bhutto and what he rather caustically called "his democracy," and then he talked of General Zia ul-Haq. "On Zia's death, I think a referendum was held," he said. "Five hundred thousand people attended his funeral, and they are continuing to visit his grave."

As I left Haroon's office, I was struck by the realization that the upcoming elections would, in a sense, be a contest fought from the grave—between Zulfikar Ali Bhutto and Mohammed Zia ul-Haq.

Sahabzada Yaqub Khan, Pakistan's then Minister of Foreign Affairs, who is a retired lieutenant general and a former ambassador to the United States, was highly respected both inside his country and by government leaders abroad. In contrast to the generals in ISI, who were solely responsible for operating the CIA arms pipeline to the mujahideen and for carrying out Zia's Afghan-jihad policy, Yaqub Khan was a thoughtful and cautious man, and was increasingly concerned about Pakistan's growing involvement in the Afghan war.

He worried that Zia's insistence that the mujahideen should push on to take major towns, with the help of ISI "advisers," would embroil Pakistan too deeply. It was also leading to growing accusations from Moscow—seventy-three in the previous six months—that Pakistan was violating the Geneva Accords, signed in April of 1988 by Pakistan and Afghanistan and guaranteed by the Soviet Union and the United States, which provided for the phased withdrawal of the 115,000 Soviet troops in Afghanistan—a withdrawal that had begun successfully in May of that year. But Moscow was now hinting that the withdrawal could be stopped and had issued increasingly strident warnings to Islamabad in recent months to stop allowing arms for the mujahideen to be moved through Pakistan and then across its border into Afghanistan. Pakistan's actions could "no longer be tolerated," the Kremlin had warned only days before Zia's death.

I called on Yaqub Khan late one afternoon shortly before he left for New York to attend the United Nations General Assembly and meet with Soviet foreign minister Eduard Shevardnadze and Khan's old friend George Shultz. A tall, erect patrician, who favors three-piece suits, Khan is a courtly insider, equally at home with Pakistan's zealous mullahs and with chiefs of state abroad.

He was particularly troubled that afternoon. Hours earlier, Soviet warplanes had dropped bombs twelve miles inside Pakistan. "Since 1980, there have been 2,363 air violations; ground violations by Soviet and Afghan troops have numbered 806." He paused for a moment and shook his head.

I asked him if he anticipated a change in U.S. policy toward Pakistan in the light of General Zia's death and the beginning of the withdrawal of Soviet forces from Afghanistan.

"I anticipate no change, and I certainly hope there will be none," he replied. "The withdrawal of Soviet forces"—leaving a large infrastructure behind—"will not materially affect the degree to which American national interests are involved. The Carter Administration is an example of how American errors in various hot spots of the world—Ethiopia, Angola, the Iranian hostage crisis, and Pakistan—

sent signals to Moscow about American resolve. These, taken together, created in the minds of Brezhnev and his advisers an impression of appeasement and weakness in the United States. The invasion of Afghanistan was one of the results."

As both ambassador to Washington and Minister of Foreign Affairs, Yaqub Khan had seen the highs and lows of Washington's often strained relationship with Islamabad.

He reminded me that in 1979, months after the Carter Administration cut off economic and military aid to Pakistan because of its nuclear program, the American embassy was burned to the ground by mobs. The demonstrators, angry over Washington's confrontation with Iran, attacked the embassy for seven hours, and Zia ul-Haq, whose Army was responsible for the embassy's protection, did little to disperse the crowds. Indeed, Zia had gone bicycling as the American embassy burned.

There had been considerable speculation since Zia's death that President Ghulam Ishaq Khan, an old associate of the foreign minister, might heed Yaqub Khan's concern over the implications of the ISI's strategy in Afghanistan and tighten the reins of the intelligence organization, so I asked the minister about this. Not surprisingly, at the time he refused to comment. Posing the question another way, I asked him if there would be any change in Afghan policy.

He said that no major changes were likely as a result of President Zia's death, but that, as the "situation has evolved," the seven-party alliance of Afghan resistance groups could begin moving toward an agreement with Kabul on a broad-based government of transition in Afghanistan.

Next, I called on Kamal Matinuddin, another retired general, who was the director general of the Institute of Strategic Studies in Islamabad. He articulated a widespread Pakistani fear: that when Afghanistan was "over," Washington would abandon Pakistan—which was then the world's fourth-largest recipient of American economic and military aid—in favor of Pakistan's giant neighbor and longtime adversary, India. "We are fighting this war for the United States, as much as we're fighting for Pakistan. And if Washington thinks the Soviet withdrawal from Afghanistan is the end of Soviet influence in the area, it is being very naïve," General Matinuddin said. "If we are abandoned, is that morally right? This war has created enormous problems for Pakistan. We are spending roughly a million dollars a day out of our own pocket looking after three million Afghan refugees. We have over five hundred thousand drug addicts—a spillover from the war—and daunting geopolitical problems. We can't protect the Afghan border; we can't see over the hills. Our relations with the Soviet Union are at their lowest ebb." He paused and then said, "Now, when the Americans think it is nearly over, we are seeing the first signs that the small irritants in our relations, like the nuclear issue and human rights, could come to the fore. How can America do this to a friend?"

Karachi, the capital of Sindh Province and the former capital of Pakistan, is the country's financial and political heart. A sprawling city of more than nine million set on the Arabian Sea, it leads a life of its own, frequently erupting into violence—often to the astonishment of the country's leaders in placid Islamabad. (On only one weekend when I was there, in the weeks after Zia's death, almost three hundred people were killed in ethnic violence in Karachi and in a massacre by unidentified gunmen in nearby Hyderabad.)

The only sustained rebellion against Zia's rule had also been here, during the summer of 1983, when thousands of demonstrators, in the interior of Sindh, defied the Army and for two months vented their frustration and anger over Zia's rule by demonstrating, attacking government property, and "courting arrest."

I remember what it had been like then.

They had come from across the province: young bearded students, carrying the Koran; feudal landlords, protected by phalanxes of heavily armed guards. Sardars, or traditional tribal chiefs, had also come; as had pirs and mirs, the hereditary religious leaders of volatile Sindh. It was a surprisingly strong rural mass movement—the first such political movement outside the cities that Pakistan had seen. I had spent a weekend here, in the interior, watching the demonstrators as they defied police lines and were beaten back, by lathi charges or tear gas. I watched as they burned government buildings, tore up railway lines, broke into Sindhi jails. And I also watched them as they "courted arrest."

"Please go home," a young police sergeant, armed with an old Lee-Enfield rifle, had pleaded with them one afternoon in the dusty courtyard of Dadu jail, set in the center of one of Sindh's most violent, upriver market towns. "I cannot arrest you! I simply have no more room!"

A friend and I were able to enter the overcrowded and extremely dirty jail only because of the total chaos that prevailed outside it. There we found seventy-seven political prisoners, most of whom were supporters of the Pakistan People's Party or of Sindhudesh, a small separatist organization that favored Sindhi independence and whose followers—not unlike most of the Pathans in the North-West Frontier—had never wanted to be part of Pakistan. They suggested that I meet their leader, G. M. Syed, the father of Sindhi nationalism and a hereditary pir. He had been under house arrest in his village for twenty years.

As we left Dadu and drove toward Syed's remote village of Sann, we passed through slate hills that turned to desert and scrub, then through tracts of land where fields of cotton, wheat, and rice had been flooded by the capricious monsoon. We traversed narrow village lanes crowded with horse-drawn carts. Army trucks, mounted with machine guns, often blocked our path. The soldiers in the trucks stared at the Sindhis in the lanes, and they stared back: fierce-looking men who carried daggers and wore embroidered skullcaps. Poverty visited us everywhere.

When we finally reached his stucco villa, we found the seventy-nine-year-old G. M. Syed, a small man with a large white beard, receiving a stream of guests. The temperature had soared to more than a hundred degrees, and Syed and his friends were huddled under straining ceiling fans. He was delighted, he told me before I could ask, that Indira Gandhi, the prime minister of India (who would be assassinated the following year), had given her tacit approval to the uprising here, and had called for the restoration of political rights in Pakistan.

"Why are the Sindhis so angry?" I asked.

"Because we are dominated by Zia's Punjabis," he said.

Zia never succeeded in breaking the hold of the tribal and feudal chieftains in Sindh, and they resented the fact that, ever since the creation of Pakistan, the government and the military had been dominated by those from the Punjab. Theirs was Pakistan's most populous province, its breadbasket, and it was set in a crucial spot: hugging the border with India.

Using his fingers, G. M. Syed ticked the figures off: only 2 percent of Pakistan's armed forces came from Sindh; only 5 percent of federal civil servants were from Sindh. Of two thousand industrial units now operating here, Sindhis controlled only five hundred of them. And of the province's total population, Sindhis represented only 45 percent—the rest were Punjabis, Baloch, or *mohajirs* who had migrated from India. In the capital, Karachi, the percentage was even less.

Now I had returned to Sindh to meet the daughter and the political heir of Zulfikar Ali Bhutto, Benazir, who lived in a spacious Karachi villa surrounded by twelve-foot-high walls. A simple brass marker at the entrance read ZULFIKAR ALI BHUTTO, BARRISTER AT LAW. Bhutto, who was Pakistan's foreign minister from 1963 to 1966, administrator during a period of martial law, president between December of 1971 and August of 1973, and prime minister beginning in August of 1973, was convicted of having conspired to assassinate a political enemy and was hanged in the courtyard of Rawalpindi's central jail on the morning of April 4, 1979. How people viewed the case depended on their position in the political spectrum.

Benazir Bhutto, who had been a student at Radcliffe and Oxford, was under house arrest at the time of her father's death; Zia made her a political prisoner for four years, under house detention or in jail. In December of 1987, she married Asif Ali Zardari, a wealthy Karachi businessman—a marriage that had been arranged by the two families. When Zia announced the date of the 1988 elections, Benazir was pregnant with her first child, and many people (most notably Zia) had assumed that she would not be able to campaign. But she gave birth to a son a month after Zia died and was back on the hustings not long after that—to the collective irritation of Zia's military establishment.

Before I called on Benazir Bhutto, many Pakistanis had told me that even though she had never run for office she would probably win the election—and she did, to become the first woman to govern Pakistan—if she could hold her party together. Doing so, however, was clearly not an easy task. Over the previous two years, she had tried to move the Pakistan People's Party toward the center, but many of her most active supporters were anti-Army, anti-business, and anti-American—opposed, in other words, to those very forces that she was trying to enlist.

A tall, vibrant woman of thirty-five, Benazir Bhutto received me in a small anteroom of the villa in which she had been detained off and on for nearly three years, until a group of American senators pressured Zia to release her in January of 1984. She then left for London, and returned to Pakistan in April of 1986.

Her father's legacy was a key component of Benazir's election campaign, for the November ballot would be the first party-based election in eighteen years, and Zulfikar Ali Bhutto had won the last. I asked her whether, in her view, the Army would permit her to come to power if she won.

"There has never been a conflict between the Army and the Pakistan People's Party," she had said then. "After the 1971 defeat"—when India defeated Pakistani forces and Bangladesh was born—"my father restored dignity and honor to the Army. During the time my father was in power, there was not one violation of Pakistan's airspace. Under Zia, Afghanistan was crossing our borders and violating our airspace nearly every day." Her eyes flashed as she went on. "In eleven years under Zia, we became a drug culture, a country where people were killed in the streets. Corruption reached a new high. And the Army saw this, too."

A bearer entered the drawing room with cans of Diet Coke balanced precariously on an antique silver tray. As we drank, Benazir expressed hope for improved relations with the United States. "The United States has traditionally been a friend of Pakistan and given us tremendous assistance," she said. "I would hope that the United States would continue its support, for the rebuilding and reconstruction of Pakistan. Our infrastructure deteriorated badly during Zia's years, and Washington can help us to rebuild. I would hope for a relationship based on mutual strength. During Zia's dictatorship, the United States did not put enough stress on those things for which it stands—things I saw and learned about during my Radcliffe days: human rights, clamping down on drugs. The Americans must also understand our nuclear program. I hope these doubts"—about the nuclear program—"will be cleared up."

Benazir Bhutto had often been compared to Corazon Aquino, the dynastic successor to her husband in the Philippines, but Benazir acknowledged that the comparison was not correct. Mrs. Aquino had come to power with the support of the Army, the business community, and the Catholic church. For Benazir, the daunting triumvirate of the generals, the multimillionaire industrialists, and the mullahs still had to be won.

As a result, part of her election strategy was to challenge Zia's interpretation of Islam. "Zia's Islamization was a hoax," she said. "And his dictatorship was contrary to the Koran. The Koran says there should be government by consensus—*ijma*. The very notion of military dictatorship is contrary to the Koran."

She ensconced herself more comfortably on the sofa, and then she said that her optimism about the future was such that it even extended to Pakistan's relations with India. "I'm sometimes told that I'm being naïve—that the Indo-Pakistani rivalry is as old as our country," she said. "Still, there's no reason that relations can't be improved." She then spoke of India's prime minister, Rajiv Gandhi, who had, dynastically, succeeded his assassinated mother four years earlier. "Rajiv Gandhi is young—part of the post-Partition generation, as I am," she pointed out. "So perhaps we are freer of the prejudices and the bitterness of that time. Look at the European Community. France and Germany had age-old rivalries, but slowly they've come to terms with each other. Why can't we?"

Peshawar—the winter residence of Afghan kings until the early nineteenth century—has been a battleground for imperial armies and tribal warlords for centuries. When the Soviet Union invaded Afghanistan, it was transformed into the key staging area for the jihad. It had previously been visited only by drug dealers and spies, but during the jihad it had burgeoned. Now there were gunrunners, smugglers, freedom fighters, and war victims—and drug dealers and spies.

Before the Soviets arrived in Afghanistan, Peshawar had been home to some 750,000. Now there were thousands more mujahideen, hundreds of Western aid workers, and over two million Afghan refugees. Its densely packed mud houses, pastel villas, and streets crowded with four-wheel-drive vehicles and donkey carts also became temporary home to the thousands of Afghan Arabs who fought in the jihad. It was easy to find them during the 1980s, when I first covered the war, in the posh neighborhood of University Town, or in a string of hostels along one of the city's main thoroughfares, University Road.

For this was not only the capital of the North-West Frontier, it was also the capital in exile of the anti-Soviet Afghans. I discovered on a recent visit that, twenty years later, it still is.

Looking back on those early war years now, it struck me that the mujahideen were never really an army but, rather, a mosaic of fifteen hundred separate "fronts," based on tribal or ethnic or linguistic membership. They sometimes came together to resist the Soviets, but rarely to initiate combat. Warlords led them, more often than not, and they recognized allegiance to no one but their tribal chiefs. Thus it was that when they transported CIA weapons out of Pakistan to their base, they were far more likely to be attacked by a rival than by the enemy. As a result, at least 30 percent—perhaps as high as 50 percent—of the U.S. arms never reached the battlefields of Afghanistan. They were siphoned off, either by the ISI, the political leaders in Peshawar, individual commanders, or by a combination of the three.

Nevertheless, as the jihad progressed, ever-more sophisticated weapons were dispatched to Pakistan. In 1986, the United States sent its first consignment of Stinger antiaircraft missiles, and the British, at the same time and at the urging of the United States, sent their own ground-to-air missile, the Blowpipe. But according to an article in the September 1987 issue of *Armed Forces Journal International*, of the 1,150 Stingers and Blowpipes sent to Pakistan, between September of 1986 and August of 1987, only 863 actually reached commanders inside Afghanistan.

Over the years, things became progressively worse. Some five hundred Stingers had gone "missing" by the end of the war.

The CIA had attempted to buy them back, Lieutenant General Hamid Gul, a former director of the ISI, and one of its most influential figures during the jihad, told me one morning in 1996 over coffee in Islamabad. It was a joint endeavor with the ISI called Operation Trojan Horse, but it was rather muddled and highly flawed, he said. "The CIA told us we could pay $100,000 each, and $75 million was set aside. It was ridiculous from its inception: you don't bargain for Stingers *below* the going black market rate!" The ISI and the CIA were consistently outbid, and some of the missiles—which are capable of destroying aircraft at a range of three miles—were purchased by the revolutionary government in Iran; others appeared on display in the tiny emirate of Qatar in a military parade. At least two of the Stingers were bought by Islamic fighters in Tajikistan, and another two were purchased by a militant separatist group in the Philippines called Abu Sayyaf, a group that grew out of the CIA's jihad.

Now I had retraced my steps, returning to Peshawar, in order to get a sense of how the death of Zia had been received in what, for all intents and purposes, had become a salient of Afghanistan.

In May of 1988, five months before I arrived, a dozen or so majors from the ISI had been arrested for selling the mujahideen's military supplies. And a month before that, twelve thousand tons of CIA weapons had been blown up. It had happened on the morning of April 10, with a massive explosion at the Ojhri army camp. Set in a densely populated, thin greenbelt connecting Rawalpindi and Islamabad, the camp was a key installation of the ISI. As panicked civilians ran for cover, thousands of mortars, ground-to-ground missiles, and antitank rockets ignited and rained from the sky. They fell for more than an hour: into school playgrounds, into cinemas and banks, and into embassy compounds in Islamabad six miles away.

More than a hundred people died, and more than a thousand were injured that day. And although Zia's government was quick to blame KHAD, a commission of inquiry would later also fault two of Zia's generals from the ISI—the agency's former director, General Akhtar Abdul Rehman, who died aboard Zia's plane, and his deputy, then Major General Hamid Gul, who had replaced him that March—for having stored weapons in a civilian neighborhood. The Ojhri camp, on the day that it imploded, had held more than 75 percent of recently arrived CIA arms, which had been flown in on a massive scale as a last-minute attempt to reinforce the mujahideen before the Soviets, on May 15, began withdrawing from Afghanistan. The mujahideen were furious.

The Central Alliance—the seven major resistance groups based in Pakistan that, together with four others based in Iran, were fighting the Soviet forces in Afghanistan—had its headquarters in the center of Peshawar, in a four-story, dun-colored building that seemed about to collapse. When I arrived late one morning, I found it bursting with at least a thousand Afghans, who overloaded its balconies or spilled out into its halls. There were laughing children, occasionally leapfrogging with goats or sheep; a sprinkling of women, eyes darting from behind black veils that covered their faces. Steely-eyed men in billowing trousers, some just back from the war, argued, gesticulated, and prayed in corners—or shot a rifle skyward, presumably to make certain that it worked.

The preferred nomenclature of U.S. officials, at the time of the jihad, loosely divided the resistance forces into two groups: the "fundamentalists" and the "moderates." Few of us who covered the war were at all certain who the "moderates" were. All seven of the groups were a cantankerous and deadly lot, who had quarreled with each other for years. In some cases, they had killed each other on Afghanistan's battlefields. Nevertheless, they were still, in a manner of speaking, coordinating the ISI, CIA-financed jihad of the 1980s in Afghanistan.

From the beginning of the war, Zia had been emphatic that he favored the most fundamentalist of the groups, the Hizb-i-Islami, led by the ruthless Gulbadin Hekmatyar, for Hekmatyar not only protected Pakistan from the resurrection of the call for Pashtunistan but was also the preferred candidate of the Jamaat-e-Islami, one of Pakistan's most fundamentalist political parties—and the only one that had given Zia a political constituency. It was imperative that Pakistan win this war, Zia admonished his generals. As a result, the policy of "strategic depth" was launched: the policy meant to secure a friendly northern and western border as a bulwark against India—in effect, to create a client state, which, if war broke out between Pakistan and India again, the generals in Islamabad could use as a military hinterland. The ISI, which had helped to fashion "strategic depth," was, of course, convinced and, as a result, it gave priority to Hekmatyar's needs and, according to Western officials, turned over roughly 50 percent of the CIA supplies to him.

A former engineering student who had been in Pakistan since the early 1970s, having arrived as part of the guerrilla army that Zulfikar Ali Bhutto would raise, Hekmatyar was a stocky man of forty-one, with a black beard and black eyes, and he had been a source of controversy over the years: neither Washington nor Pakistani officials were certain of how much strength he actually had inside Afghanistan. What everyone did know, however, was that Hekmatyar counted as his friends the Egyptian cleric Sheikh Omar Abdel-Rahman, the most extreme leaders of Pakistan's religious right, generals from the ISI, and many Saudi officials and financiers who passed in and out of Peshawar during the war years—including Osama bin Laden. Because of Hekmatyar's Islamic militancy and anti-Western views, John Schulz, the Voice of America correspondent in Islamabad, told me, "Gulbadin personifies a thirteenth-century vision of Islam. He gives the Moghul Empire"—India's great Muslim dynasty—"no credit for anything, except introducing dancing girls and diaphanous skirts."

In late 1986, I had asked U.S. Congressman Charles Wilson, one of the most enthusiastic supporters of the jihad on Capitol Hill, why the anti-American Hekmatyar was getting the largest share of the CIA's arms.

"Personally, I think Gulbadin's a pain in the ass, and that's on the record," he had said. "But he's a strong leader who inspires his people to fight. I've had these fundamentalists tell me to my face that they're not going to give the Americans credit for giving them the arms. But they're killing Russians, and that's in everyone's interest, ours and theirs. We had fifty-eight thousand dead in Vietnam and we owe the Russians one. I'll begin to feel a little better when there are sixty thousand funerals in Moscow and Leningrad."

I went in search of Gulbadin at his private villa, hidden behind towering, beige-colored walls. The street was heavily guarded, and sentries stood at the gate. After a good deal of conversation, I was finally ushered into the house, only to be told by one of Hekmatyar's aides that he was "inside"—meaning inside Afghanistan, a place into which he had not ventured for at least a year. (I discovered later that that day had not been an exception to the rule. Gulbadin was, in fact, at the Sukhrob refugee camp, attempting to disrupt a meeting of the mujahideen's "moderates.")

When I finally met him a few days later, he proved to be as disagreeable as he had always been. First he insisted that I sit on the floor at his feet; then he insisted that I wear a veil. I accepted the former but refused the latter, reminding him that he was neither a cleric nor a priest. It was only after one of his advisers remarked that he had seen me earlier, interviewing Zia ul-Haq, that Hekmatyar relented. I was offered a chair.

He basically said little during the hour I was there, lurching from one rhetorical outburst to the next. He had the reputation of being charismatic, a religious populist, in a sense.

He would continue fighting, he told me that afternoon, and he would never accept a coalition government in Kabul.

"But what will you do for arms?" I asked. "The CIA is about to close its weapons pipeline down."

Hekmatyar peered at me from behind his glasses, and then he smiled.

He went on to tell me that he would "liberate Afghanistan, at all costs," and establish a fundamentalist, theocratic government.

We said our good-byes, and as I stood to leave, he told me to sit down. Then he said that he had a message for the West: "Once Afghanistan is liberated, the war will go on until the Muslim republics of the Soviet Union are liberated as well."

As I left Hekmatyar's villa and waited outside for my car, I remembered something that a Pakistani professor had told me a few days earlier. "Theocracy is at the heart of the mujahideen's ideology," he had said. "But it is totally alien to Afghanistan. Afghans fight because they have always opposed foreign domination. But nationalism has always been their driving force. What Zia has done has been to transform an essentially nationalist struggle into a holy war."

As we made our way through Peshawar's cacophonous streets on that autumn afternoon in 1988, I had no way of knowing that in the years to come the same lethal formula would be applied by Pakistan but, this time, 175 miles away in the disputed state of Kashmir.

On the eve of the Soviet departure from Afghanistan, new splits were appearing within the Afghan resistance groups. Not only was there antagonism between the moderates and the fundamentalists—and, because of his fanaticism and attempts to dominate the jihad, an almost universal antagonism toward Hekmatyar—but some of the best and most successful commanders in the field were now acting independently of their political leaders in Peshawar, many of whom had not entered Afghanistan since the war began. Their most distinguished member was Ahmed Shah Massoud, known as the Lion of Panjshir. He would ultimately capture Kabul in April of 1992, three years after the Soviets withdrew. Not a shot was fired. No one was more stunned than the ISI, for after its long years of support of Hekmatyar, it was denied the final prize of the jihad.

There was also a growing belief among the field commanders, including Massoud, that the seven Peshawar-based leaders had made money out of the war. One ranking Pakistani government official had said to me, "If and when the mujahideen can form a government in Afghanistan, I will be surprised if these seven Peshawar leaders, without proper escort, can reach Kabul alive."

The Afghan Information Center was a required stop for foreign journalists covering Peshawar during the years of the jihad. It was independent of the seven mujahideen groups and had been founded by Sayd Baha'uddin Majrooh, an erudite former dean of the philosophy department of Kabul University. In February of 1988, Sayd Majrooh was killed. He left his bungalow early one evening and, outside, assailants shot him at point-blank range. The assailants could have come from KHAD or, according to Western diplomats, from Gulbadin Hekmatyar.

Sayd's son, Naim, an engineer with a pleasantly boyish face, who greeted me warmly when I arrived, now directed the office. Following an exchange of pleasantries, he introduced me to two field commanders, who had just arrived from the eastern Afghan city of Jalalabad, not far from the site where the CIA had recently completed the construction of an elaborate network of caves. They were in a place called Tora Bora, and one of the commanders, a man named Ahmed, said that he was superstitious about them. *Tora Bora*, in Pashtu, meant "Black Widow," he explained. "No good will come of those caves." He then went on to tell me that the tension in

Afghanistan between the field commanders and the ISI had reached a high point, sharpened by Zia's insistence that the mujahideen give priority to capturing a major town—preferably Jalalabad—as a base for a government in exile.

"We simply don't want set-piece battles," Ahmed said. "Nearly all of us favor a slow erosion of Soviet defenses. We just are not *capable* of taking major towns. We've tried repeatedly, without success. We've had the same experience we had in Kunduz: we captured it; Soviet and Afghan aircraft, as a result, retaliated and bombed it heavily. Then the civilians asked the mujahideen to leave."

Four months earlier, in May of 1988, there had been a showdown between the field commanders and Gulbadin's supporters along with the ISI. Forty-two commanders, led by Abdul Haq, the powerful commander of Kabul, had simply refused to try to seize Jalalabad. "This was sheer stupidity," Abdul Haq told me afterward. He was clearly angry about the ISI's increasing determination to hijack the jihad. "Are we expected to take massive casualties? To be so exhausted that we are unable to capture Kabul? Kabul should be our first set-piece battle. We're not interested in talking provincial capitals and killing ourselves."

Zia had been furious, a Western diplomat said to me. He had been determined to seize Jalalabad by June 1 in order to give it to Congressman Charles Wilson for his birthday.

Leaving Naim's office, I traveled down a dusty path that followed a stream to the headquarters of the Jamiat-e-Islami, another of the fundamentalist groups, which had some of the best commanders inside Afghanistan—including Ahmed Shah Massoud. The leader of the Jamiat was Burhanuddin Rabbani, a Tajik scholar who in 1993 would become, in a manner of speaking, Afghanistan's president. In the years that followed he would head the Northern Alliance, the opposition force that battled the Taliban and then, with American military support, became Afghanistan's interim government at the end of 2001. Outside his office, a poster advised: "In our point of view, conquerist America and bloodthirsty USSR are both enemies of the great revolution of Iran and Afghanistan." Rabbani, nevertheless, expressed the hope to me that, with Zia's death, the distribution of arms among the guerilla forces would become more equitable. He then dashed off, depositing me in the office of Masood Khalili, Jamiat's political officer, who is now Afghanistan's ambassador to India. I asked Khalili if the mujahideen were now willing to share power with Najibullah and accept a broad-based government in Kabul.

His answer was blunt: "With traitors there will be no compromise." Khalili then predicted that "within four months of a full Soviet withdrawal, the present Kabul government will collapse"—a claim that Western officials and the government of Pakistan viewed with skepticism, even then.

A handsome man with a black beard, Khalili wore a U.S. Army combat jacket over his *shalwar kameez*. Outside his office, children played on the banks of a canal. In the distance, a muezzin chanted from the minaret of a mosque.

I asked Khalili about reports that the mujahideen were still fighting each other inside Afghanistan.

"In one or two places," he replied. "I don't remember where."

"What effect will the death of Zia have on the war?"

"His death was extremely tragic for everyone," Khalili said. "For Zia, Afghanistan was a crusade. He was a friend right from the beginning—a bridge between the Western world and Afghanistan. But we could have fought the war without him, and we'll do so now. It would have been very, very difficult if Zia had been killed six years ago. But now the mujahideen are far better equipped and trained, our morale is much higher, and our casualties are much lower. I see no changes in the war's course."

I asked if he thought that Zia had been killed by KHAD.

"I don't think KHAD is that effective," Khalili said. "The only one that comes to mind is the KGB itself. It could have hired someone locally. I also can't rule out the Pakistani Army. It's large and diverse. Without Zia, there's got to be a power struggle going on in the Army now. Out of the chaos, a revision of policy toward Afghanistan could come."

That revision never came and, over the next thirteen years—whether under Pakistani dictator or democrat—ISI's influence continued to expand, as did its involvement inside Afghanistan. "It is imperative that Pakistan have a friendly government in Kabul," Zia ul-Haq had told me shortly before he died. And that day finally came in September of 1996, when the Taliban, which had grown out of the chaos left by the CIA's jihad, swept into Kabul and declared it theirs. But by then, as General Matinuddin had predicted in 1988, the United States government had walked away.

CHAPTER 3

IN THE TRIBAL LANDS:

BALOCHISTAN

TWELVE YEARS PASSED before the United States returned to Pakistan, which was again transformed into a key staging area for America's newest Afghanistan war. And if Pakistan thus became one of the most strategically sensitive countries in the world, one of its most strategic parts—as it had been during the years that the British and Russian Empires clashed in the first "Great Game" in Afghanistan—was Balochistan. By the autumn of 2001, it was in the eye of the storm once more.

Vast, underpopulated, inaccessible, and remote, its ordered chaos is presided over by seventeen major tribes, led by irascible chiefs—none of whom are particularly fond of the United States. Yet three of the four Pakistani air bases that General Musharraf ceded to Washington that fall are located here—in Pasni, Shamsi, and Dalbandin—much to the collective irritation of the tribal chiefs. Thus, as American warplanes roared over their deserts and mountains and plateaus en route to Afghanistan, a major component of the bombing there to break the terrorist network of Osama bin Laden, the tribal leaders were opening their arms to hundreds, if not thousands, of bin Laden's al-Qaeda fighters and members of the Taliban. One Pakistani official told me that by March of 2002 five thousand or more had slipped into Pakistan—some through the North-West Frontier Province's tribal lands, but most through Balochistan.

They crossed the border at Chaman or Zhob, or through the district of Chagai, traversing mountains that soared to 15,000 feet, then traveled along little-known tribal trails, some of which were merely rutted donkey paths. Despite the deployment of thousands of Pakistani troops in the hidden valleys and atop the mountain peaks, only three hundred or so al-Qaeda fighters were intercepted as they crossed. They now comprised nearly half of the detainees being held at the U.S. naval base in Guantanamo Bay, Cuba. These early successes, however, included none of the top leaders of al-Qaeda. And so, as the months went on, the Afghan Arabs and the Taliban continued to come to Pakistan, which was already home to some of the most militant, and lethal, armies of the Islamic world.

Things used to be different in Balochistan, whose tribal lands had been among the most secular parts of Pakistan. That is, until the jihad in Afghanistan began. One of my most vivid memories from Balochistan dates back to 1983, when the entire staff of the ISI headquartered there was removed for trafficking in drugs and CIA arms, which were meant for the mujahideen. Under the ISI's watchful eye, the mullahs and the maulanas and the religious parties of Balochistan flourished during the war years, and more than seven thousand madrasahs quickly sprang up. Many of their graduates would later become both leaders and foot soldiers of the Taliban. Now, in a sense, they had begun returning home. By the late spring of 2002, there was growing concern in Washington that al-Qaeda and the Taliban were regrouping in the contiguous tribal areas of the North-West Frontier Province and Balochistan. And there were fears, too, that these tribal lands, stretching for 1,400 miles along the frontier, could become the world's next Afghanistan.

The accused was a small man for a Bugti. He was barely five feet six inches tall, and appeared even smaller because of the massive turban on his head—fifteen yards of muslin spun round and round, a characteristic of Baloch tribesmen. Swathed in long, flowing pantaloons and robes, the cloth is meant to keep them as cool as possible in temperatures as high as 130 degrees.

In 1890, Sir Edward Oliver, a British colonial officer who had served in Balochistan, described the Baloch tribesman as "essentially a nomad—good looking, frank, with well-cut features, black and well-oiled flowing hair and beard, attired in a smock frock, that is theoretically white, but never is washed save on the rare occasions when he goes to durbar." He went on to say, "The Bilochi is a general favourite. He is a bit of a buck, and when he finds himself passing into the sere and yellow, dyes his hair. It is not uncommon to find an old gentleman with eyebrows of deep black, and the tip of his beard gradually shading off through purple to red, to the roots of pure white." On a visit to the southwestern province in 1989, I discovered that little had changed, with the possible exception that some Baloch now trim their hair.

Akram Bugti, the man accused of murder, certainly didn't trim his, and it appeared that he rarely washed it. He could have been fifty or seventy. He stood in a tight circle of relatives, watching an old man struggle to open the gates of the walled village of Dera Bugti, which is the headquarters of the Bugti tribe, the second largest of Balochistan's major tribes. The gates were opened at dawn, as they have been for centuries, revealing a dun-colored village of low mud houses surrounded by towering mud walls. The landscape was parched and dusty. Every man was armed. The few women in evidence were shrouded in burkas, covered from head to toe. At the village mosque, a mullah chanted from the minaret. Mullahs seemed to be everywhere in Balochistan.

Akram Bugti walked slowly toward a trench in a nearby field. He had been accused of murdering a cousin in a land dispute. He had protested that he was innocent—he might have wanted to murder his cousin, but he had not. So he had decided to "walk the fire," a tribal ritual that has been practiced for hundreds, perhaps thousands, of years. If Akram walked the fire and wasn't burned, his accuser would have to pay him compensation, including the cost of firewood, and could never accuse him of this crime again. There is no appeal or recourse under tribal law, and 95 percent of Balochistan still observes tribal law. I found the figure extraordinary, but a patient government official explained that Balochistan's powerful tribal chieftains simply had never accepted any other law.

Final preparations were being made at the trench. In accordance with tribal practice, it was two feet wide, one and a half feet deep, and seven paces long. (Seven, I was told, is an auspicious number for anyone who walks on live coals.) Akram's brothers had filled the trench with wood from the *khaur* tree—only this wood would do—it burns fiercely and is quickly reduced to coals. Tribesmen, using the ends of their turbans to protect their faces from the heat, began pounding and splitting the red-hot coals. They were tall, sturdy men. Some wore intricately hand-embroidered vests; nearly all had AK-47s slung across their shoulders.

There was a stir as the figure of Akbar Khan Bugti came into view. He was an imposing man, with an imposing title: Nawab-Sardar of the Bugti tribe. He had been installed as the Bugtis' tribal chieftain by the British during the days of the Empire and had ruled the Bugtis for nearly fifty years. Tribesmen rushed toward him to touch his knees or his feet, and he clearly relished the attention. He was not a modest man. Draped in layers of clothing topped by a vibrantly colored shawl, he settled himself cross-legged on a woven mat and with a sweep of one large hand said, "Let us begin."

Akram Bugti climbed onto a stone at the east end of the trench. His feet were washed, and examined by the judges—elders of the tribe—for scars, blisters, or burns. A mullah was then given seven green leaves from a peer tree and a copy of the Koran. Three times he circled the trench, reciting the *drohi*, or oath to the fire: "O fire, in the name of God, the Holy Book, and the Saints, Akram Bugti, son of Tariq, being examined for the crime of murder, if he is truly guilty, may he be burned. If he is innocent, may the coals be as cold as ice." He dropped the peer leaves one by one on the coals, to test the heat of the fire. Two goats were slaughtered nearby, and as the blood flowed, Akram lowered himself into the trench. He walked deliberately, looking straight ahead. The heat was so intense that Akbar Khan Bugti, perhaps fifteen feet away, found it necessary to shield his face. The walk seemed to take forever, but it must have been less than a minute before Akram climbed out of the trench. His feet were washed, immersed in the goats' blood, and then examined again by the elders. There were no blisters or burns.

Celebratory shots rang out from the AK-47s as Akram collected ten thousand rupees (about $500) from his accuser as compensation for the false murder charge. His honor restored, he reminded his accuser that he must also pay him for the cost of the wood.

Balochistan is a brooding and melancholy place. Its martial people fought the British to a standstill during the days of the Raj; Kipling wrote here; and Field Marshal Bernard Law Montgomery taught at the Staff College in Quetta for three years, beginning in 1934. Most of the province was normally off-limits to foreigners, but I finally received permission to tour it, along with a security guard.

In Quetta, the provincial capital, a 340-mile drive from Dera Bugti, I asked the nawab of the Bugti about tribal law.

"Well, fifteen days ago, in the village of Usta Mohammed, a chap was getting married," he said. "It was, of course, an arranged marriage. The bride and groom would not lay eyes on each other until her veil was lifted on their wedding day. But the day before the wedding the girl's brother became suspicious that the two had had relations, and he killed them both. *Siahkari*, 'black work'—adultery. The brother will not be judged. Under tribal law, when a man kills for passion or honor there is no punishment. The killing is justified."

I had been told that no lawyers are permitted in the Bugti tribal lands. The nawab himself presides over many of the cases. His judgment is final.

"Killing for honor is not murder," he went on. "Of course, there are cases of common murder, where blood money and compensation must be paid. Adultery, without exception, is punishable by death."

We were sitting in his receiving room. I was the only woman permitted in the room, where sardars, mirs, hajis, and maliks, a few smugglers, and a man who had recently killed his wife sat cross-legged on a magnificent Bukhara rug or lounged against pillows piled against the walls. The nawab used to serve vintage Russian vodka, but for health and political reasons he now served only 7UP.

I returned to the unfortunate couple in Usta Mohammed, and asked what the grounds for suspecting adultery were. What would happen if it had been merely suspicion?

"Well, that may be looked into," the nawab replied. "If any question arises, the parents of the boy who popped off the adulterers will have to find witnesses to support his case. But that's highly unlikely. Indeed, he will be lauded for what he did."

The others nodded agreement. Outside the door, standing at attention, were heavily armed guards. A diminutive servant in an embroidered prayer cap entered, carrying a cistern of water and a bar of Lux soap. He moved from guest to guest as we washed our hands. Two towels hung over his arm—one was for the nawab, the other for the rest of us. The servant went out and returned juggling platters of food: the traditional *sajji*, or roast lamb; curries and rice; vegetables heaped with chilies. Then he brought platters of hot nan bread.

The dinner conversation moved quickly, from Benazir Bhutto, who had recently been sworn in as prime minister, to the price of AK-47s or Kalashnikovs; from Yeats and Wordsworth to Ayatollah Khomeini and the ongoing Afghanistan war.

I asked the nawab why Akram Bugti hadn't been burned when he walked the fire.

"According to Saadi, 'You grow old and learn you are still a student, at birth and at death.' I can't explain it," said the British-educated nawab of the Bugti tribe.

Akbar Khan Bugti is an Anglophile. His grandfather Shahbaz was knighted by the British in the nineteenth century. His father, Mehrab, who had prospered under the Raj, died when Akbar was twelve, and the boy became a ward of the British Crown. He had a German surrogate mother, who recited nursery rhymes and taught him table manners. On instructions from the governor-general, he was sent to Aitchison College in Lahore, where Oxford-equivalent degrees were offered to the sons of the princely rulers of British India. It was a privileged life of indulgence, and the young Akbar embraced all that was fashionable at the time—cricket, Fabian Socialism, and tea sandwiches with the crusts cut off.

Then there was a revolt in Dera Bugti. Determined tribesmen refused to acknowledge the regent and demanded that Akbar return. At the age of nineteen, in the presence of the British political agent, he was installed as Nawab-Sardar of the Bugti tribe. In 1947, he ceded his tribal fiefdom to the new state of Pakistan, but only reluctantly. Since then, he had been in and out of favor, in and out of government, in and out of jail. He had been charged, exonerated, then charged again, with murder, insurrection, treason, and various misdemeanors. He had served as a minister in the central government of Pakistan and as governor of Balochistan. Now, he was the province's chief minister—its highest elected official—and one of its most powerful men.

I had first met the nawab in the parking lot of a Karachi hospital in the summer of 1983, when Sindh Province—on Balochistan's eastern border—was in revolt. I had asked him then if Balochistan would join the protest.

"How can we protest by demonstrating?" was his rather tart reply. "We're too few people in too vast a land. When the Baloch protest, we take up our arms, go to the mountains, and fight."

Indeed, Balochistan has been fighting for centuries. When the Baloch tribesmen have not been fighting each other, or fighting the heat or the land, they have fought the Arabs, the Turks, the Tatars, the Persians, the Hindus, and the British. Most recently, they have fought the far superior Army of Pakistan. Yet they have never been fully conquered or subdued—not by the armies of Genghis Khan, Lord Curzon, or Pakistan. Four times since Pakistan's creation, the Baloch, who—like many Sindhis and Pathans—never wanted to be part of Pakistan, have rebelled, demanding greater autonomy, or even an independent state, which would reunite the five million Baloch in Pakistan, Iran, and Afghanistan under one flag. With 147,000 square miles, Balochistan has nearly half the landmass of Pakistan. Were it anywhere else, it probably wouldn't warrant much attention at all, but it sits astride the oil lanes of the Persian Gulf. Squeezed into the triangle where Pakistan, Iran, and Afghanistan meet, it is geopolitically and strategically the most important part of Pakistan. It commands nearly all of the country's coast—470 miles of the Arabian Sea. On the west, it borders Iran, and, after Peshawar, its northern border was the key staging area for the jihad. It is a land that is ruled so autocratically by its nawabs that, in the words of the historian Charles Chenevix Trench, "an oath of innocence taken with one's hand on the Nawab's head was always accepted." Historically, it has twice been a loose tribal confederacy—and then four princely states—loyal, at various times, to the Persian emperor and the Afghan kings.

But for all the conquerors who passed through it, none left relics or landmarks of empire except the British, and, in a sense, Balochistan is still a relic of the British Raj. In the nineteenth century, the British needed to control it if Afghanistan was to remain a buffer between British India and the armies of the czar, for one of the major routes to Afghanistan lay through Balochistan. The British spent more than forty years trying to subdue its tribes and, in the end, declared a truce. The terms were quite generous, and in 1876 the British entered into an unusual arrangement with the nawabs (the rulers of the larger tribes and of the princely states) and the sardars (who ruled the smaller tribes). In exchange for stationing troops at critical points—which meant, in effect, along the Afghan border and along the roads and rail lines leading to it—they made treaties, backed by handsome subsidies, which gave the tribes autonomy as long as they behaved. The British settled into a military cantonment in Quetta and circuit houses near the frontier, but they administered nothing else in Balochistan. The nawabs and sardars, now supported by the empire and with their powers considerably reinforced, had total jurisdiction over their lands.

Then came Partition in 1947, when British India was cleaved in half, at the insistence of a group of Muslim intellectuals—living largely not in what would become Pakistan but in the cosmopolitan centers of Bombay and New Delhi—who demanded a separate Muslim homeland. They were led by the secular and erudite Mohammed Ali Jinnah—a barrister who smoked cigarettes, wore hand-tailored suits and spats, and married a Parsi, a non-Muslim. Known as the Quaid-i-Azam, or "Father of the Nation," Jinnah had been agitating for nearly ten years to take his co-religionists out of Hindu-dominated India. What he was awarded by the Raj, however, was, geographically, an artificial state—from 1947 until 1971 its eastern and western parts were separated by more than a thousand miles of India. Another set of lines was drawn upon the map by another set of Englishmen. There was immediate chaos in Balochistan.

The nawabs and sardars insisted on their right to independence; the British refused. Ultimately, the tribal chiefs succumbed to blandishments, bribes, or threats, and, with the exception of the Khan of Kalat, yielded their princely states and tribal kingdoms to the new state of Pakistan. The khan, to the annoyance of the British and the bewilderment of Pakistan, declared independence. It lasted only eight months. The Pakistani Army moved in and crushed the insurrection, and the Baloch were transformed. Born warriors, they became nationalists, and they have never fully forgiven Pakistan.

Wherever I went—and I traveled more than 1,500 miles, sometimes in jeeps, once in a Mercedes, and twice in armored cars—I was told stories, by angry students and by angrier nawabs and sardars, of the three rebellions that followed, especially the last, which was also the most violent, when Benazir Bhutto's father ruled Pakistan. From 1973 to 1977, the elder Bhutto not only unleashed the Army in force but bombed and strafed the Baloch at random—with U.S.-manufactured Chinook and Huey Cobra helicopter gunships, some of them on loan, along with pilots, from the Shah of Iran. Thousands died—according to most estimates, 3,300 Pakistani soldiers and over six thousand Baloch. Nearly everyone in Balochistan, whose population is only four and a half million, was in some way affected by this little-known war. The defeated guerrillas, who had been armed only with bolt-action rifles and homemade grenades, retreated to the mountains, or to Moscow or Afghanistan.

Quetta has the reputation of being a rather dreary place, and it was with some apprehension that I checked into the Serena Hotel. It had opened only a few months earlier and was owned by the Aga Khan. I was pleasantly surprised to find such a symbol of contradiction in this ramshackle frontier town. The hotel was stylishly decorated and had a telex and twenty telephone lines. Its bookshop featured titles by Richard Nixon and Che Guevara, and there were recent issues of *The Economist*, *Vogue*, and *Vanity Fair*. In the coffee shop, flushed men in business suits, wearing ill-fitting toupees, talked in whispers to a heavily bearded group of Afghan mujahideen. Outside, an old man struggled to load wood onto a donkey cart, and the visiting Sri Lankan cricket team was doing calisthenics in the hotel parking lot. Behind the Sri Lankans, a handwritten sign warned PARK YOUR CAR AT YOUR OWN RISK. Shortly after my arrival, the American ambassador checked in. He was followed by the Soviet ambassador, and then the Chinese Vice-Minister of Geology. Officers of the Saudi Arabian Air Force checked in and out. Quetta was decidedly not a dreary place.

Camels and pony-drawn carts, Japanese motorbikes, jeeps, and scooters clogged its streets. A traffic policeman dressed in the traditional Raj uniform of blue beret, blue sweater, and smart white belt stood all day on his elevated perch, blowing his whistle and waving his arms about. I tried to imagine the tiny outpost that the British had transformed into this Victorian sector of cricket fields, sprawling bungalows, and street lanterns that once burned coconut oil. Quetta was, after Aldershot, the largest garrison-station in the empire, and there was also the Staff College—one of only two in the entire empire.

From their cantonment, the British drew another sweeping line across the map. This side of the line, they said, would be British territory, and the laws of the Raj would apply. That side would be tribal territory, and the nawabs and sardars would rule. This curious land apportionment was inherited by Pakistan, and, to this day, it survives exactly as it was then. I had been told that things were changing, and that I was probably seeing the last of the "real nawabs." (Only seven nawabs were left today, and some twenty sardars.) In addition to dispensing justice and administering tribal law, the tribal chiefs raised private armies and channeled much of Balochistan's development aid. If a nawab or a sardar disagreed with a government project on his land, he simply blocked the roads or sent out snipers and didn't permit outsiders in.

One morning I roamed through the narrow lanes of Quetta's smugglers' bazaar, where if you had enough money and the proper contacts you could find anything. Scores of tiny stalls hugged each other under a corrugated-tin roof. The faces of the merchants were friendly, but weathered and tough. Some of the men wore the traditional Baloch turban; others, with falconlike faces and less elaborate turbans, were Pathans from the north.

Piled high on shelves or neatly arranged along the lanes of the bazaar were American cigarettes for $4.00 a carton; Soviet refrigerators; Black & White Scotch; designer jeans from Hong Kong; and Cuisinarts and tape recorders from the Persian Gulf. I was told that I could also buy antitank rockets and launchers, AK-47s, light cannon, land mines, and grenades—all "slippage" from the CIA's arms pipeline to the mujahideen. For these, however, I was told that I must drive to the nearest Afghan refugee camp, just outside town. It was only the middlemen who sat in the Quetta bazaar. Some of the arms were being sold to Balochistan's nawabs and sardars. What was already most worrisome to Washington, however, was the significant number of sophisticated Stinger missiles that had been lost.

One night over dinner, I asked the nawab what the Iranian consulate—one of only two foreign diplomatic missions in Balochistan—was doing here.

"Buying Stingers," he answered matter-of-factly. He then told me that it was in Quetta in June of 1987 that the mujahideen had sold their first large consignment of Stingers to Iran. After days of protracted negotiations between two mujahideen commanders and four Iranian Revolutionary Guards, the two commanders, mullahs from the Khash Rud area of western Afghanistan, agreed to sell sixteen Stingers from their stock of thirty-two, and received a million dollars. "They were also told they'd be remembered in Heaven," the nawab said. Although he is a Muslim, he can be rather casual about Islam.

The Iranians had long considered Quetta a key diplomatic post for monitoring insurgency along the Iranian-Balochistan border by secessionists from Iran's own population of a million or so Baloch. With the jihad in Afghanistan, the Iranian diplomatic presence in Quetta grew, and, by 1989, Teheran was widely believed not only to be courting maverick commanders of the mujahideen but also to be funding a militant new force of pro-Iranian Shiites who had recently entered Balochistan's turbulent political scene. Over recent years, the Shiites (largely ethnic Hazaras, originally from Afghanistan), led by Iranian Revolutionary Guards, had killed opponents of Ayatollah Khomeini who had fled to Balochistan, and had carried out attacks against Sunni Muslim Afghan refugee camps.

And even though the Soviets had withdrawn from Afghanistan by now, the war—along with the Iranian attacks—continued in ever-more lethal form, now fought between the Soviet surrogate government of Najibullah and the increasingly fractious mujahideen. It had always seemed ironic, at least to me, that it was here, on the Afghan border, less than two hundred miles from the Iranian frontier, that the CIA had embarked on one of its most clandestine projects during the jihad. By the winter of 1984–85, everyone knew, of course, that perhaps as much as 50 percent of the agency's arms had gone missing during the early years of the war. So it was decided, as an experiment, to circumvent Zia and the ISI and to dispatch a test shipment directly to a commander inside. That commander was the Lion of Panjshir, Ahmed Shah Massoud.

The shipment was delivered near a gloomy border town, a place called Chagai in the middle of nowhere that had been inhabited by only the heartiest of smugglers for hundreds of years. Buttes and sand dunes abounded. So did vipers and snakes. Quite by accident, my husband (the South Asian bureau chief of *Time* magazine) and I happened to be in Chagai on that particular night.

We were having dinner, at what was politely called the "government guesthouse," when our driver pounded on the door. "Something is happening in the desert," was all that he said. We jumped into his car and drove down a narrow, pitted road, whose only distinguishing characteristic was a string of telephone poles looming from desert scrub. As my eyes adjusted to the darkness, the twinkling lights of Chagai now out of sight, a brightly painted lorry with tinsel and pop art decorating its doors overtook us and careered along. It halted silently a few yards ahead. Twenty or so men, dressed in huge floppy turbans and the bloused pantaloons of the Tajik tribe, appeared suddenly from the sand dunes, tall, silent men, who took possession of the sensitive cache: recoilless rifles, grenades, and mines. We learned later that the shipment had crossed three continents in eighteen days. It had originated in West Virginia, was flown to West Germany, where the American markings were removed, and then repacked, concealed in ten steel containers that bore the labels of electronic equipment, fertilizers, and television sets. It was next sent to a CIA airfield in the Persian Gulf Sultanate of Oman, and finally shipped across the narrow straits to Balochistan's Makran coast.

The maze that the arms pipeline traveled was said to be run almost exclusively by a hard core of a hundred Afghan exiles, trained by the CIA, who operated through shipping companies, travel agencies, and Islamic organizations in the Middle East and the Persian Gulf. One was a former Manhattan taxi driver; another, a millworker from Ohio; still another, a judo instructor from the Southwest.

As we (along with fifty or so villagers who, like us, were concealed by the sand dunes) looked on, Massoud's lieutenants gently transferred the containers into a commandeered Soviet Army truck. They then shared a cup of tea with the lorry driver, and they were off. *"Allahu akbar!"*—"God is most great!"—were their parting words. Then under the cover of darkness, they rattled off toward the rugged mountains and, beyond them, Kabul.

I couldn't help but remember that evening, a year or so afterward, when I was in Peshawar having tea with Abdul Haq, the irascible Kabul commander of the mujahideen. The CIA delivery we had witnessed in Chagai appeared to have been a success. Yet, as we chatted now, Abdul Haq's story was less sanguine, more apocalyptic. He had received two cases of SAM-7 missiles that spring, and went on to say: "This was something we had never seen. But how to work them?" He explained that concealed in the wrapping was a neatly printed instruction manual. It was written in Chinese! "We expended five missiles before we got the hang of it," he went on. "A 60 percent loss before we even got the bloody missiles out of our camp!"

As I traveled through Balochistan now, I thought of Abdul Haq and also of that night in Chagai so many years ago. No, I decided Chagai was definitely not a place that one revisited. I remembered, in particular, the vipers and snakes. In the years to come, however, my resolve would yield, most dramatically in 1998. For it was in the western desert of Chagai district that Pakistan exploded its first nuclear device.

Khan Dawood Jan Beglar Begi is an immense man with a close-cropped beard, who looks somewhat Levantine. As the Beglar

Begi—or sardar of sardars, king of kings—he was at the top of the structure of nawabs and sardars. He thus presided over the grand jirgas, or councils of chiefs, which settled tribal wars and disputes between the often unruly nawabs and sardars. He was also the ruler of the former princely state of Kalat. He and his wife, Jamila, had invited me to the Kalat palace for two days. The town of Kalat is only a two-hour drive from Quetta, but it is a journey backward in time. The rooms of the palace are filled with regimental silver, rusted muskets, and Kashan rugs. Paintings and faded photographs speak of the glamour and power of the nearly three centuries (beginning in 1666) when much of Balochistan was ruled by Kalat.

The khan, dressed in a white *shalwar kameez* topped by a black silk waistcoat, rushed into the drawing room, his hands outstretched. Though he was of sizable girth, he never seemed to walk; every time I saw him, he was rushing about. A jolly man in his mid-fifties, he seemed to love to talk.

"You know, Balochistan has always been a buffer, a bridge," he told me before I could ask. "To understand the future, you must see the past. Before the British, and well before anyone even thought of creating Afghanistan, this was an independent area. My point is, if Afghanistan is now independent, why isn't Balochistan? We were not in the Stone Age when the British arrived. We had two Houses of Parliament, our own constitution . . . I still get furious." He picked up a pack of Marlboros and began to chain-smoke. "We've had successive rebellions to gain our rights," he said. "On October 6, 1958, the Pakistani Army raided this very house. There were twelve thousand soldiers fanning out all over Kalat. Twelve thousand soldiers, can you imagine? They took away my father and installed me as khan. There were many more Army operations—and then you ask us why we are anti-Pakistan."

Jamila urged him to keep calm. She is a striking, outspoken woman, who brought all the palace women out of purdah when she married the Khan. Theirs was not an arranged marriage, which is almost unheard of here. But the khans have traditionally married into the royal family of Afghanistan, to which Jamila belongs, so the match was considered acceptable.

An old servant entered, pushing a silver trolley piled high with tea sandwiches, dried fruit, cakes, and, since I was an American, a tin of Nescafé. He wore white gloves and a green waistcoat with a tiny Kalat coat of arms, and on his head was a cockade turban. He told me that he had served the palace for fifty-six years.

"First the British, then the Pakistanis, now the Americans," the khan went on. He began gesticulating vehemently. The United States, concerned that the Soviet Union might attempt to further destabilize Pakistan by supporting another Baloch revolt—either to retaliate against U.S. funding of the mujahideen or to extend its own influence south from Afghanistan, through Balochistan, to the Arabian Sea—had recently begun trying to woo the Baloch tribes, with over $200 million in development aid.

"The U.S. government is always looking for a diversionary way of coming in," the khan said. "In Balochistan, we are allergic to the United States. We are against you. You never try to understand us. You always try to be a nanny, or come marching in with a big stick."

The howling of dogs and the chanting of mullahs woke me at dawn; tangerine skins that Jamila's maid had put on top of a wood stove in my room scented the air. Kalat is 6,800 feet above sea level, and it was cold. The Khans chose this as the seat of their kingdom—which was spread over 134,000 square miles—because it straddles the mountain area of Sarawan in the north and the searing deserts of Jhalawan to the south. Temperatures in Balochistan soar in the summer and in the winter plunge in some areas to below freezing. Only three to twelve inches of rain falls yearly, and it usually falls all at once.

I could hear the palace coming awake outside my room. I knew that the khan and Jamila would already be up, saying their prayers. In

Kalat and the northern Pathan areas, people take their religion much more seriously than in other parts of Balochistan. People always seemed to be saying prayers.

After breakfast, the old servant, Syed Bahar Shah, walked me through the palace, which has forty rooms. He took me first to the fourth story, where the khan's father had weighed Mohammed Ali Jinnah in gold. The money was for the creation of the new nation of Pakistan, which the khan's father had supported.

"I did the weighing," Bahar told me. "It was a glorious day. Mr. Jinnah weighed exactly ninety pounds, and he got his weight in gold. Then I weighed his sister, Fatima, and His Highness presented her with a chain that was worth $1 million at that time. It was gold, with diamonds, emeralds, and rubies."

We walked on. "Here is where His Highness raised the flag of independence in August 1947," Bahar explained, pointing to the highest minaret on the mosque. He went on telling me of Kalat's glittering past through its furniture, photographs, and rugs. Then came the abrupt interruption of the present: unmistakable pockmarks of bombings in the palace courtyard, broken benches, scattered rubble. The khan keeps the courtyard this way as a reminder that Baloch nationalism had its origins in Kalat.

Later in the day, Jamila and I got into a Pajero—a Mitsubishi jeep, which was the new status symbol of Balochistan's elite—and drove around Kalat, visiting some of her projects, which include health programs, cottage industries, and a school. She introduced me to Zuleah, a short woman with a ring stud in her nose. Zuleah had been accused of adultery and sentenced to death under tribal law. Jamila was outraged—she knew from her maids that the woman was innocent, that her husband simply wanted her out of the way—so she had confronted the sardar of Zuleah's tribe. It was a bold and unusual step. "Women have no rights here whatsoever," she told me. "I had a terrible time getting this woman out"—and, later, two others. "I was able to do it only because I am the wife of the khan." She went on, "The khan has been very liberal with me, allowing me to meet men. My mother-in-law had to do even her shopping inside the house."

Jamila moved among the women with grace and ease. They kissed her hand, then placed it to their eyes. It was part of the khanate's code of honor; they would, if necessary, give her their most precious possession—their eyes. "If only I could do more," she said. "But we just can't do anything for our women unless the men agree. First I have to talk to their husbands and fathers, then to their nawabs and sardars. We're living in the jet age. Why won't the sardars let their women out?" She told me that during the November 1988 elections she had campaigned among Kalat's women for two of her brothers-in-law. Both were defeated by mullahs. I was surprised to learn that Balochistan was the only place in Pakistan where the electoral strength of the mullahs had grown.

We returned to the palace, so that I could say good-bye to the khan.

"We have a saying here: 'A Baloch child may be born without socks on his feet, but when he grows, every step he takes is on gold,'" he told me. "We have vast amounts of minerals, copper, marble, uranium, gas, and oil. One day we'll be prosperous, and that's the day that we'll be listened to by the world."

I asked him if he thought there would be another insurrection in Balochistan.

"We don't know what's going to come, but we can judge from our past," he replied. "No one is going to give us anything on a plate. We will have to fight for it. The Baloch have always gotten things for themselves."

I asked if that was why everyone was so heavily armed.

"Good gracious." He chuckled. "How can we not be armed? There are so many American weapons just floating about. A Stinger costs only twenty lakh rupees"—about $100,000 then—"though the Iranians are paying more. A Redeye missile costs the equivalent of only $35,000. A SAM-7 is about the same. Antitank rocket launchers, at $1,250, are very reduced these days."

I was driven back to Quetta in one of the khan's bulletproof cars, through mountains that dropped to desert and then onto a plateau. Balochistan has a fortresslike feeling about it, or so it seemed to me, as though the Baloch would go to any lengths to shut out the rest of the world. When they leave their deserts and mountains, they say they are going to "Hindustan." For most people Hindustan means India. For the Baloch it also means anyplace else in Pakistan. Unlike the rest of the country, Balochistan had only thirty-one people per square mile. (Its people were outnumbered by sheep and goats three to one.) Now every fifth person was an Afghan refugee, and the Baloch were bitter that they were losing their identity.

I had insisted to the nawab that I wanted to see Balochistan, and finally he arranged for me to travel from Quetta to the Arabian Sea with Mir Humayun Khan Marri, his son-in-law. Humayun was also the nephew, and possible political heir, of Khair Bux Marri, the powerful Nawab of the Marri tribe, who had lived in Afghanistan under various Communist regimes since shortly after the last insurgency. Humayun was Balochistan's Minister of Communications and Works. He had been the finance minister, holding the most important portfolio in the provincial government, but the nawab, perhaps with more force than tact, had snatched that ministry away and given it to a mullah whose only formal education was in a Koranic school. Otherwise, the mullahs had threatened to leave his government and form a coalition with Benazir Bhutto, and that would have sent the nawab into the political wilderness again.

Humayun, a shortish, bearded man in his late thirties, was an economist and engineer, and had spent time in Colorado and Arizona on an AID grant. The purpose of the trip, he told me, was to inspect road-building projects, bridges, and schools. Two engineers from his ministry—along with his bodyguard and his secretary— were also making the trip.

As we left Quetta, Humayun pointed out an old signpost beside the road. It had an arrow pointing west and bold white lettering that read LONDON, 9,470 KM. We traveled straight down the center of Balochistan to the Arabian Sea. We went from the Pathan areas through the lands of the Baloch and those of the Brahuis (whose language derives from Dravidian), and we ended among the Makranis, some of whose ancestors were brought to Balochistan from Africa during the Middle Ages as slaves. We traveled nearly a thousand miles, during the last part retracing the route of Alexander the Great, zigzagging between the desert and the sea. There was no coastal road in Alexander's time, and there was none now.

Speeding along the national highway, we passed nomadic tribesmen migrating to lusher lands—a long camel train of herds, bedding, and children. The Baloch, too, have always disdained the artificial lines of the British mapmakers, who literally quartered their tribal nation in the nineteenth century. Today the tribesmen come and go as they always have, migrating between their traditional homelands in Pakistan, southern Afghanistan, and the eastern fringes of Iran.

As we went south, the temperature rose. Customs officials with M-16 rifles searched a brightly painted truck—filled, I guessed, with electronic items smuggled via Iran from the Persian Gulf. A hunched old man pulled a hand plow across a parched field. A smuggler roared by him—at least, Humayun said he was a smuggler—in an air-conditioned Mercedes-Benz. Students were plastering anti-American slogans on baked-mud walls.

I asked Humayun why the Baloch had such bitter feelings about Pakistan.

"Just look at the figures," he said. "They speak for themselves." As he pulled a raft of documents out of an attaché case, I thought of what G. M. Syed, the Sindhi leader, had told me during the 1983 revolt. There were scarcely any Baloch in the Pakistani Army, civil service, or diplomatic corps. Of a total of fourteen provincial government secretaries in Quetta, only four were Baloch; of a total of 3,200 students at Balochistan University, fewer than five hundred were Baloch; of a total of 180 faculty members, only thirty were Baloch. Balochistan's coal was sent to the Punjab, so the Baloch had to burn wood trucked in from Sindh. Its onyx and marble were shipped to Karachi for finishing, and its natural gas was piped to industrial belts in the Punjab and Sindh, returning in cylinders to Balochistan. The largest gas fields in Asia were then in Sui, on Nawab Bugti's tribal lands, and although he denies that he receives more than a "stipend" in royalties, many people told me that he had become a millionaire. (In 1983, after threatening the Pakistani government for nearly thirty years, he finally succeeded in getting a pipeline that connected Quetta—but no other major towns—to the southeastern Sui fields.)

"So, you see," Humayun went on, "we're being exploited and neglected. We're bitter, we're angry, we're armed."

We began to climb through lofty passes of the Brahui mountains, between peaks covered with mist. In the midst of the rock-strewn mountains, there was a burst of unexpected color—the white, pink, and lavender blossoms of apricot and almond trees. I watched a herd of sheep grazing under a radar device. A sign announced that we were passing through a PROHIBITED AREA—a surveillance center, Humayun said. Military aircraft flew in formation overhead. We were now on the road to Iran. More than thirty thousand troops were garrisoned in Balochistan's major towns. It seemed to me that they were watching Afghanistan and Iran, but the Baloch insisted, twelve years after their last rebellion was suppressed, that the Pakistani Army was still watching them.

"You know, we have the area, the resources, the strategic points, and the coast," Humayun said. "If you think about it, we *are* Pakistan."

A solitary figure sat on a craggy rock, playing a *nar* flute as he watched his flock. Ahead, a large group of tribesmen waited along the desolate road. We were about to have our first *hal*, or exchange of news, as integral a part of tribal life as respect and honor. We were just outside the town of Zawa, the home of the Zehri tribe, the largest tribe in the southern desert of Jhalawan, and the bloodiest, Humayun said. I glanced ahead at their walled compound ringed by rifle sights. I had met their previous sardar, a hunchback named

Doda Khan, in Quetta some years earlier. He had explained to me that he hadn't always been a hunchback, but that his uncles, to deprive him of the sardarship, threw him out the window of a moving train. He was fortunate, he had told me; he had survived and become sardar. He had two wives, who had given him a number of sons, but he totally distrusted all of them except Rasool Bux, who was to be his heir, and so Doda Khan had the rest of them locked away in jail.

"Poor Doda Khan, poor Rasool Bux," one of the tribal elders now said to me. "When Doda Khan died, all of his sons were let out of jail, and Sanaullah"—a brash young man, who was a member of the provincial assembly—"and his three brothers murdered Rasool Bux. Sanaullah thus became our new sardar." (During Pakistan's elections the previous year, Sanaullah's campaign slogan was that he had already killed fifty-six men and wouldn't mind killing others if they didn't vote for him.)

The Zehris wanted to exchange gossip and news: How was the nawab balancing his fragile coalition government of mullahs who were loyal to Libya and Iran, and energetic students who were loyal to Marx? Would the Khan of Kalat call a grand jirga to dispense punishment for the murder of Rasool Bux? What was the news of the Afghanistan war? Most important, though, the Zehris wanted jobs. Humayun's ministry was the largest in Balochistan and employed some twelve thousand workers; a laborer could make a thousand rupees ($50) a month—three times what most of the Zehris were making now.

Early that evening as I sat on the terrace of the Las Bela Circuit House, a Victorian structure with wide verandas and spacious lawns, a group of students joined me and began to talk. In Balochistan's tribal society, which lacks a significant middle class, the students and former students filled the vacuum and were a strong political force. Since Washington had an enormous stake in Pakistan, I asked the students what they thought of the United States. They didn't like it much at all, they said. The conversation jumped from Angola and Central America to Afghanistan and Vietnam. They might have been able to overlook those excesses, they said, if they had been able to study in the United States, but they hadn't even been able to do that.

"All the American scholarships are based on patronage, and whom you know," a medical student named Halim said. Consequently, most students went to the Soviet Union, or to Czechoslovakia or East Berlin. Every year since the late 1960s, Halim went on, a hundred or so Baloch had gone to Moscow's Patrice Lumumba University. Some came back to Balochistan, but they usually couldn't get jobs. Others now went to Kabul to join Khair Bux Marri or the Baloch Liberation Movement or the Baloch People's Liberation Front.

The students suggested that we go into town. Town was really little more than a few dusty streets leading to an elaborately inlaid arabesque mosque. Outside tea stalls, men sat cross-legged on rope charpoys, smoking opium pipes. A line of silent women walked home from the well, balancing earthen jugs of water on their heads. The students talked of Marx as the mullahs chanted evening prayers. (The students said they didn't like the mullahs any better than they liked the United States.) As we walked, Balochistan struck me as a contradiction once again. There were no roads, but for only $10 you could buy a bottle of forbidden Black & White Scotch; there were no schools—illiteracy here was 95 percent—but everyone seemed to have a radio, and in the most isolated villages tribesmen were agile in discussing world affairs. Undeveloped Balochistan certainly was; backward it certainly was not.

We stopped to watch camels being auctioned under a cluster of palms. "Camels!" A young economist named Tariq was clearly outraged. "We still ride camels in the twentieth century. The world totally ignores Balochistan. We need electricity, water, hospitals, roads, and schools."

"What we need is a revolution," said his friend Ayub.

The students argued a bit, then explained to me that the Baloch

Students Organization (which was funded by the Soviets) had recently split. The more conservative Marxists supported the nawab; the more radical supported Khair Bux Marri and the Baloch who were now organizing, just across the border, in Kabul and Kandahar.

Mir Ghaus Bux Bizenjo was one of four great names in Baloch politics, the others being Khair Bux Marri; Nawab Bugti; and Ataullah Mengal, the Sardar of the Mengal tribe. Unlike the others, however, Bizenjo was neither a nawab nor a sardar; he had the birthright but had chosen politics instead. Until his death in the summer of 1989, he was the undisputed elder statesman of Balochistan. His village of Nal, where we met, was close to Mengal's home village of Wadh; both were walled compounds in the heart of Jhalawan.

In his youth, Bizenjo had been a firebrand orator and the most articulate proponent of an independent Balochistan. He was a courtly man with a handlebar mustache and a mane of white hair. I asked him what he and his nationalist party wanted now.

"Pure and simple," he replied. "Greater autonomy within Pakistan. Why can we not have the right to keep our traditions, history, language, and culture alive? All we're demanding is what you have in America—it's called states' rights. We have been demanding this for forty years, but in Islamabad it falls on deaf ears." He hesitated. "That's what I want, in any case," he went on. "But the students, the young people, they're frustrated and angry, and have become increasingly vocal of late. They say, 'We have no future in Pakistan.'" He paused for a moment, then he smiled. "They're becoming rather like I was then."

Bizenjo remained a 1930s-style Communist—a legacy of his student days at Aligarh University, which was known as the Cambridge of the East. He was also an internationalist and a securalist. In his Nal study, images of the Buddha and Zoroaster shared equal space with Marx, Lenin, and Ho Chi Minh. His library was said to be one of the finest in Pakistan. He had been Balochistan's governor in 1972 and 1973, when Khair Bux Marri led the National Awami Party and

Ataullah Mengal was chief minister. Theirs was the first popularly elected government that Balochistan had ever had.

I asked Bizenjo how long he thought the nawabs and sardars could survive. He himself had often said they were an anachronism in the twentieth century.

"For better or worse, as long as we're a tribal society they have to exist," he said. "They're the final arbiters, the executive authorities of the tribes; they safeguard the tribes' interests. You can't legislate them out of being, as Bhutto tried to do. You've got to change the system. Otherwise there will be chaos, and our entire social organization will break down."

Balochistan had always been one of the most secular parts of Pakistan, or so it seemed to me. So I asked Bizenjo why, in his view, the mullahs had made such surprising electoral gains.

He said that they had been funded, and their campaigns run, by the ISI. "The mullahs are not nationalists or anti-imperialists," he said with a loud laugh, taking a pinch of snuff from a small leather pouch.

Before I left, he expressed concern to me over the continuing American and Pakistani sponsorship of the mujahideen, warning that "You are playing with fire. The Afghan civil war is already spilling across our borders, and could become a regional war. It could also bring the pro-Kabul Baloch insurgents out of the hills."

Turbat is a sprawling town of whitewashed adobe houses, a hundred thousand people, and a booming black market economy. It was also home to the man known as Ramzi Ahmed Yousef, who organized the 1993 bombing of the World Trade Center in New York. (Yousef's fellow assassin, Mir Aimal Kansi, who opened fire outside the headquarters of the CIA, was also from Balochistan, though he lived in the north, dividing his time between Quetta and the Pathan border belt.) Turbat, in addition, was the administrative center of the Makran coast. After three days, we had finally reached Pakistan's geopolitical heart. Makran's harbors—Pasni, Gwadar, Sonmiani, and Ormara—are considered among the best of the Arabian Sea's natural warm-water ports, and Makran also shares a land border with Iran.

We were picked up at the guesthouse in Turbat one morning by two silent, handsome men with strong, chiseled faces and jet-black beards. They wore Baloch turbans and carried Kalashnikovs. I told Humayun that I couldn't bear to look at one more bridge or road. He smiled sympathetically and told me we were taking the morning off. We could now concentrate on his uncle and were going to have breakfast with the Marri tribe.

Like the Nawab Bugti, Khair Bux Marri had been installed by the British as nawab of his tribe. He, too, had been sent to Aitchison College and had been a ward of the British Crown. But he had not embraced all that was British, as the Nawab Bugti had done. During his days at Aitchison, I'd been told, Khair Bux prided himself primarily on his dress. He favored Savile Row jackets and Gucci shoes, loved flashy sunglasses and even flashier cars. His one dream during that time, Humayun said, was to go to Hollywood and meet Errol Flynn. Indeed, it appeared that everything he did—the way he clipped his mustache, the way he combed his hair, his speech, his mannerisms—was an expression of loyalty to the Errol Flynn mystique. Then in 1958 the Pakistani Army crushed Balochistan's second revolt, and Khair Bux, a budding politician, became a Marxist. He was a powerful speaker with a lively intellect, I'd been told, and was largely responsible for the sweeping victory of the nationalists in the December 1970 poll. The government that came to power then didn't last long, however—only nine months—and its abrupt dismissal by Zulfikar Ali Bhutto was what provoked the 1973–77 insurgency. Now Khair Bux was in Kabul, with a well-trained, well-armed guerilla force of at least five thousand men. His choices could well determine the future course of Balochistan.

We left the road and traveled along a sandy tract. A volley of shots rang down from a sand dune. It was the traditional Marri welcome, and we were now inside their camp. The men embraced Humayun, nodded somewhat hesitantly at me, and then led us to a thatched *joug* hut. It reminded me of an old-fashioned bandstand, with open sides and thick bamboo columns supporting a conical roof. Its sandy floor was covered with carpets, and pillows of gay colors were neatly arranged. Before we entered, we removed our shoes. Above the seat of honor, at the head of the *joug*, was a large tinted photograph of the old guerrilla fighter "General" Sher Mohammed Marri, who now led a group of Baloch insurgents based in southern Afghanistan, only twenty-three miles from the border of Balochistan. Next to it was a photograph of Khair Bux. His face was strong and sympathetic, though he did not smile. I was told to take the seat of honor, and a shy little boy brought me a glass of water, an apple, cigarettes, and a box of matches. The apple was Iranian, the cigarettes were British, and the matches Soviet. Then the *hal* began.

As Humayun inspected a new delivery of American rifles—Winchesters, I was told—I looked around at the nomadic encampment of some thirty families. They had traveled on foot for more than a thousand miles from the northern Marri area to the Arabian Sea. Tents of black goatskin blended with other *jougs*. Everything was shaded by groves of palms. Beyond us, a fire was being laid in a pit dug in the sand, and men with rifles over their shoulders began preparing food and large cisterns of thick, pungent tea. They scooped dough out of elaborately painted earthenware bowls, wrapped it around stones, and laid the stones on the coals; then they put other stones on top of them, to make the traditional Baloch bread. I saw flashes of embroidery and vivid colors inside the huts and tents, and I knew that women were watching, but I would probably not meet them. I never did.

Humayun asked me if I wanted to listen to Baloch music. I expected a bard; instead, one of the Marris brought a four-speaker Sony tape recorder into the *joug*. It was in an exquisite hand-embroidered case, with golden tassels and tiny mirror inserts. A large man with a red mustache and a long white beard explained, "Our poets no longer sing of roses but of cries for justice and revenge."

The tape began playing. The shrill, haunting *nar* flute accompanied the storyteller's rhythmical chants:

> *I sing of the mountains which are our natural forts . . .*
> *I sing of the red rose which is the color of our blood . . .*
> *May Allah curse the Pakistani government and martial law . . .*

Three generations of Marris sat cross-legged on the floor. Some had fought the British; some had been jailed and tortured during Zulfikar Ali Bhutto's time; some were waiting to hear from Khair Bux Marri, to see what would happen next. I asked them to tell me about their nawab, and the fierce-looking faces finally beamed with smiles.

First they told me about his grandfather Khair Bux the Great, who had led resistance against the British at the turn of the century, and then about his father, Meherullah Khan, who had also been in the forefront of anti-British activity. The Marris, who control 3,400 square miles of land and are Balochistan's largest tribe (they number about 134,000), also consider themselves Balochistan's master race.

The tribesmen were joined by a civil engineer. He had gotten his master's degree at the University of the Punjab, but, as a Marri, he had returned to work in Balochistan. A tribesman interrupted to tell me about his grandmother, who had fought on a battlefield. "She fought like a general," he said proudly. It had been a tribal war to avenge the death of her son.

Scores of children sat quietly outside the hut, listening intently to the stories.

A large man with a stern mouth partly hidden by a beard leaned over and told me to eat. The breakfast was enormous: grilled lamb and chicken, more Iranian apples, sweet cakes and bread—all cooked over charcoal in a pit dug in the sand.

Most of the tribesmen hadn't seen Khair Bux Marri in years, but that appeared merely to fuel the legend. He had been imprisoned after the insurgency was put down, and following his release had gone to London and into exile. In 1981, he moved to Kabul, where large numbers of Marri guerrillas were already being trained by the Soviet-supported regime. Since then, thousands of other Marris had moved to Afghanistan.

One man remarked, as he filled his pipe with tobacco from a bright embroidered pouch, "Just last year, when Khair Bux issued a call for the tribe to join him, some fifteen thousand tribesmen responded, selling their belongings and herds, and crossing the border." The Balochistan government had found it impossible to stop the exodus.

I asked him if he would still take an oath of innocence by placing his hand on Khair Bux's head.

He seemed somewhat startled. "Of course, why not?" he said.

"What do the Marris want?" I asked, glancing around the *joug*. Independence? Greater autonomy? A unification of the Baloch tribal lands?

There was only a temporary hesitation. Then one young man said, "Whatever our nawab tells us."

In Turbat, young men from the Baloch Students Organization, the BSO, told me how wonderful the Afghan Communist "revolution" had been. Old mullahs told me how wonderful the Iranian Islamist revolution had been. Provincial government officials (mostly Punjabis, I learned) told me they found absolutely nothing wonderful about being posted to Balochistan's hinterland. Over 50 percent of Balochistan's annual budget of $325 million went for public services and salaries of civil servants, I'd learned. Most of these civil servants, of course, were comfortably in Quetta, not here in the hinterland. Less than $75 million went for development. I had learned that the literacy rate of women in the interior was only 1 or 2 percent, and that the murder rate, on average, was one or two a day. I had watched Balochistan's main forms of entertainment, cricket and cockfights, in dusty towns; watched men congregate in the tea shops, to chew or drink a powerful concoction of hashish and marijuana known as *bung*. I had also seen towering volcanic mountains and tranquil desert oases, with herds grazing under palms. Turbat means "grave." Makran's second city, Panjgur, means "five graves."

Makran, which is spread over thirty thousand square miles, is Balochistan's second-largest division and has less than sixty miles of metalled roads. They had meant to build roads, provincial officials told us, but one problem was superseded by the next. Much of the money had gone into contractors' pockets, and, once that was sorted out, angry tribesmen, or angrier students, had blocked construction sites, throwing rocks at the work crews who were courageous enough to arrive. As far as I could figure out, the students and tribesmen considered road building part of a "plot" by the Pakistani Army and the Americans to take over the Makran coast. The Americans may say that they came here to improve irrigation systems and build bridges and roads, but the Baloch were convinced that they were building bases and landing strips.

One afternoon, we went out to an AID project—road building, again—and were told by the supervising engineer, Mike Marra, an American, that the project, part of a $107 million U.S. effort to develop the Makran region, was "a total mess." It was one of AID's largest road projects in Pakistan, but he couldn't get the materials he needed from the Pakistani contractor—whose company was owned by relatives of President Ghulam Ishaq Khan—and 60 percent of the time had elapsed with only 6 percent of the work done. It didn't help that his engineers had to be escorted by armed guards. When the project began in 1987, students had pelted the engineers with rocks. "I've never seen anything like this place," he said. He seemed about to weep when he told us that he had been here for eighteen months; his replacement had arrived the week before but had had a heart attack his first day on the job.

Next, we went to an American bridge-building project over the Kech River, which regularly floods during the rains, often claiming scores of lives. This project seemed to be going well, but Naim Baloch, a BSO leader, took me aside and told me to look around.

"See the way they tie their turbans," he said, pointing to the labor-ers scurrying about the site. "Ninety-nine percent of them are Afghan refugees. The Americans have never trusted the Baloch."

When I asked an American why Afghans had been hired, he told me that they worked more cheaply and that the Baloch wouldn't do manual jobs. I thought of the Zehri tribesmen we had met along the road.

Makran is different from the rest of Balochistan. Nearly 95 per-cent of its people—who number about 650,000—live on less than 5 percent of the land rather than in isolated tribal pockets, as many of the Baloch do. The area prides itself on its level of education (though even among men the literacy rate is only 12 percent), and, to all intents and purposes, there is no tribal hierarchy here. The sea has meant openness—conquerors have come in, and Makranis have gone out. The principal port, Gwadar, once belonged to Oman. It was given to the Sultan of Oman by the Khan of Kalat in the eigh-teenth century and was sold back to Pakistan for about $10 million in 1958. The sales agreement gave the Sultan recruiting rights, and large numbers of Makranis serve in Oman's Army and Navy. Those from Gwadar retain dual nationality with Oman, and each year thousands of other Makranis continue to go and work in the Gulf. For those who remain behind, the mainstay of the economy is smuggling, and Makran was emerging as an important transit center for Afghanistan's heroin trade.

One morning, I went to Turbat Hospital, hoping to find out what impact remittances from the Gulf had had on Balochistan's most sensitive geopolitical slice of land. I met three doctors, Shafi, Mohsin, and Hamid, who ranged in age from the early thirties to the mid-fifties. They told me that the impact had been immense, and that people were now returning after twenty years with, accord-ing to Dr. Shafi, "great expectations and little reality." Those with money had no place to invest it; those without money couldn't find jobs. Turbat still had no electricity—the town's center operated on generators provided by the Chinese—and the Gulf workers couldn't even plug in their VCRs.

We met Major Ghulam Mohammed, who had served in the Omani Army for twenty years and had recently returned. He was riding a new red Honda motorbike, and he told us that he had been luckier than most. He had gone into business and built a market and a hotel. "But most of these workers are uneducated," he said. "What are they to do when they come back? They've also been exposed to the most conservative Islam on earth. We in Makran have always been secular. But many of these returning workers are hard-core fundamentalists."

He told us that the Baloch in the Omani Army used to number some twelve thousand. (The total strength of the Army was only eighteen thousand men.) Now, however, that number was being dramatically cut, to some four thousand men. "And what happens to these chaps—both armed and Islamist—when they come back?" he said.

"Will they join the Pakistani Army?" I asked. Nonrepresentation in the Army was, after all, one of the Baloch's complaints.

"I doubt it," Major Ghulam replied. "An unskilled, uneducated private in the Omani Army makes the equivalent of $550 a month; a lieutenant colonel in the Pakistani Army makes $175 a month."

Our last night in Turbat, Humayun and I called on the Nawab of Makran, Khalid Khan Gichki. He was not a tribal leader; his title derived from the fact that his family had ruled Makran for five hundred years. An intelligent, thoughtful man of forty-five, the nawab was surrounded by a group of lively relatives when we arrived. We sat in the old Durbar Hall, where the nawab once gave audiences from a princely looking chair. Lofty arched doorways led to a spiral staircase, and there were touches of rococo and Chippendale.

The nawab, who was basically pro-American, was immensely concerned about what was happening in Balochistan. "Just as in the days of the British, we're considered no more than a buffer, a toy on the chessboard, being popped about," he told us. "The Americans and the Russians both have their eyes on our warm-water ports. But what is the benefit to the people of what the Americans and the Soviets are doing here?"

The benefits could be quite substantial, I suggested. The non-Communist world was pouring hundreds of millions of dollars into Balochistan. Not only were the Americans building bridges and roads but Canada and Kuwait were funding electricity and power projects. The Asian Development Bank was constructing fishing ports. The World Bank, the Saudis, and the Japanese were all attempting to counter Soviet influence with crash programs of development aid.

"Ah, but are these the projects that we need?" the nawab said. "For thirty-three years, we have been discussing the Mirani Dam. If this dam were built, it would cultivate nearly fifty thousand acres of land, and Makran would bloom. But did the Western countries think of doing this? No. We Baloch are never consulted on what we need." (In fact, a week after I visited the nawab it was announced that the Soviet Union had agreed to finance the Mirani Dam.)

"In the old days, Balochistan was so simple," the nawab went on. "Now the pressures, the tension, the fissures—everyone has become so extreme, especially the students and the mullahs. And they are the ones who are posing the most serious challenge to the nawabs and sardars."

He paused for a moment, and then said, "I fear that we are sitting on an ammunition dump and that at any moment it could explode."

I asked him what he meant, and a cousin answered from across the room. "Balochistan, especially Makran, could become another Afghanistan, another Beirut. Look at the arms inflow. A bullet costs only one rupee; an egg costs two. There is a lot of money, combined with a lot of illiteracy. We are driving Mitsubishis, but we're still in the Stone Age. Old family feuds are still going on. And there are all these special militias floating about. There are also some four thousand Iranian Baloch living in the Central Makran Range, fully armed and supported by Iraq, who are running cross-border operations into Iran. No one can touch them—not the Army, not the government. They do whatever they want." (A provincial government official later told me that the Iranians—who were mainly royalists, as well as Baloch—probably numbered closer to five hundred. But then *he* had never been to Makran.)

When I returned to Quetta by plane, I found that the usually sleepy airport had been jolted alive by the arrival from Peshawar of the political leaders of the mujahideen. They had come to meet the American ambassador, who had come to meet the Nawab Bugti. It seemed to me that, in a sense, much of what was now happening in Balochistan sprang from what was happening in Afghanistan: the radicalization of the students and former students, the rise of the mullahs in politics, Khair Bux Marri's uncertain future, and the emergence of increasingly vocal Pathan nationalists. All of Pakistan's provinces had been gerrymandered to avoid tribal dominance, so the Baloch in the south were offset by nearly two million Pathans who dominated the north. Since the days of the British, there had been suspicion and antagonism between the two groups.

One morning just after dawn, I left Quetta with my driver and headed north. A government official had provided a security escort and told me that when I reached the town of Pishin, an hour's drive away, the deputy commissioner would be waiting and would show me around. As we drove out of Quetta, I was struck by the way that the towns and the villages to the east and north blended more naturally into Afghanistan, of which they were once a part. The Pathans, who make up nearly half of Balochistan's population, control many of the province's businesses and much of its trade, and are generally more prosperous and better educated than the Baloch. Their nawabs and sardars also don't rule nearly as arbitrarily as their Baloch counterparts, but settle things through the traditional jirga. "We are far more democratic," one Pathan told me. "If you want to weigh a Baloch tribe, you weigh its nawab. If you want to weigh a Pathan tribe, the whole tribe must be weighed. And we are far better fighters. A Baloch has never captured any Pathan land." It was a rather ominous statement, since Baloch-Pathan clashes, primarily over jobs, had become a pattern over the years.

Once I reached Pishin, it became apparent that, for all practical purposes, Balochistan's northern border with Afghanistan had disappeared. Afghan refugees now dominated the northern towns, and the mujahideen had transformed Pishin, Zhob, and Chaman into key staging areas for the war. Like the Baloch, many of the Pathans who normally lived here had never wanted to be Pakistani and from time to time had renewed their call for self-determination within their own Pashtunistan. The desire for Pashtunistan, I discovered, had been made considerably stronger by the jihad in Afghanistan.

Shahbaz Khan Mandokhel, Pishin's deputy commissioner, was a pleasant, lively man. A government civil servant who came from the area, he was also a Pathan. He suggested that I first go to one of the tribunals, where the laws of the Pakistani government, rather than tribal law, were enforced. The tribunals dispensed justice in Balochistan's towns—5 percent of the land area, where 30 percent of the people live—and although I'd been told that they were singularly unsuccessful, Shahbaz said I should see for myself.

The tribunal was in the same building as Shahbaz's office, a dilapidated frame structure that seemed about to collapse. The magistrate, Mohammed Jalal, who was sitting behind a rickety desk, asked me to join him. On the other side of the room, eleven men accused of murder stood side by side. It was another land dispute within a family, and these men were from the Achakzai tribe. The father and a cousin of the murdered man had come to give evidence that day. They seemed to stand much too close to the magistrate's desk. A small man with a long pen and an inkwell sat at one side to transcribe the evidence, and the proceedings began.

The accused were rough-looking men. Their turbans and *shalwars* were covered with dirt and dust. Within moments, everyone was shouting, and the accused surged toward the magistrate's desk, surrounding the hapless witnesses, who stood their ground. The accused wanted to interrogate the witnesses.

"Move back, get away from my desk," the magistrate warned. It did no good. There were more shouts and gesticulations. A guard entered, carrying a stick. He didn't use it, but the men moved back.

"You know, they really prefer their own laws," the magistrate said. "Look out the window. See, just across the field, on that ridge, tribal law begins. Under tribal law, they are judged by their own people, and they accept the verdicts, because of their loyalty to their nawabs and sardars. Also, the penalties are comparatively light. In some murder cases, a man might receive a maximum sentence of fourteen years in a nawab's private jail, but that rarely happens. They pay compensation instead. But here, in the tribunals, murder is punishable by hanging." He paused for a moment, and then he said, "Would anyone in his right mind kill someone in town?"

I went in search of Shahbaz, and he asked me what I thought. He said that the tribunals were even more chaotic in the Baloch lands. He had an armored jeep, and in it we drove toward Chaman, from whose rooftops one could watch the Afghan jihad. Balochistan's northern Pathan areas had always been a free-trade zone, where smuggling thrived. Now the growing black market economy was supplemented by lucrative heroin and arms trades. We passed five lorries from the Army's National Logistics Cell—the biggest freight carrier in Pakistan. They were ferrying arms and ammunition to the mujahideen. Shahbaz told me that since the Soviets withdrew from Afghanistan earlier that year, as many as fifty trucks at a time arrived from Quetta, and they arrived every week. We passed the ammunition depot at Yaru, which was a major training center for Gulbadin Hekmatyar. Nearly half a mile long, it stood prominently along a ridge—a huge, medieval-looking fortress that was run by the ISI. Shahbaz remarked that it had been featured on Radio Moscow's English-language service the previous night.

Such broadcasts would be repeated in the years to come; the war in Afghanistan would go on; and Pakistan would continue to be haunted by the policies pursued by Zia ul-Haq—not only along the country's border with Afghanistan generally but also here in Chaman particularly.

The lorries ferrying arms would continue to arrive, as would commandos and trainers from the ISI, whose powers had proved formidable not only during the jihad but also in the years that followed it, and whose generals, under the tutelage of Zia ul-Haq and then his heirs, politicized the ISI as it had never been politicized before. A victory, of sorts, for Pakistan finally occurred when Gulbadin Hekmatyar was named prime minister of Afghanistan in 1992, three years after the Soviets withdrew, when the puppet Communist government in Kabul finally fell. But the fighting continued, in the form of a fratricidal civil war in which Hekmatyar unleashed a deadly offensive against President Burhanuddin Rabbani and other factions of the mujahideen, using a formidable arsenal of arms—all of them supplied by the United States and Saudi Arabia.

Even by the standards of Afghanistan, chaos and carnage thrived. From 1992 until September of 1996, when the Taliban hurtled into Kabul, at least thirty thousand Afghans died.

When I returned to Quetta, I went to see the leaders of the Pathans, of the mullahs, and of the students to try to find out what might happen next in Balochistan. Much depended, or so it seemed to me, on whether in the coming years the mullahs or the Marxists would assume the upper hand. The three men whom I was about to meet were linked by the common thread of their opposition to the old order of nawabs and sardars, and they all knew Khair Bux Marri. They traveled frequently between Balochistan and Afghanistan or between Balochistan and Iran.

Mahmood Khan Achakzai, whose Pashtoon-Khuwa was the strongest political party in the Pathan belt, was the most important political leader of Balochistan's Pathans. He was also the most important spokesman for Pashtunistan. I met him in the bungalow of relatives of his; students were meeting in another room, and older, turbanned men were unloading a shipment of weapons in yet another room.

A large, partly bald man of forty-one with a mustache and an easy smile, Mahmood is a Marxist and an engineer, and had lived underground in Pakistan or in exile in Kabul for the previous five and a half years. He had returned to Balochistan only recently, when Benazir Bhutto had given him amnesty. (A murder charge had been registered against him, something he called a "misunderstanding" between General Zia and the Pashtoon-Khuwa.)

Mahmood was born into nationalist politics. His father, Abdul Samad Khan, had been a relentless fighter, along with the Frontier Gandhi, Khan Abdul Ghaffar Khan, for Pathan autonomy. (A true Pathan—or Pashtun—nation would include not only much of Balochistan but also Pakistan's North-West Frontier Province and about half of Afghanistan.) Such was the bonding of the Pathan tribes that when Abdul Ghaffar Khan died in 1988, both sides in the jihad declared a truce so that his funeral cortege could travel safely for his burial in the eastern Afghan city of Jalalabad.

I asked Mahmood what Pashtunistan meant now.

"A Pathan homeland," he answered. "Within Pakistan if possible, and out of Pakistan if we must. And we shall get it, by strength of words, strength of numbers, and strength of arms. It is not we who will decide whether we break Pakistan or keep it intact. It is the Punjabis and the government of Pakistan."

Most recently in 1985, the Afghan government, wanting to upset Pakistan, had resurrected calls for Pashtunistan. Kabul had summoned tribal chiefs from both sides of the frontier to call for Pashtun unity under Afghan sovereignty. Mahmood had been one of those summoned, so I asked him if the Achakzais, who numbered more than half a million and whose tribal lands spread across the border into Afghanistan, would accept Afghan sovereignty.

"Afghanistan is our homeland, Pakistan is our country," he replied. "The boundaries of countries change. A homeland remains one."

As Afghanistan grew increasingly chaotic, there was a growing fear, especially in the Pathan areas, of a Pakistani-Afghan war. I asked Mahmood if this was possible.

"If Pakistan and America continue arming and supporting the

mujahideen, it is not only possible, it will become a necessity," he replied. He paused for a moment, and then he said, "And if a war starts how can Pakistan expect our support—and I mean the support of both the Pathans and the Baloch, including Khair Bux?"

What would happen next, I wondered.

"What happens in Balochistan over the coming months and years will be tied to what happens in Afghanistan," he said. "If the Afghans are allowed to decide their fate, without U.S., Pakistani, and other outside interference, we will keep quiet, both the Pathans and the Baloch. But, if they're not, we will do whatever is necessary to support the government that the Afghan people want in Kabul."

When I called on Maulana Mohammed Khan Sheerani, the leader of the largest fundamentalist party in Balochistan, everything seemed destined to go wrong. He was staying with Maulana Ismatullah—the new Minister of Finance—and Ismatullah seemed to move on average once a week, each time to a bungalow larger and grander than the last. When I finally reached his residence, I was nearly an hour late, and twenty or so mullahs who had assembled were obviously displeased. The moment I entered the drawing room, someone objected that I had not covered my head. It was nearly a hundred degrees outside, and the bungalow was stuffy and hot. I glanced around and saw that a number of men—who were not mullahs—had not covered theirs. I said that I was not going to cover my head until the men covered theirs.

Maulana Sheerani listened, stroking his gray beard, but did not participate in the dispute. Finally, the supreme negotiator, he gave me his handkerchief and ordered a servant to bring appropriate head coverings for the men. All that the servant could find was blankets. Within minutes, the men had begun to perspire, and I had been introduced to mullah politics.

Maulana Sheerani, who was forty-nine, was a member of the National Assembly, and of the Jamiat-i-Ulema-i-Islam (JUI), which was headed by the Maulana Fazlur Rahman, and which was said to be heavily funded by Libya and Iran. It also held the balance of power in the fragile coalition government of the nawab. For the fortunes of the JUI had increased palpably during the jihad. Fazlur Rahman was already one of the strongest religious leaders in Balochistan and now his influence had spread into the North-West Frontier Province and the Punjab—thanks, in large part, to the largess of Saudi Arabia, Tripoli, and Tehran. He had established an elaborate network of madrasahs, where jihad was preached. And in the process, he and hundreds of other like-minded clerics across Pakistan would help to train and arm what eventually became a Pakistani network of highly disciplined and effective Islamic militants—and a new breed of terrorists as well. Fazlur Rahman and the JUI were, in a sense, a portent of what lay ahead: a dangerous convergence between Pakistan's clerical and radical Islamic political trends. For as Zia ul-Haq, and now Benazir Bhutto, had accommodated the religious right, and thus emboldened it, the clerics had begun adopting political ideas from Pakistan's Pan-Islamic militants.

In the years to come, this highly combustible mix would present itself most lethally in the proxy war being waged in Kashmir.

After an exchange of pleasantries, Maulana Sheerani made it clear that he did not consider the Soviet-supported government in Kabul to constitute a "revolution," as the students and former students did. "The students' militancy is fed by unemployment and boredom," he said. "We shall provide jobs for them, and then they'll quiet down." He looked at Afghanistan, he told me, as a jihad. "It has also made the people here much more religious." He smiled.

But did this apply to the Baloch, I asked, or only to the Pathans? The maulana was a Pathan from the border area of Afghanistan, and it was in the Pathan areas that the mullahs had made their greatest electoral gains. "It applies to everyone in Balochistan," he said. "The only reason that we did not sweep the board is that the nawabs and sardars wouldn't let us campaign on their turf. Every time we tried to enter the Bugti or Marri area, or the Jhalawan, we were turned back by sticks, stones, and rocks." He went on. "Balochistan is poor, and Islam addresses the problems of the poor. The cruelty of the nawabs and sardars against their people, and their so-called socialism, which has given the people nothing, is a thing of the past."

"What do you think of Khair Bux Marri?" I asked.

"He's a nawab, and the nawabs have to go. They discourage education; they discourage their people from joining government service or moving to the towns. They won't permit development in their areas. They have kept their people locked up in a medieval world." The maulana was dressed in a handsome brown robe trimmed with gold, and he fingered a set of yellow prayer beads as he talked.

I asked him what the JUI thought of the United States.

"We oppose all imperialists," he said. "The United States has taken advantage of the peculiar geographical position of Pakistan. You signed the Geneva Accords"—the accords which had provided for the withdrawal of Soviet forces from Afghanistan—"but now you've disavowed them by continuing to arm the mujahideen. In principle, we support the mujahideen's cause, but we do not agree with direct interference. You are destabilizing the entire region."

I asked him what the most powerful force in the region was.

He smiled cheerfully. "The Iranian revolution, of course."

Dr. Kahur Baloch, a twenty-eight-year-old dental surgeon, was the leader of the more militant faction of the Baloch Students Organization. It had been somewhat difficult to find him, for he was living underground. (There had recently been a shootout between students supporting Khair Bux Marri and those supporting the nawab.) He was finally found, however, and he came to meet me at my hotel, with a group of enthusiastic supporters.

I asked him why his group supported Khair Bux.

He said that Khair Bux was honest and willing to defy the authority of anyone; he was also the only Baloch leader who had not "deviated, withdrawn, or sold out."

"What have Khair Bux and the Baloch been doing all these years in Afghanistan?" I asked.

He explained that there were now a number of Baloch groups in Afghanistan, which were roughly aligned with the Baloch People's Liberation Front, or BPLF, an old guerrilla army that had fought in the 1973–77 insurgency. It remained essentially an army, and had recently been pressed into service by the Afghan regime to fight limited engagements in and around Kandahar against the mujahideen.

The group that Dr. Kahur favored, however, was the Baloch Liberation Movement, or BLM. Its members were the ideologists of the movement, he said, and many of them had studied at Patrice Lumumba University or in Afghanistan. They had underground political cells in Quetta and military contingents in Afghanistan. They ran Balochi-language broadcasts that originated in Kabul and were aimed at "mobilizing the people," he said. (The broadcasts were listened to with rapt attention, I had discovered during my trips.) They also wrote revolutionary literature and tracts, which local student leaders read to the tribesmen if the tribesmen couldn't read.

Dr. Kahur, a small, intense man, was wearing granny glasses and, over his *shalwar kameez*, a jacket; he was also chain-smoking British cigarettes. His face resembled Lenin's, and he was extremely well read. He was part of Balochistan's newly emerging intellectual middle class. "We became convinced after the dismissal of the nationalist government in 1973 that there was no way to obtain our rights through the democratic process in Pakistan," he went on.

I asked if there would be another insurrection.

"Yes, it could happen," he said. "When you block the way of evolution and development, then people rise up and there's an insurrection. And insurrection leads to revolution." The entire group smiled.

Dr. Kahur told me that the BSO and the pro-Kabul Marri insurgents in Balochistan's hills were organizing reinforcements to send to Afghanistan. They crossed the border at Zhob or Chaman, then went to Kandahar on camelback or on foot. (A military officer had told me that the border was "highly permeable.")

Six or seven hundred Marri guerrillas from the BPLF had quietly returned to Balochistan over the last nine months, so I asked Dr. Kahur what they were doing now.

He said they were simply "roaming about" in the Marri tribal lands.

I had been told that the guerillas were blocking government efforts to bring in electricity and roads by sealing off large areas or shooting at the engineers; other than that Khair Bux Marri had given them instructions "not to create trouble now."

"Well, what do you think?" the nawab asked me on my last night in Quetta. We were having dinner in his receiving room, sitting cross-legged on the exquisite Bukhara rug. The usual friends were there.

It seemed to me, I told him, that as only the second powerful tribal leader to govern Balochistan, he was in a way being put to the test. He would have to build roads, open schools, bring development; and these very reforms would break the tribal system and erode his absolute authority as a nawab.

"Hmm," he said. He seemed a bit taken aback. I waited with some trepidation. But that was all he said. "Anything else?" he finally asked.

I told him that everyone seemed angry, frustrated, and armed.

"Well, I'm also angry and frustrated," he thundered, "and we've always been armed." He calmed down somewhat, and then went on. "Granted our arms are now far more sophisticated than they've ever been before."

"Why *is* everyone armed?" I asked.

"For protection," he replied. "A woman wears bangles, a man's ornament is his weapon. When the Russians first arrived in Afghanistan, people would sell their herds of sheep—their only possession—to buy a Chinese AK-47, which cost the equivalent of about fifteen hundred dollars then. A weapon is a man's badge of honor, and a Baloch will take a life or give his life for three things— his woman, his weapon, and his land."

I knew that part of his moodiness centered on Khair Bux. As

chief minister, the nawab was under increasing pressure from the Baloch to negotiate conditions that would allow Khair Bux Marri to return. The two men, though they had been friends in earlier years, basically distrusted each other now. A few years earlier, the nawab had said to me that Khair Bux could not sustain his guerrilla movement without an outside base, whether in Kabul or in the Indian state of Rajasthan. Then he had said bitterly, "You can't say from Pakistan, 'I will break up the nation.' It's far easier to have romantic illusions of revolution from a comfortable base abroad. But what are his real choices? Does he battle for a dream he'll never realize? Or does he come back to Balochistan, his tail between his legs?"

Now I reminded him of those remarks, and he said, "Why doesn't he tell us what he wants? Then we could talk. The government could have hard-and-fast conditions. But we have to know what he wants."

The nawab's favorite grandson, Brahum Dagh, a sweet-tempered boy of eight, was eating dinner with us, and, thinking of how often he sat quietly with the men, I realized that the nawab was teaching him *Rajniti*, the philosophy of being a nawab. As I left his house that evening and waited outside for my car, the nawab, as his German surrogate mother had done with him a half century before, began singing softly to Brahum Dagh, "Twinkle, twinkle, little star."

CHAPTER 4

HUNTING WITH THE SHEIKHS

ONE FRIDAY MORNING in January 2002, just before midday prayers, I went to the falcon market in Doha, the capital of the Persian Gulf Emirate of Qatar, with a friend. It was the falcon season and the birds were selling swiftly, and for a substantial price: a blond, nearly white, shahin from Iran had fetched the equivalent of $30,000, a dealer from Balochistan named Hussein exclaimed with a broad smile. We then ensconced ourselves in overstuffed armchairs arranged in a large circle in his shop, which brought a traditional majlis to mind. A young boy served Bedouin coffee, which is bitter and has the consistency of tea, in thimble-sized porcelain cups. A sheikh and his family joined us.

Normally, at this time of the year, scores of Qataris—and Saudis and other elites from the Persian Gulf—flock to Pakistan to hunt the houbara bustard, an endangered species of a fast-flying and cursorial desert bird that migrates there each fall from the former Soviet Union and from the Central Asian steppes. But the number of houbara was dramatically reduced this year, and the royal falconers were convinced that the U.S. bombing of Afghanistan had disoriented it.

No one was more distressed, I later learned, than the Minister of Defense of Saudi Arabia. For his private airport at Dalbandin—which he had constructed precisely for his royal hunts—was one of those that General Musharraf had ceded to the United States for its air war.

Pakistan certainly could not afford to antagonize the House of Saud. The kingdom had poured billions of dollars into Pakistan over the years: in aid and debt relief, for military purchases, and for Pakistan's program to construct what became known as the world's first nuclear "Islamic bomb." It had underwritten Pakistan's sponsorship of the Taliban, as it had financed thousands of madrasahs spread across Pakistan, including those in Balochistan presided over by the JUI's Maulana Fazlur Rahman, and the largest madrasah in the North-West Frontier, whose chancellor was the JUI's Maulana Sami ul-Haq. None of this, of course, was a totally selfless undertaking by the Saudi royal house, for it all formed part of the kingdom's conscientious policy to export its radical and puritanical doctrine of Wahhabi Islam.

In this respect, the darker side was that the Saudis, too—as they were doing across the larger Islamic world—were the primary financiers of Pakistan's militant sectarian and Islamist groups. Sunni supremacists came under their sway, as they had for twenty years, a legacy of Saudi Arabia's proxy war with Shiite Iran for ascendancy in the Islamic world—a war that was being fought to most lethal effect on the streets of Karachi and across the Punjab. Washington had attempted, in a delicate way, to restrain the Saudi leaders over recent years, but to no avail, for whether it was to fight Iraq, or to fight terrorism, or to keep the oil flowing, Saudi Arabia, like Pakistan, was deemed to be, at least on the surface, a crucial American ally. It was only after the September 11 attacks that Washington begrudgingly began to concede that it knew little about the militant Islamist movement inside Saudi Arabia itself—a movement that had produced not only Osama bin Laden and his primary financiers but fifteen of the nineteen young men who, on that day, brought terror to the United States.

Now America was at war with these men, a war that was concentrated, by January 2002, along the Pakistani-Afghan frontier. Yet not a day passed when one or another of the members of the House of Saud did not call Pakistan for any news, however tenuous, of the spotting of a bird.

Abrar Mirza, the conservator of wildlife for the Province of Sindh, is by nature a rather doleful man, and he always appears to be in a state of crisis. When I first met him, late in November of 1991, he was especially anxious because he had been waiting for weeks—waiting for the full moon, and waiting for the rains, and waiting for the houbara bustard. A good many Arab sheikhs and princes were also waiting—discreetly—in opulent Karachi palaces.

Mirza dreads November, he has often said, because his entire life is put on hold. The responsibilities of his position include the delicate job of monitoring the Arab royal hunts. He is a bit puzzled by them and can't really explain why, with the arrival of the houbara, scores of Middle Eastern potentates—presidents, ambassadors, ministers, generals, governors—descend upon Pakistan in fleets of private planes. They come armed with computers and radar, hundreds of servants and other staff, customized weapons, and priceless falcons, which are used to hunt the bird. Mirza considers it all a little excessive. But then the houbara bustard has been a fascination to the great sheikhs of the desert for hundreds of years. Poets have written about it. Old men of the desert have sung of it in tiny tea stalls. Even today, Arab diplomats, in well-appointed embassies abroad, discuss the advent of the season, and discuss it endlessly.

"The bird is a month late!" Mirza announced one morning when I stopped by his office in Karachi and found him at his desk, which was covered with mounds of papers and half-finished cups of tea. He would make a fine Inspector Clouseau: middle-aged, wiry, although with a bit of a paunch. "Only a handful have arrived. And I am being held responsible, as though it's all my fault. Look at these telegrams!" He threw a mass of papers into the air. They were urgent messages from the Pakistani government—the majority of them from the Ministry of Foreign Affairs, which was most distressed.

It is the foreign ministry that awards the visiting Arab dignitaries special permits to hunt. Pakistanis themselves have been prohibited from killing the houbara since 1972. Yet each season, which lasts from November until March, their countryside is carved up like a giant salami into ever smaller parts. Some sheikhs—among them Zayed al-Nahayan, the President of the United Arab Emirates and, until its collapse, the chief shareholder of the Bank of Credit and Commerce International, or BCCI—receive permits that cover thousands of square miles. No other hunters may cross the invisible line that separates Sheikh Zayed's personal hunting grounds from those of, for example, the Saudi Princes Naif and Sultan, or the Dubai leader, Sheikh Maktoum. At least, that is so in principle.

"Look at this!" Mirza nearly shouted, flailing a piece of paper before my eyes. Across the top was stamped CONFIDENTIAL MOST IMMEDIATE; it was a message from Colonel S. K. Tressler, the chief of protocol. Sheikh Maktoum would soon be arriving from Dubai, and a party of royal Bahrainis was hunting on his turf—not even Dubaians but *Bahrainis*. Mirza was instructed to sort the muddle out. Then, there was a party of hunters from the royal family of Qatar "sneaking around," Mirza said, on Saudi Arabia's turf. And a member of the Dubai royal family was reported to have bagged two hundred birds in a protected national park, in the company of the honorary game warden, who was a member of the Pakistani parliament.

For the moment, however, the greatest concern had to be the royal Bahrainis, since they were Colonel Tressler's concern. Mirza's men had attempted to evict them, but "they had been insistent— they refused to budge," Mirza told me. "There will be another Gulf War, you mark my words. And I am confident that not a single bird will return to its nesting grounds this year. The only back migration to the Soviet Union will be those birds who are clever enough to escape from Pakistan, either crossing the border into India or remaining in Iran and Afghanistan."

I asked how many sheikhs and princes were expected this year.

Mirza said that the foreign ministry had "officially" allotted some twenty permits thus far. Then, there were the "unofficial allotments," made by Pakistan's chief ministers and governors to their Arab friends, plus any number of "special favors" awarded by the Army's general staff. "And then there are the others." Mirza threw up his hands. "And these are the worst offenders—those who have no permission, and who come by totally illegal means. They cause colossal damage, and we don't even know where they *are*."

He calmed down momentarily. "None of this would have happened if it hadn't been for Abedi." He meant Agha Hasan Abedi, the Pakistani who had founded BCCI. "He was the one who first arranged hunting outings in Pakistan for the sheikhs. He set up everything for them—from doing their shopping to providing bribes and geisha girls. The more he provided, the more their deposits filled his bank."

Agha Hasan Abedi died in 1995, a few years after BCCI collapsed in what may be the greatest financial scandal in banking history. Once a $20 billion financial empire, the bank was in tatters when its international operations were closed down following discoveries that it was involved in fraud and theft, in secret weapons deals, in money laundering and drug trafficking, and in financing terrorist groups. Osama bin Laden had used the bank to move some of his fortune around; so had the CIA to conduit money and weapons to the jihad; and so had the ISI and General Zia ul-Haq. How did Pakistan become so enmeshed with the interests of one bank? The answer did begin, in a sense, with Mirza's unfortunate bird.

I had my first inkling of the royal houbara hunts during a visit to Pakistan a few years earlier when, late one evening, I entered the elevator of my Karachi hotel and, to my astonishment, found myself in the company of two Arabs with falcons on their arms. After a bit of research, I sought out a friend of a friend from the Ministry of Foreign Affairs, a man I will call Ahmed, and he agreed to let me accompany him to the Karachi airport on a night when he was to receive an advance party of one of the sheikhs. He made me promise not to reveal that I was a journalist.

The sheikhs are obsessive about their privacy. Some—like the Saudi Minister of Defense—have built personal airfields to protect themselves from public view. Some have constructed huge desert palaces, surrounded by fortresslike walls. Some live in elaborate tent cities, guarded by legions of Bedouin troops. They have their own communications equipment, road networks, security forces, and police. Totally closed off to outsiders, their hunting fiefdoms are, in effect, Arab principalities. They sprinkle the vast deserts of Balochistan, Punjab, and Sindh, covering hundreds of miles. The sheikhs move in and out of them like phantoms, giving rise to any number of outlandish stories, many of which turn out to be true. There is, for example, the story that the late King Khalid of Saudi Arabia transported dancing camels in a C-130 to join him on his hunt. There is the story that Prince Sultan, the Saudi defense minister, slaughtered seventy sheep and lambs every day to feed his royal entourage. There is the story of the late ruler of Dubai who built one of Pakistan's most modern and most expensive hospitals near his hunting grounds. It had twelve operating theaters, and only three were being used, so the Pakistani government requested that the others be relocated to remote areas, which have little medical care. Sheikh Rashid refused, explaining, "I hunt my birds here."

It was well past midnight when Ahmed and I reached the airport. (The sheikhs of the desert have always preferred to travel in the middle of the night.) A Pakistani Army major met us in the VIP lounge, where a small group of Arab diplomats, in tailored silk suits, sat in a corner sipping cups of sugary tea. They shook hands with Ahmed and nodded politely to me. Then black stretch limousines whisked us to a remote section of the airfield, which had been cordoned off by Pakistani troops to assure the sheikh's entourage of total privacy.

As we waited on the tarmac, the arriving planes lit up the night sky. Flying in formation—observing protocol, apparently—an executive Learjet was followed by two customized Boeings and a fleet of reconfigured C-130s, which flew two abreast. They had all been designated "special VVIP flights" by the Pakistani government. There would be no customs clearance, no passport control—the royal entourage enjoyed extraterritorial status in Pakistan. The lead planes touched down, and a red carpet was hastily unrolled. We all hurried to it and stood in a slightly dishevelled line.

"This is the sixth flight this week," one of the Arab diplomats told me, exhaustion in his voice.

"Do you accompany them on the hunts?" I asked.

"Good heavens, no," he said, smoothing one of his silk lapels. "I'm basically a fisherman myself."

Two military officers in dress uniform got off the executive jet and walked briskly toward us, carrying attaché cases and swagger sticks. They were followed by other members of the sheikh's personal staff—a purser, a physician, a royal chamberlain—all in kaffiyehs and flowing camel-colored robes. Security men in khaki uniforms hurried from one of the Boeings and fanned out across the field. The doors of the C-130s opened, and immense vehicles began rolling down the ramps.

From a distance, the vehicles were merely dots of color—canary yellow, bright red, black-and-white. Then they lumbered by us: two-thousand-gallon water tankers and eight-thousand-liter fuel tankers—dozens and dozens of them—in militarily precise lines. Now planes were landing all around us, ramps were quickly dropped, and jeeps, Range Rovers, and Land Cruisers raced down. They had all been customized for the royal houbara hunts, so that areas once inaccessible were now easily accessible. They had open backs and convertible tops, and were equipped with special gauges, special shock absorbers, and special tires. Their drivers were dressed in Bedouin robes and wore exceedingly dark glasses, even though the night itself was exceedingly dark.

There was a din, deafening at times, as camp managers shouted instructions in Arabic, as gears ground and brakes slammed, as more and more heavy equipment was disgorged. Security men dashed back and forth. Cranes labored across the runway and carefully unloaded satellite dishes and communications equipment. From time to time I glimpsed generators, air-conditioners, mobile bars, VCRs. "They're totally self-sufficient in the desert," the diplomat who preferred fishing said. "Some of them even drill their own water holes. Providing water for an entourage of three hundred people is a problem." He shook his head.

During all the commotion on the runway, I had become separated from Ahmed, and now I went in search of him. I found him among a group of agitated officials, standing in a tight circle beneath a wing of one of the planes. "The mobile palaces are new," he told me, "and they don't know how to get it down." Looking up, I saw an unwieldy dark-blue structure, about fifty feet long and perhaps thirty feet wide, stuck at the top of the ramp. It was a customized Mercedes, and prominent on its hood was a now slightly askew gold-plated royal crest. "When they first began coming," Ahmed said, "even King Khalid and Sheikh Zayed slept in a tent."

In 1929, H.R.P. Dickson, a British colonial officer who had served in Kuwait, described the houbara's yearly arrival on the Arabian Peninsula as "a season for rejoicing." He wrote, "The rains are close at hand and . . . the hubara have arrived. They are verily, like the manna of old, Allah's reward to those who have endured the summer heat."

By the 1960s, the houbara had been hunted almost to extinction in the Middle East. "There was near hysteria when the bird disappeared," an Arab ambassador told me. The kings, sheikhs, and princes hurriedly dispatched scouting parties abroad. They recruited British and French scientists to attempt to breed the houbara in captivity. They called upon Japanese technicians to develop special tracking devices and customized vehicles for the hunt. It was the beginning of what would become a multimillion-dollar industry. But none of their endeavors solved their most pressing problem: Where could they hunt the houbara bustard *now*?

Pakistan, Afghanistan, Iran, and North Africa seemed the most promising hunting grounds. But the sheikhs quarreled with Colonel Qaddafi, and he forbade them to come to Libya to hunt; they quarreled even more strongly with the Iranian mullahs, who, in a sweeping proclamation, banned the houbara hunts. So did the government of Tunisia. Egypt was more accommodating, but the houbara population had been severely reduced there, too. Afghanistan had an abundance of houbara, but then the Soviet Army invaded, and the ardently anti-Soviet Persian Gulf sheikhs simply refused to deal with the Communist infidel. Only Pakistan and Morocco—and, to a lesser extent, Algeria—remained as preferred hunting grounds.

Pakistan was believed to have one of the largest migratory populations of houbara in the world, but no one was quite certain, then or later, how large it actually was. For although the houbara was declared an endangered species in 1975, largely as a result of the high-tech hunting of the sheikhs, no international conservation group had ever done a comprehensive study on the bird's distribution worldwide. After a good deal of debate, experts at an international symposium in Peshawar in 1983 finally agreed that Pakistan's houbara population probably numbered somewhere between twenty and twenty-five thousand birds. In retrospect, the figure seems extremely low. The houbara reproduces at a rate that increases its numbers by only about 5 percent a year, and the conservation officials I spoke with on this trip told me that the Arab hunting parties were bagging at least six thousand birds a year, and even that figure was considered a very conservative government estimate. (Sheikh Zayed alone brings 150 falcons with him.)

And although General Zia, who had been in power for six years, had supported the Peshawar symposium, he ignored its unanimous appeal that houbara hunting be banned in Pakistan altogether for at least five years. For while the number of Arab royal falconers was small—perhaps two or three dozen men—they were all immensely powerful, and immensely rich, and they put millions of dollars into their hunts. They also provided Pakistan—whose per capita gross national product at the time was only $350 a year—with some $3.5 billion annually in military and economic aid and in remittances to two million Pakistanis working in the Gulf. And as important as anything else, the House of Saud alone had committed some $5 billion—the only commitment larger than Washington's—to the jihad. Millions of more Saudi dollars flowed into Pakistan for the establishment of not only madrasahs and mosques but also banks and welfare groups, all of which was a key component of the export of Saudi Arabia's austere school of Wahhabi Islam. The lavish infusion from Riyadh served Zia ul-Haq's own vision well: for in the process he, like Pakistan itself, was transformed into a leading figure in the world of militant Islam. (In the years to come, not only the inheritors of Zia's legacy but, indeed, all governments of Pakistan would use and nurture Islamic militancy for reasons of state: not only in Afghanistan but also in Kashmir, even more self-consciously.)

So despite appeals from Prince Philip, the president of the World Wildlife Fund, and from other conservation groups, the sheikhs and princes continued to hunt. Over the years, their numbers have increased, and so has the number of houbara they bag and ship back to their kingdoms, in specially designed refrigerated trucks aboard the C-130s, which have been reconfigured expressly for the houbara hunt.

Veru is a dun-colored village of low mud houses, parched fields, and dust, hidden away in the interior of Sindh, where dacoits roam more or less at will. Some thirty gangs were now said to be in control—armed with dynamite, rocket launchers, and Kalashnikovs. It was in the desert outside Veru that members of the royal family of Bahrain were encamped, and where Mirza was determined to stage a lightning raid. I went to his office one morning and found him most distressed. Sitting with him was Dr. Mohammed Hasan Rizvi, a leading eye surgeon who had recently received an international award in recognition of his efforts as one of Pakistan's most committed conservationists.

"The program has changed," Mirza told me. "The authorities won't permit an arrest. So we will simply visit the sheikh, and while we are there we will attempt to count his bag. Dr. Rizvi will join us. The only problem is, we've lost the sheikh!"

He shuffled through the growing pile of papers on his desk and found another MOST IMMEDIATE telegram. "All of this has caused extraordinary difficulties for this office," Mirza said.

"How could you lose a sheikh?" I asked.

"There was a shoot-out near his camp a few nights ago. The Rangers"—a federal militia force—"were attempting to arrest some dacoits, and the entire royal party fled. Their camp is deserted, except for a few vehicles and some jerricans."

Since Dr. Rizvi was said to be extremely close to the sheikhs, I asked him to tell me what a royal hunt was like.

"The sheikhs fall apart when they see the houbara," he replied. "They follow the bird helter-skelter in their customized cars— brand-new Mercedes 250s is what they used to bring. I hunted with the then Crown Prince [now the ruler] Sheikh Maktoum of Dubai. Within twenty minutes, our muffler broke off. Even with a vehicle that the sheikh had had so carefully customized—it had special springs and shock absorbers, and higher, heavy tires—a Mercedes is not meant for the desert, and we traveled, or so it seemed, at the speed of sound." He paused for a moment, and then he said, "In the old days, it was so much more refined. You would see their caravans for miles along the roads, and the roads were perfumed. King Khalid. Prince Naif. Sheikh Rashid. They were real falconers."

Why was falconry so important to the sheikhs? I asked.

"It's their tradition—it's in their blood," he replied. "From the very earliest times, falconry has been the sport of kings—the Moghuls, European nobility. And that special brotherhood between falconers still exists based on ancient and honorable codes. They even have a special terminology—it's like rhyming slang, a trick they have invented to keep outsiders out. The sheikhs claim it is one of the purest forms of hunting in the world. They are passionate in its defense. The falcon is a quick learner and a thrilling flyer, and there's a certain magic involved. The magic is the force that brings a trained but untamed bird down out of the sky and back to her trainer's arm.

"All their falcons have names. They're named either for great Arab heroes or famous falcons of the past. Some years ago, when I went out with one of the sheikhs, his favorite falcon was lost. He sat for four days in the middle of his camp, calling out his falcon's name. Can you imagine? This was the president of a country, and he did nothing but sit and shout 'Mubarak' into the wilderness."

The following evening I was invited to a dinner for one of the visiting sheikhs. It was held at the elegant Karachi home of the Talpurs, one of the great feudal families of Sindh. They were the ruling family of the district of Mirpur Khas and controlled vast tracts of land, where members of the royal families of Dubai and Qatar had begun to hunt, including Sheikh Muhammad, a Dubaian prince for whom the dinner was being held. None of the guests seemed certain of precisely who he was, although they all assured me that he was definitely a very influential sheikh.

A billowing *chamiana* tent of red, white, blue, and yellow had been set up in the middle of the Talpurs' lawn. It was filled with imitation Louis XV wing chairs and upholstered settees arranged in a large rectangle. Bearers in starched white jackets served whiskey and gin in tall glasses that had been wrapped delicately in paper napkins. (Alcohol is forbidden in the Islamic Republic of Pakistan.) As everyone waited for the sheikh to arrive, I greeted a number of Pakistani ministers and former ministers. It was an impressive gathering of Karachi's feudal, political, and financial elite. If the Arab sheikhs and princes were attaching greater urgency to the houbara hunt this year, so, in a sense, was the government of Pakistan. It had vacillated during the Gulf War the previous year, agonizing over what it could do that would be acceptable at home and yet would not displease its Arab patrons or the United States. In the end, ten thousand troops were sent to the Gulf with orders not to fight. Officially they were sent to Saudi Arabia to guard its religious shrines. But no sooner had the troops been dispatched than Pakistan's zealous mullahs—the majority of whom Saudi Arabia had been funding for years— announced, with some flourish, that they had recruited thirty thousand volunteers to fight on the side of Iraq. Nobody knew for certain where Pakistan stood, and no government was more irritated than the government of Saudi Arabia. The houbara bustard was now a pawn on the geopolitical chessboard.

"We must find a proper seat for you," my host, Nawab Abdul Ghani Talpur, said to me. "You must not be so close to the sheikh as to be conspicuous, but you must not be so far away that he can't see you and invite you to join him on his settee." It was finally decided that I should sit between a feudal landlord and a member of parliament. The landlord was a short, plump man with betel-stained teeth who was wearing a reddish-orange toupee. He said that the sheikhs had been hunting on his private lands for nearly a decade. We all hurried to sit in our assigned places as the sheikh's arrival was heralded by screeching sirens and guards scurrying to take up positions along the perimeter of the tent, their Kalashnikovs at the ready.

"His Majesty," the nawab announced, and we all jumped to our feet.

"He's not 'His Majesty,' " the landlord whispered dismissively. "He's merely the brother-in-law and the cousin of the ruler of Dubai, and he's not a very good hunter either. When he didn't find any houbara in my desert tracts, he moved his entire camp—servants, vehicles, falcons—into Kirthar National Park. He killed more than two hundred houbara in ten days, and he killed gazelles and ibex, too."

"Why was that permitted?" I asked.

"No one has ever written, either Jesus or the Prophet Muhammad, that Pakistan must be poor."

That was the way many of my conversations in Pakistan went. I met game wardens wearing jeweled watches that were gifts from the sheikhs. Politicians, chief ministers, and former chief ministers received lavish residences or customized cars. Some of them shopped frequently in London—flying back and forth in one or another of the sheikhs' private planes.

Sheikh Muhammad bin-Khalifa al-Maktoum swept into the tent. His face showed no emotion as he went from guest to guest. A slight man with a Vandyke beard, he was dressed in a black robe trimmed with gold and a white kaffiyeh. For some reason, he carried a shepherd's wooden crook in his hand.

After I introduced myself, he asked me if I lived in Pakistan.

"No, Your Excellency. I've come for the houbara hunt."

"We're not hunting," he said, rather tartly. "We're only training falcons." And he moved on.

I asked the landlord how much a typical royal hunt cost.

"Well, when you take everything into account—the hunting vehicles, minus their electronic fittings, cost at least $20,000 each; then add the costs of their falcons and private planes; and, of course, there are the out-of-pocket expenses." He laughed a guttural laugh. "The controller of Sheikh Muhammad's household told me that he paid about $200,000 out-of-pocket for this particular trip. He's spent a total of about $9 million thus far, and he bagged about six hundred birds. That works out to about $15,000 a bird."

He then quickly added that that figure was low. The sheikhs normally spent between $10 and $20 million for a typical royal hunt.

I glanced at Sheikh Muhammad, now sitting on a gilded sofa at the head of the tent. He sat rigid, seemingly bored, with the shepherd's crook held upright in his hand. The etiquette of the evening was that one was not permitted to leave one's seat unless summoned by the sheikh. We sat for over two hours, and only three of the sixty-odd guests were invited to the royal settee.

"Have you ever been with a sheikh on a bustard hunt?" the landlord asked me as the evening dragged on. "It's the craziest thing I've ever seen, but it's like a religion to them. They're out in the desert from dawn to dusk, covered with dirt and dust. The driver is submerged in one of those jeeps, as if he were in an APC"—armored personnel carrier. "The sheikh sits next to him in an elevated seat that swivels at 180 degrees. I guess it's a good hobby, if you're into that kind of thing."

"What kind of thing?" I asked him.

He looked somewhat startled, then said, "My lady, these Arabs eat the houbara for sexual purposes—it's full of vitamins."

Some days later, the rains began in Balochistan. "They're in retreat," Mirza announced in triumph when I arrived at his office that afternoon. "We've had reports of spottings all along the border—the sheikh's caravans are clogging the roads. They're abandoning Sindh Province, and converging on Balochistan."

"But it's only just begun raining," I said.

"That doesn't matter," he replied. "One day is enough. The houbara needs only very sparse vegetation. Now do leave me in peace. I have no more time. I'm sending you to the beach."

"The beach?"

"Yes. There are some Bahrainis or Abu Dhabians—I'm not sure who they are—training falcons. Report back to me immediately on what you see." (Apparently, in return for agreeing to help me learn more about the houbara hunts, Mirza expected me to become a member of his team.)

So with his deputy, Beg Mohammed, and another conservation official, I headed for the beach. It was on the outskirts of Karachi and was deserted when we arrived; only scattered sand dunes and desert scrub broke the monotony of the pebbles and salt marshes, which stretched for many miles.

In a matter of minutes, from behind a sand dune, four men appeared. They looked somehow menacing as they walked toward us across the empty sand. They walked in cadence, silently in single file. Their long robes were the color of the desert: gray and brown. They wore red-and-white checked kaffiyehs, and brown leather gloves covered the right hand and wrist of each of them. When they came closer, I could distinguish falcons on their wrists.

Perched immobile and erect, the birds were hooded to keep them calm before the hunt. Only occasional tremors of alertness, and their hooked bills and talons, distinguished them as birds of prey. They were creatures taken from the wild that could never be truly tamed.

One of the falconers chanted softly to his bird. The rhythm was that of the hoofbeats of a camel crossing the desert sand. The four men were now directly in front of us. None of them spoke; they only stared. I studied the face of the one closest to me: the color of tanned leather, with a craggy nose and piercing dark eyes, it bore an uncanny resemblance to the face of the saker falcon he carried on his arm. The bird was in perfect feather—golden and dusty brown, with perfectly drawn white spots on the tips of her feathers and extraordinarily large talons.

"Where is she from?" I asked the trainer.

"Abu Dhabi," Beg Mohammed interrupted.

"Northern Balochistan," the trainer replied.

"But isn't it illegal to trap falcons in Pakistan?" I asked.

The two men looked at each other, and then they laughed.

Now a customized Range Rover hurtled toward us, its driver, a thickset man in a white kaffiyeh and robe and very dark glasses, bouncing up and down. The car screeched to a halt, and the driver, jumping to the ground, introduced himself to me as Khalil al-Mazoor, the chief falcon trainer of the president of the United Arab Emirates, Sheikh Zayed. Then he embraced Beg Mohammed, in the traditional Arab-Pakistani way.

"When is Sheikh Zayed arriving?" I asked Khalil.

"In January, *inshallah*. May Allah give us rain. We've surveyed every inch of our hunting grounds. The deserts are barren, and we need flat areas to hunt. We cannot hunt in the mountains, because there we risk losing our falcons, and that is very costly." He smiled.

"How costly?" I asked him. "What did you pay for this saker, for example?"

"No comment," he said. (I learned later from a falcon dealer in Balochistan that Sheikh Zayed bought fifty falcons in Pakistan that year. Their average cost was $20,000 each.)

I asked Khalil if he could arrange for me to travel with Sheikh Zayed and his entourage when they arrived.

"Are you crazy?" he said. "You don't know what the hunt entails. We travel hundreds—*hundreds*—of miles in the desert each day. It is blistering hot one minute, freezing cold the next. Your color changes from the desert. So does the color of your clothes."

He abruptly returned to his Range Rover, and we followed him and watched as he carefully removed four woven wicker baskets from the backseat. He lined them up in a row on the sand, and I peered inside.

"That's the houbara bustard," Beg Mohammed said, perhaps a bit too sharply. He sounded a bit like an auctioneer.

Each basket contained one houbara, its legs tied to the wicker with twine. The birds were buff and sandy-gray, and their undersurfaces were white. A black-and-white crest topped each head, and unique black-and-white frills adorned their necks. They were about the size of chickens, and I guessed that they weighed perhaps three pounds. One of the birds attempted to crane forward, its long neck outstretched. I was amazed to see how its contours and coloration fused so naturally with the desert and its shrubs, and remembered something that a friend had told me earlier—that the houbara is such a master of camouflage that special effort is needed to pick it out even at fifteen yards and even when you know all the time that the bird is there.

I stared into the basket. The houbara stared back. The look was somehow disarming; I can't recall another bird ever looking at me quite that way.

Khalil issued orders and fingered a set of amber prayer beads. His white robe and white kaffiyeh wafted gently around his pudgy body in the late-afternoon breeze.

"How do you train falcons?" I asked.

"On the houbara," he answered, as though stating a simple fact. He then explained that the houbara is not the falcon's natural prey.

"But the Arab royal houses have hunted the houbara with falcons for centuries," I said.

"I know that," he answered, and walked away.

One of the falcon trainers roughly broke the twine holding the houbara's legs. He pulled it out of its wicker basket and clipped its wings. The houbara looked back at us before it was released. It seemed reluctant to fly, although the tight binding of its legs now made it difficult for it to run. (It normally prefers running—at speeds of up to thirty miles per hour, as fast as a galloping horse.) Its wingbeat seemed shallow as it finally took to the air, flying in the direction of the open sea, only some ten feet above the sand.

Next to me, the trainer removed the saker's leather hood, and the bird twitched her head, scanning the horizon. On spotting the houbara, about two hundred yards away, she bobbed her head in expectation, three or four times, up and down. In less than a minute, she left her trainer's arm and soared toward her prey, flying swiftly and deliberately. The trainers broke ranks and dashed behind the birds; the other three falcons remained on their trainers' arms. Khalil, Beg Mohammed, and I followed at a walk. Flocks of nesting birds, flapping and screaming, soared from the dunes in front of us and into the air. Then all was quiet, and I saw a white flutter of feather and tail from behind a mound of sand. The saker made her final swoop, and white feathers flew in the air.

A falcon trainer told me that if I really wanted to see a hunt I should go to Balochistan, to Chagai district. It was a Saudi hunting area—a place called Yak Much. Since it bordered Afghanistan and Iran, Chagai was on one of two migratory paths by which the houbara entered the country, and was thus one of the most preferred hunting areas in Pakistan.

A sixteen-hour car ride through desert and mountains and tribal lands brought me back to Quetta, and to Balochistan—the only province in the country where the houbara is known to breed. In increasing numbers each year, eggs, chicks, and birds were being smuggled out, primarily to Taif, Saudi Arabia, where French scientists—in a multimillion-dollar effort of limited success—were attempting to breed the houbara in captivity. In the autumn of 1991, Mirza had confiscated five such consignments—some five hundred birds in all—in just six weeks.

Shortly after my arrival in Quetta, I called on the provincial wildlife minister, Jam Ali Akbar. He told me that he really wasn't much of a wildlife person himself. He wrote pop music and was the president of Balochistan's Roger Moore Fan Club. I asked him if the provincial government was doing anything to protect the houbara.

"It's impossible—it's a federal-government matter," he said. "And these sheikhs are extremely attached to this little bird. It's not a simple matter." He shook his head. "The wildlife people say this shouldn't be permitted. But then the sheikhs' agents come, bringing priceless gifts, like diamond-studded gold Rolex watches. And sometimes, I've heard, they dispense briefcases containing a couple of thousand dollars—and you can keep the briefcase, too. The sheikhs say that these are migratory birds, so we lose nothing. And if we don't permit it, they'll simply go somewhere else."

Quite by accident, I met Balochistan's largest falcon dealer, Mir Baz Khetran, one afternoon in my hotel. His presence there shouldn't have surprised me. Royal hunters had begun arriving, en route to their hunting grounds, and guards with AK-47s stood watch in the parking lot, which was increasingly occupied by Land Cruisers, Range Rovers, and customized jeeps with Arabic license plates and green vinyl tarps that were covered with sand and dust. Most of the vehicles had horizontal bars across their backs, on which hooded falcons perched. Falcons had become a familiar sight throughout the hotel. Two shared the room next to mine with their Saudi royal trainers, who were en route to Yak Much. Three more were in the room across the hall. You could track them easily by the green-black stains they left in the carpeted corridors. The falcons seemed at home in the lobby (I happened upon one of them under the hotel's Christmas tree) and blended naturally with the Afghan mujahideen fighters back from the jihad and with the highly perfumed men in business suits who were buying or selling drugs, arms, or birds. Mir Baz and his brother, Lal Muhammad, dealt in falcons together, which was largely illegal in Pakistan. Lal Muhammad also served as one of the chief minister's key advisers—on wildlife.

It was Lal Muhammad who trapped the falcons, Mir Baz explained, their servants trained them, and then he himself sold them to the sheikhs. His falcon empire had ensured him a seat in parliament, and he had been a cabinet minister in Benazir Bhutto's recently dismissed, short-lived government. Mir Baz was in his early forties, and had a round, puffy face and dark hair. He wore sparkling rings and a good deal of cologne; gold chains covered his chest, which was half exposed.

"Such hectic times," he said, slumping in his chair. "The falcon season lasts for only four months." (The most expensive falcons migrate with the houbara from Siberia.) "But fortunes, madam!— fortunes can be made. There is a huge competition between these Arab sheikhs. And if a sheikh sees a falcon that he judges to be *hurr*," or noble and free, "and if that bird is nearly white or totally black—both are extremely rare—that sheikh, madam, nearly has a heart attack. He simply must buy it, and will pay *such* money for beauty."

"How much?" I asked.

"Nothing less than the equivalent of $8,000. The record price for Balochistan this year was twenty-five lakhs"—$120,000—"for a shahin, which was caught in the northern border area, near Zhob. By the time it reaches the Middle East, it will bring much more."

All the sheikhs hunted their falcons only through March, he said, and then released them to the wild, each man keeping three or four favorites for the following year's houbara hunt. Mir Baz then explained that the peregrine, the shahin (a subspecies of it), and the saker were the sheikh's falcons of choice, and that their price— which was sometimes negotiated over an entire day, sometimes pleasantly, sometimes not—was based on a complicated system involving color, age, pedigree, and size.

"The shahin is more valuable than the saker, and it is particularly rare," he said. "It is also the fastest bird on earth. It dives at the houbara at 250 miles an hour, hits its body, and breaks its bones. But it's not a very persistent hunter. The saker is; it is slower, but it attacks again and again and again. When the saker and the houbara struggle on the ground, it's an uneven match. A defect in the houbara is that its claws are very small."

Mir Baz then said, "You know, madam, these Arabs consider the houbara an aphrodisiac."

"So I've heard," I replied.

"But some of them, madam, eat one houbara a day—sometimes two, if it's a special occasion. That means they may eat as many as *five hundred* birds a year!"

Several nights later, I was invited to dinner by the Nawab Akbar Khan Bugti, who was now the leader of the opposition in the Provincial Assembly, having been defeated in elections the previous year after the mullahs withdrew their support for him. Nevertheless he remained one of Balochistan's most powerful men.

When I arrived at his home, I found his receiving room crowded with his usual friends. Sardars, mirs, and maliks sat cross-legged on the Bukhara rug and lounged against pillows piled along a wall. The nawab greeted me warmly; he then went from guest to guest, and each reported on the site of one or another of thirty or so royal parties hunting in his tribal lands. Depending upon the number of hunters and their falcons' pedigree, each party was bagging between ten and thirty houbara a day.

"Where is Yak Much?" I asked the nawab, after he had spoken to his guests.

"In the middle of God's country," he replied. "It's miles and miles from nowhere—nothing but tons and tons of sand. And it's totally off-limits to everyone except the Saudis. Ask *them*." He pointed out two men on the other side of the room, and then introduced me to Ali Mohammed Notezai and Sakhi Dost Jan. They were the kingmakers of Chagai district, of which Yak Much was a part.

Notezai was a member of the Provincial Assembly and was allegedly involved in the drug trade. He reminded me of a penguin with stubble on its face. Sakhi Dost was a rather more distinctive type: a large man, he had a broad, menacing face, and his teeth were betel stained. He wore a brown waistcoat over his *shalwar kameez* and a white turban, cockaded and lofty, that tied from behind, so its folds of soiled cloth streamed down his back. His wealth, which was considerable, was also said to be grounded in smuggling and drugs, and he had the reputation of being a bit of a Robin Hood. He robbed only the rich, he told me, explaining with unchallengeable logic that there was no point in robbing the poor.

Both men (who, in April of 2000, were sentenced to life imprisonment for drug trafficking) had known the Saudi defense minister, Prince Sultan, for years—ever since he began hunting in Chagai district, where he held exclusive sway over nearly twenty thousand square miles. They told me that the Saudi hunters would be led by one of the prince's sons: Prince Bandar, the ambassador in Washington, or Prince Khalid, who had commanded Saudi forces during the Gulf War, or Prince Fahd, the governor of Tabouk Province. But it would definitely be a son. "In this wild mavericking, they don't trust even their brothers," Notezai explained.

"What *is* so fascinating about the houbara?" I asked.

"The sheikhs tell me it is the ultimate challenge for the falcon," the nawab replied. "Much of the fascination is in the flight, it can go on for miles. The falcon is the fastest bird there is, and the houbara is also fast, both on the ground and in the air. It is also a clever, wary bird, with a number of tricks. Part of the lure is in *finding* it. You can spend half a day following its tracks. It's a contest—your wits against its. Then there's the contest between the two birds. The houbara tries to stay on the ground, where it is difficult, sometimes impossible, for the falcon to strike. The falcon tries to coerce it, cajole it, frighten it into the air. There the falcon reaches for the sun, and then comes down on the houbara—but it must stay above. Otherwise the houbara, whether as part of its defensive armor or in its reaction to fear, emits a dark-green slime violently from its vent. Its force is so strong that it can spread for three feet, and it can temporarily blind the falcon, or glue its feathers together, making it unable to fly. The sheikhs have told me that once that happens, many falcons will never hunt the houbara again."

The nawab called for a servant and gave him instructions in Balochi. The servant left the room, and he returned carrying a custom-built leather case. He placed it at my feet.

"Open it," the nawab said.

I did. Nestled inside, protected by a fur lining, was a 24-karat-gold-plated Kalashnikov. It was a gift to the nawab from the Minister of Defense of the United Arab Emirates, who hunted in Balochistan each year. It was the size of a normal Kalashnikov but was perhaps three pounds heavier, because of the gold. It was engraved with the royal coat of arms, and its two magazines were also plated in 24 karat gold. The nawab handed it to me. I had held a Kalashnikov before, but I had never held three pounds of gold.

"In the old days, we would hunt the houbara on foot or camelback," the nawab said. "We would try to outsmart it, using the camel as a shield. The houbara knows the camel, since the camel grazes in the areas where the houbara feeds. You couldn't go directly for the bird, or it would flee. So you circled it on camelback, making the circle ever smaller. The houbara would watch, mesmerized, confused. But now customized vehicles have replaced camels, palaces have replaced tents. They use radar, computers, infrared spotlights to find the bird at night. What is the challenge? What is the thrill? The odds have changed immensely for the houbara. The poor bird doesn't stand a chance anymore."

Early one cold December morning, I headed southwest for Yak Much. Prince Fahd, the governor of Tabouk Province, would be leading the Saudi royal hunt, and he was about to arrive. Arrangements had been made for me to stay at the government guesthouse in Dalbandin, which is the closest town to Yak Much, thirty-five miles away.

As we sped along the highway, we passed tiny villages hidden behind towering, dun-colored walls. Watchtowers and sentry posts sprang into view unexpectedly along the desolate road. The mountains dropped suddenly onto a plateau, then onto desert, which rose and fell in mounds and dunes. A tiny black line stretched across it— the railway line to Iran. In addition to pilgrims and smugglers, it ferried immense water tankers, which Sakhi Dost Jan then trucked from the station to Dalbandin. He controlled the town's entire water supply—and about everything else there, it seemed.

Dalbandin is a little desert town of some five thousand people with mud-baked streets and a teeming bazaar. Its mud houses are dwarfed by the soaring minarets of a white marble mosque, which had been built a few years earlier by Prince Sultan. The town's economy was based on grazing and smuggling, and every man seemed to be armed. Dalbandinians were now outnumbered by Afghan refugees two to one. The guesthouse was a low-slung building with peeling green walls and a concrete floor, covered here and there by straw mats. There was no heat, and everything was freezing cold. There was no running water, no electricity, no coffee, no butter, no herbal tea. "But if we are fortunate, madam, we may have a few hours of electricity tonight," Rahim Bux, the caretaker of the unfortunate building, told me as soon as we arrived. He explained that Dalbandin had no electricity; the town's center operated on generators provided by the provincial government and by Prince Fahd. "But the Saudi generators stopped working after a year," he said. "And the government generators never worked at all."

As we drove out of town that evening, the lights came on at the preappointed hour of six o'clock. Then, at precisely 6:15, they all went out.

Yak Much (One Date Palm) is a desert village of about a hundred people, one gas station, and a few little food stands and shops. Actually, it now has five date palms, though its most distinctive feature is a large green board at the village line, which in bold lettering announced NO HUNTING PERMITTED. Since the houbara breeds here, Yak Much is, in principle, a protected sanctuary.

A mile or so beyond the sign was the Saudi royal camp. My driver was the first to spot it. There was nothing around us except desolate miles of sand, but then, stretched along the horizon, we saw lines and lines of tents. If we hadn't been looking for them, we could easily have passed by. The camp was deep in the desert, five miles off the road, and as we continued along the highway we could see the tents one moment, and the next moment they would disappear.

We left the highway at an unmarked point—there was no road—and careered across the desert, lurching around bushes and shrubs. Then the camp came into focus—scores and scores of black, brown, and white pyramidal forms. Against the flat emptiness of the desert, the tents suggested a gathering of giant dinosaurs. The camp sprawled over some ten acres in two concentric circles, bringing a medieval city to mind. The inner tent city, of forty-four *chamianas*, was surrounded by perhaps sixty smaller tents. They stood like a wall, as if to keep all outsiders out. The perimeter was guarded by Pakistani levies and border militiamen, dressed in blue or gray sweaters and berets. Some were swathed in blankets against the desert chill. The inner city was guarded by security men in the retinue of Prince Fahd.

Vehicles were lined up in neat patterns on the perimeter of the camp: water tankers, oil tankers, petrol tankers, and a fleet of customized hunting jeeps. There were immense yellow cranes to pull the vehicles out of the sand if the need should arise; a mobile workshop, which was fitted with everything necessary to overhaul a car; and huge refrigerator trucks to carry the hunting bag out. Silver satellite dishes were anchored in the desert rock. From inside the camp, you could make a phone call to anyplace in the world. I spotted two royal falcon trainers whom I had met in Quetta earlier. They carried mobile telephones, and their falcons were perched upright on their arms.

There were now about a hundred falcons inside the camp for the seventy or eighty royal hunters who would accompany Prince Fahd. Only the prince's favorite falcons would arrive with him. I asked the chief of the Pakistani security detachment how long it had taken to assemble the camp, and he said only four days. The hunting vehicles—there were sixty—and the heavy equipment, tents, generators, and fuel had all been transported from Jidda by C-130s to the airport in Dalbandin.

"Where is Prince Fahd's tent?" I asked.

"There," he replied, and he pointed to a white *chamiana* on the far side of the camp. Its inner lining was of cashmere cloth, hand-stitched, he said, and its entrance panels were brocaded with gold thread.

Officials in Dalbandin had told me that the Saudi royal parties—which usually hunted two to three thousand birds during their month long stay—had no beneficial impact on the local economy: they'd given residents only two generators (which, of course, didn't work), a mosque (which they didn't need), and the airport (which was used almost exclusively by the hunters themselves—exclusively, that is, until the season of 2001–02, by which time the government of Pakistan had granted the U.S. military proprietary use of it as a staging area for Washington's newest Afghan war).

As we drove out of the tent city, only some two hundred yards beyond the last security ring, my driver pointed to eight baby houbara, strutting across the desert unperturbed. Their bare legs were spindly, and their heads were held high. As we came closer, they soared into the sky. Dusk was approaching, and I looked out the window, back at the camp, where generators had switched on the lights. The tents glittered against the darkening sky. Small campfires flickered, silhouetting men in flowing headgear and long, flowing robes. The last thing I saw as the camp disappeared from view were the satellite dishes, which hung in the night like giant moons.

At the camp the following evening, after Prince Fahd himself had arrived, I sat in a Land Cruiser next to the dining tent, whose vast brown folds with intricate gold stitching billowed in the wind. The tent was surrounded by some twenty-five security men, who stood at smart attention with their Kalashnikovs.

I sat in darkness, my head covered with the hood of my cape. It was bitterly cold, and the wind was ferocious. Land Cruisers and Range Rovers began to arrive. As I waited for Prince Fahd's personal physician, whom I'd met earlier in the day, I watched Dalbandin's notables saunter toward the dining tent, where they had been invited to dine with the prince. The visiting wildlife minister, Jam Ali Akbar, was flanked by servants and guards carrying two carpets, which were gifts for Prince Fahd. Ali Mohammed Notezai strutted like a peacock as he entered the tent. Sakhi Dost Jan, wearing his brown waistcoat and white turban, shouted instructions here and there. Earlier that day, I had spoken to both men about the possibility of my meeting Prince Fahd.

"Impossible," Notezai said. "The prince doesn't want to meet any women this time."

"I'm not a woman. I'm a journalist."

He shrugged. "It's all the same," he said.

The prince's personal servants ferried bottles of mineral water and huge trays of food between the tents: roast lamb with dates and rice; hot nan bread; hummus; tahini; baskets of fruit. I watched two trainers open a large wicker basket near my jeep and pull out two baby houbara with clipped wings, to be used for training falcons. Carrying the little birds in their left hands, they walked off, each with a falcon perched on his right wrist.

I left the jeep and stood in darkness near the entrance of the dining tent. Inside, Prince Fahd, dressed in a camel-colored woolen robe embroidered with gold thread, sat cross-legged on an Oriental carpet, receiving his guests. The floor of the *chamiana* was covered with exquisite Kashan and Persian antique carpets and rugs; bolster pillows, in silk cases sewn with gold thread, lined the walls. In a far corner, there was a network of cellular phones and other communications equipment hooked to a satellite dish. Behind the prince, like a ceremonial guard, thirty-five hooded falcons stood at attention. They perched on specially designed, hand-carved *mashrabiyya* stools, etched with ivory and gold. The falcons were of three different kinds—different in color, age, and size. Despite their magnificence, however, all were dwarfed by a peregrine that stood at the prince's side, on the arm of his chief falcon trainer. The peregrine had traveled with Prince Fahd on the royal flight, and during the entire evening she never left his side.

No drinks were brought from a mobile bar affixed to the prince's tent, much to the annoyance of his heavy-drinking Pakistani tribal guests. Prince Fahd spoke mostly in Arabic, which none of his guests understood. He spoke English only with his guest of honor, Jam Ali Akbar.

Then, in a toast of sorts, Price Fahd said, "There is brotherhood in this tent. We are all brothers in Islam."

The guests waited for him to say something else—perhaps that he would build a hospital, or install tube wells, as the Dubai royal family had done in nearby Kharan. But Prince Fahd said nothing more. Instead, he stood up and led his guests out of the *chamiana* and into a smaller tent nearby where dinner was served.

The Saudis walked apart, with the Pakistanis behind, across the short stretch of desert separating the two tents. Between the two groups, the chief falcon trainer walked alone, Prince Fahd's peregrine perched on his gloved arm.

Sakhi Dost Jan was the last of the VVIP guests to depart. He stood outside the dining tent, flanked by bodyguards and aides. He gesticulated, then shouted. A Saudi intelligence officer flailed his arms. Other Saudis came up and encircled the two men. "What is happening?" I asked one of the guards.

"Rupees, madam," he said. "Lakhs of rupees." He rolled his eyes.

After some ten minutes of negotiations, an aide of Prince Fahd's appeared and presented Dalbandin's godfather with two bulging leather saddlebags. Sakhi Dost smiled his toothy smile. He then got into his Range Rover and roared away.

One of the guards brought me a plate of food and a cup of tea. I looked down at the dark meat, which was surrounded by rice. "Is this the houbara?" I asked.

"Yes," he replied.

I hesitated momentarily, and then took a few bites. The meat was tough and stringy—it reminded me a bit of goat—and left a bitter aftertaste. Far from arousing amatory impulses, it had an irritating tendency to stick in my teeth. How could anyone eat five hundred of these birds a year? As I pondered the mysterious ways of the desert, Prince Fahd's physician came over to chat.

"Is it true that the houbara is an aphrodisiac?" I asked.

He looked amused and shrugged his shoulders. "No," he replied. "It's basically a diuretic. But they *think* it's an aphrodisiac."

The howling of dogs and the chanting of mullahs again woke me at dawn. No sooner had I started a fire in my tiny fireplace, in Dalbandin's guesthouse, than one of the royal trainers whom I'd met in Quetta the previous week—I'll call him Farouq—pounded on my door. "We're taking the falcons out!" he said. I was to accompany him back to the Saudi camp.

We left the highway before we reached the main turnoff to the camp and drove into the desert for perhaps a mile, to a spot where another trainer and a driver waited in a customized, carpeted Range Rover. Both men carried hooded falcons—one a shahin and one a saker—on their gauntleted right arms.

I was instructed to sit in the backseat of the open jeep, with the other trainer and the hooded saker, which seemed dangerously close to my left knee. Farouq—with the hooded shahin now perched on his black-gloved wrist—took the revolving bucket seat in the front. He adjusted it to its maximum height, and towered some three feet above us in midair.

The sun was just beginning to rise, and the sky was violet pink. All around us the flat emptiness of the desert stretched endlessly. The silence was broken only by the wind and the grinding of the Rover's gears. From time to time, we passed black slate formations that resembled giant marshmallows burned in a bonfire.

The trainer next to me, whom I'll call Mahmud, wore sandals and bright Argyle socks. "Her name is Ashgar," he said of the hooded saker on his arm. "And she's just a year old. That is the perfect age for this particular bird."

Ashgar was extremely light in color, almost blond, and measured perhaps thirty inches from her head to the tip of her tail. White spots on the tips of her feathers, which resembled polka dots, blended quite smartly with the red leather hood and jesses she wore.

"Her talons are like steel if she grabs you. That's why we wear gloves," Mahmud said, stroking Ashgar and giving me a pleasant smile. He then told me that Ashgar was from Iran and had been a particularly sought-after bird, not just for her color but for her "soul."

I studied the falcon more closely. A tiny solar cell, covered by glass, was attached to her tail feathers, and a thin metal aerial affixed to it rose from her feathers up the bottom of her back. It was a French-made radio transmitter, a tracking and homing device slightly larger than a watch cell; it had an especially sensitive receiver that had been devised purely for the houbara hunts. Mahmud said that the transmitter weighed about five grams and had a radius of some eight miles. It gave off a constant beep once the bird was on the wing. "If she is lost during the hunt, we can retrieve her by the next day, maximum," he said. "Even when she parks for the night, we get a constant signal in our jeeps."

"Can the transmitter be used to track a houbara?" I asked.

"Only indirectly," he replied. "If the falcon catches a houbara, the beeper tells us where they are. But basically, we track the houbara by radar or two-way radio."

The wind became fierce as we raced across the desert at eighty miles per hour, searching for houbara tracks and knocking down everything in our path: shrubs, bushes, even tiny trees. I glanced ahead at the driver, who was wearing goggles and a crash helmet and was bent over the wheel intently. I suspected that at one time or another he had driven a tank.

A friend had told me earlier that the Yak Much desert was more like the Middle East than anywhere else in Pakistan was; you could travel for days without seeing another human being. We had traveled for more than forty miles, and although I'd seen no human beings, I had certainly seen their traces: plastic bags, abandoned jerricans, and discarded tires. There were some areas where the hunting vehicles had so flattened everything in sight that a plane could have landed with ease.

Then Farouq shouted, "There are the tracks!"

They were unmistakably those of the houbara—three-toed footprints dotting the sand.

Farouq stroked the shahin's underbreast, whistled softly in her ear, then raised his gauntleted arm above his head.

"A-hoh, a-hoh, a-hoh," he chanted, above the noise of the wind, as he removed the shahin's jesses and hood with a single quick movement of his free hand. "Strike! Strike! Strike!" The shahin cast her piercing eyes incessantly around, bobbed her head, and then lurched forward, leaving Farouq's arm. She soared into the air, her radio transmitter and aerial visible in the feathers of her tail. She flew low—barely off the ground—to conceal herself, and was often out of our sight as we raced across the desert, following her path. We were guided by her radio beeps.

"It should be four or five minutes," Mahmud said, and he explained that the shahin had extraordinary vision: she could sight for over a mile. But we raced along for twenty minutes before we spotted the shahin and a houbara on the ground. At first they were tiny, indistinct forms in a mustard field. Then, as we surged ahead, I lost sight of the houbara.

"There she is!" Farouq shouted.

"Where?"

Even with high-powered binoculars, I couldn't find the houbara, and it was perhaps only ten yards away, concealed and camouflaged— its contours and buff-and-sandy-gray coloring blending perfectly with the desert and the bushes and shrubs. When I finally did spot it, it was frozen behind an absurdly small bush and uttered no sound. It was a baby, weighing perhaps two pounds. The shahin circled over- head, then swooped down, attempting to frighten the houbara off the ground. The houbara tried to enlarge itself by spreading its wings, and watched our every movement with unblinking yellow eyes. In an instant, it had taken off. It darted across the desert like a roadrunner; its long legs seemed not even to touch the ground. Its tail was spread like a peacock's, and its chest was thrust out.

We raced, dashing, lurching, and jolting, in huge zigzag circles, following the two birds. Then both took to the air—an absolutely cloudless blue sky. You could distinguish the houbara by its white undersurface and wings. The shahin soared and dipped, her vast wingspan spread majestically. The houbara eluded her and tried to gain altitude. From time to time, the birds almost disappeared, be- coming tiny, inky webs, but they were never completely out of sight—we had our high-powered binoculars in addition to our radio beeps. This hunt was a far cry from the romantic image of the lone Arab walking across the desert in his flowing robe with his pet fal- con perched nobly on his arm.

The shahin soared for the sun and came down on the houbara, attempting to break its neck. The houbara flew on furiously, and the shahin struck again. The two birds spiraled downward. We found them near a tamarisk bush, struggling on the ground. The baby hou- bara lay exhausted but was still trying to kick. The first thing that the shahin had done was blind the houbara's yellow eyes, so that it could not run or fly away. Farouq cut open the houbara, retrieved its liver, and fed it to the shahin. He then hooded the falcon and ritually slit the baby houbara's throat, to conform with dietary laws.

"Now it's halal," he said—permitted in Islam.

There was a time, Wahajuddin Ahmed Kermani, Pakistan's retired Inspector General of Forests, told me, when the houbara had been so plentiful in Pakistan that you could count them from the roadways "like butterflies in a field." But that was in the 1960s, before the great sheikhs and falconers began hunting in Pakistan.

I called on Kermani, one of his country's most respected environmentalists, at his Karachi bungalow. If any Pakistani had attempted to save the houbara, he was that man. As we sat in his drawing room one morning, sipping cups of tea, he described his efforts to save it as "the only failure of my life." He went on to say, "For a quarter of a century, the hunting has been intensive and sustained. They go through the desert like an invading army. It's slaughter, mass slaughter. They kill everything in sight."

When I asked him why the government of Pakistan had done so little to deal with the situation, he replied, "Because we lack the moral fiber and the moral courage."

Kermani applauded the efforts of Tanveer Arif, the president of the Society for Conservation and Protection of the Environment, or SCOPE, a Karachi-based group that had challenged the legality of the houbara hunts in the Sindh high court. "The hunts are sheer hypocrisy, and totally contrary to our laws," Arif told me one afternoon. "Since 1912, in the days of the Raj, the houbara has been a protected species. Yet while Pakistanis are being arrested and prosecuted if they're found to be hunting the bird, Arab dignitaries are given diplomatic immunity." (Although in September of 1992 the Sindh high court ruled in SCOPE's favor, its decision has had scant impact on successive Pakistani governments.)

Like Kermani, Arif was deeply upset that international pressure to ban the royal hunts was not being brought to bear on the government of Pakistan. Twenty-three countries, including India, Iran, and the former Soviet Union, have legislation that protects the houbara, or bustards generally, and in the vast majority of these countries there is a ban on all hunting.

After returning to New York from Pakistan, I asked Paul Goriup, the leading houbara expert at the International Council for Bird Preservation, in Cambridge, England, whether he thought the international community was doing enough.

"International efforts are exceedingly scant," he replied. "The houbara is merely a distraction, not a priority. There's no doubt that in the Pakistani provinces of Sindh and Punjab the population, which was once sizable, is now terribly diminished. Balochistan is thus the only area left that is worth hunting in—and the problem there could be severe. There's a breeding population, and if the sheikhs hunt after February"—they always do—"then it's a disaster, for they impinge on the breeding population for the next year.

"It's a stalemate in Pakistan," Goriup went on. "The Pakistanis see the Arabs breaking Pakistan's own laws, yet huge sums of money are involved. As for the Arabs, they realize that the houbara is declining outrageously, yet they continue to hunt. Still they're worried, and I'm absolutely convinced that they would accept regulations if the regulations were there." He thought a moment, and then said, "I've maintained consistently that the houbara should be protected by the United Nations' Bonn Convention on Migratory Species, because such protection would elevate the problem to an international level. We could set up protected areas. Money would flow the right way. We must restore habitats and breeding grounds. This is the only way the houbara can be saved."

At the end of January, Prince Fahd closed down his camp. He had stayed in Yak Much for a month. His daily bag of houbara averaged from twenty-eight to thirty-five birds. Some days later, Prime Minister Nawaz Sharif called on the United Arab Emirates leader, Sheikh Zayed, in his two-hundred-room palace in the Cholistan desert, near his hunting grounds. He presented the sheikh with two priceless falcons—peregrines, it was said. Then, in an offering that no one understood, he also gave him a tent.

CHAPTER 5

DAUGHTER OF PAKISTAN

BY EARLY APRIL 2002, as Pervez Musharraf, with a crisp salute to the crowd, launched his one-man referendum campaign, everyone was waiting to see what Nawaz Sharif and Benazir Bhutto would do. The two former prime ministers—both twice elected, both twice deposed, both now in exile abroad—remained the only two political leaders in Pakistan with a real constituency. Sharif was entering his sixteenth month of enforced residency in Saudi Arabia, to which he had been dispatched by the general who overthrew him. Bhutto, who divided her time between London and Dubai, had been out of Pakistan for three years, since April 1999, following her conviction by a high court on charges of corruption. Now to the abiding irritation of the general who had served them both, Nawaz and Benazir were threatening to return home.

And if they did, any plans that Musharraf had for presiding over a sanitized, "grassroots" democracy, under his Army's tutelage, could be laid to rest. The general quickly reiterated that neither of the two would be permitted to stand in the parliamentary elections scheduled for October 10, 2002, and then he announced, again and again, that both would be arrested immediately if they tried to return to Pakistan. For they were the potential spoilers: the chief challengers to the ordered democracy that Musharraf hoped to sculpt. And he knew their strengths—and their weaknesses—well. First, he had served Benazir as her Director-General of Military Operations, in the mid-1990s, when the two had helped to spawn the now regrouping Taliban. Then, in turn, he had served Nawaz, as his Chief of the Army Staff, a post he had held in the summer of 1999. That was when the Kargil operation was launched, the operation in the mountains of Indian-controlled Kashmir that had provoked the world's first direct combat between two nuclear powers.

Yet it was Benazir's planned return that was more problematic to the general. For according to his intelligence reports, she was, once again, the most popular politician in Pakistan. And as had been true for many years, her Pakistan People's Party remained the country's only party with a nationwide constituency. Thus, if the October parliamentary elections were free and fair, Benazir (at least according to ISI reports in the spring) would almost certainly be returned to power again. Indeed, one Pakistani official told me that it was precisely because of this that Musharraf—over the objections of some of his powerful corps commanders—embarked on his referendum at all. The general knew that a parliament dominated by Benazir was highly unlikely to cede the country's presidency to him.

By the time that Pakistanis went to the polls, on the last day of April, the political season had not yet really begun. Far more important than the referendum was what would come next in the standoff between Benazir Bhutto, the feisty aristocrat from Sindh, and Pervez Musharraf, the increasingly self-absorbed *mohajir* general who migrated from India.

At 1:45 a.m. on April 4, 1979, four wardens entered the prison cell of Zulfikar Ali Bhutto, a waifishly thin man, nearly wasted away by malaria, dysentery, and hunger strikes. Two of them lifted him by the arms and two by the feet, and he was carried out. His back was so low that it sometimes brushed the floor. He had insisted on shaving and bathing earlier that night—and had done so, with some difficulty—and he had changed into fresh clothes. He had always been fastidious about his appearance. But now the tail of his blousy shirt, ensnarled in the cleats of one of the wardens' boots, became tattered and soiled.

Outside in the courtyard of the Rawalpindi District Jail, Zulfi Bhutto, the first popularly elected prime minister in the history of Pakistan, was deposited on a stretcher, and his wrists were manacled. There was no guard of honor and no military salute. As he was carried two hundred yards or so to a wooden scaffold, he raised his head slightly, but he said nothing. Otherwise, he didn't move. The wardens led him up the scaffold onto a wooden plank, and there a hangman put a hood over Bhutto's head, completely covering his face, and a rope around his neck.

"*Ye mujhai?*" ("This to me?") According to a book by the chief of his security detail, Colonel M. Rafiuddin, who stood two feet away, Bhutto said this in a faint voice, and the colonel believes he also heard him say, "God help me, for I am innocent!"

At 2:04 a.m., three hours ahead of schedule and contrary to the prison code, the hangman pulled a lever releasing the wooden plank, and Bhutto's body plunged into a well.

"The bastard's dead!" Zia ul-Haq gleefully told his generals when the news came.

The only family members who had been permitted to see Bhutto in the hours before he died were his daughter Benazir, his firstborn and favorite child, who was then in her twenties, and his wife, Nusrat. They had been taken under guard from a deserted police training camp where they were imprisoned and driven the few miles to the jail. Unlike previous visits, they had not been permitted inside his cell, and Benazir had sat cross-legged on a concrete floor as they received his final instructions through a thick, barred door.

"I pleaded with the jailers, I begged them to open the cell door, so that I could embrace him, and say a proper good-bye," Benazir told me in the summer of 1993. "But they refused. When I left him, I couldn't look back; I knew that I couldn't control myself. I'm not even sure how I managed to walk down that corridor, past the soldiers and past the guards. All I could think of was my head. 'Keep it high,' I told myself. 'They are all watching.' "

Some fourteen hours later, Benazir remembers, she awoke suddenly at precisely two o'clock in the morning and sat bolt upright in bed. "No! No!" she screamed. "Papa! Papa!"

In her 1988 autobiography, she wrote:

I felt so cold, so cold, in spite of the heat, and couldn't stop shaking. There was nothing my mother and I could say to console each other. Somehow the hours passed. . . . We were ready at dawn to accompany my father's body to our ancestral graveyard.

"I am in *Iddat* [mourning] and can't receive outsiders. You talk to him," my mother said dully when the jailer arrived. . . .

I walked into the cracked cement-floored front room that was supposed to serve as our sitting room. It stank of mildew and rot.

"We are ready to leave with the prime minister," I told the junior jailer standing nervously before me.

"They have already taken him to be buried," he said.

I felt as if he had struck me. "Without his family?" I asked. . . .

"They have taken him," he interrupted.

"Taken him where?" The jailer was silent.

"It was very peaceful," he finally replied. "I have brought you what was left."

Fourteen years after her father's execution, on an oppressively hot evening near the end of May in 1993, I traveled with Benazir Bhutto and her entourage from Islamabad to Rawalpindi for a *jalsa*, or public meeting—a time-honored relic of the Raj, in which rulers are presented to their subjects atop lofty wooden platforms in sweeping British gardens and public parks.

Pakistan's ever-turbulent politics were in even greater confusion than usual that night—and so they continued to be for the next six weeks, until the Army intervened and ended a paralyzing power struggle between the prime minister and the president by securing the resignations of both, appointing a caretaker prime minister, and calling new elections for the fall.

The standoff had begun in mid-April, when President Ghulam Ishaq Khan, the septuagenarian bureaucrat elevated to the presidency after Zia's death, dismissed Prime Minister Nawaz Sharif, a multimillionaire—and a former protégé of both men—on grounds of corruption, nepotism, and mismanagement; then, thirty-nine days later, to the astonishment of many and amid much fanfare, Sharif was reinstated by the Supreme Court. The wily old president, undaunted by the court's decision, was determined not to let Sharif rule. He consequently proceeded, at a dizzying pace, to dismiss two of the country's four provincial assemblies, including that of the immensely important province of Punjab—Sharif's power base. The prime minister's infuriated supporters, in a move considered less than prudent even by the rough-and-tumble standards of Pakistani politics, kidnapped the Punjab assembly's unfortunate secretary, Chaudry Habibullah, and then spirited away some 150 of its legislators—to prevent their defection from the Sharif camp—bringing them to Islamabad aboard specially requisitioned planes. They were all now living in a hotel—luxuriously, but under armed guard. The country's powerful army generals were not amused. And by the end of May they, like everyone else in Pakistan, were absorbed by how Benazir Bhutto would respond.

Since her last meeting with her father, on that morning in 1979, she had taken up the political mantle that went with her family's feudal fiefdom in Sindh. She was just two years out of Oxford and was not yet twenty-six. Against the odds, she had managed—so far, at least—to survive five years of imprisonment and house arrest and then a succession of political crises, conspiracies, and attempts on her life. In December of 1988, at the age of thirty-five, she became the first woman prime minister of a Muslim country, and one of the youngest prime ministers in the world. Her election was a vindication against a military establishment that had overthrown and then hanged the father she adored.

Her prime ministership was stormy and lasted only twenty months; now she was the opposition leader in the National Assembly, or lower house of parliament. In one sense, she was only a marginal player in the power struggle between the president and the prime minister; in another, the votes she could attract and her galvanizing popularity in the streets were of crucial importance to both men. She was playing the kingmaker's role, and her choices could well determine Pakistan's future course.

Much to her discredit in the eyes of many—including a large number of her aides—she had aligned herself with a vastly unpopular president, to unseat a democratically elected prime minister; and it was the same president who, less than three years before, had unseated her own government, and largely on the same grounds.

As one of her aides and I drove toward her residence in Islamabad, we passed the King Faisal Mosque, a huge expanse of marble topped with a golden dome, which is the burial ground of Zia ul-Haq. Benazir Bhutto lived in the shadow of his grave.

Her home—a modest two-story stucco building—was drawn up next to others in squat formation along the neatly ordered road, and it was distinguished by guards with machine guns standing at somewhat imperfect attention at the gate, a satellite dish on the roof, and larger-than-life campaign posters of her—and her father—pasted on a ten-foot-high wall surrounding the property.

Inside there was perpetual motion, as there always is in Benazir's entourage: guards strapping on their firearms; aides quibbling about an absurdly esoteric detail; fashionably dressed women rushing from room to room, Chanel bags swinging from their shoulders as they shouted into cellular telephones. On this occasion, at least, there was legitimate reason for stress. Benazir's popular support was said to be at a record low, and some aides had argued that this was no time to be testing that support by holding a public meeting.

Benazir calmly slipped a lipstick and a homemade anti-tear-gas kit—a satchel containing a wet towel, salt, and a lemon—into a black handbag, then donned her chador and swept through her office and out into the driveway where a silver truck was parked. She quickly jumped into it, and it sped off. We all dashed behind her—some hundred aides and guards and me—and weaved our way, rather recklessly, into a motorcade.

A tall, elegant, handsome woman, with large, luminous brown eyes, arched eyebrows, and a swanlike neck, Benazir is the opposite of inscrutable; she could never be a sphinx. Her skin is clear and pale, which prompted her father to call her Pinkie when she was born; the nickname is still used by her closest (but only her closest) friends.

It sometimes seems that she intentionally deemphasizes her looks, hiding behind owlish glasses, various head coverings, and bulky shawls. Some women criticize her for it; some men sympathize, because Pakistan has an appalling human-rights record on women and is among the most conservative Islamic societies in the world. Its blasphemy laws are among the most rigid, and the most misused. And its extraordinary Zina Ordinance—promulgated during Zia ul-Haq's rule—mandates that rape must be substantiated by four male witnesses, and that the victim must be able to "identify" the man involved. Only after months of sustained protest by women's groups in 1984 was a blind, sixteen-year-old servant quietly acquitted of being an adulteress, under the Zina Ordinance. (But things improved little for village women in Pakistan and, in July of 2002, a tribal council in the Punjab decreed the gang rape of a lower caste woman to avenge her brother's alleged act of illicit sex—an act that investigators found never occured.) Yet, paradoxically, in a society whose generals had spent a decade enforcing a version of Islam that would banish women from the public sphere, the people of Pakistan elected Benazir.

As we sped along the highway, I listened to her aides talk about Zulfikar Ali Bhutto and about Benazir, both charismatic populists. But he was a leftist, she is not. He was a product of the seventies, a pillar of the nonaligned world, who played the Americans off against the Soviets, and favored the Chinese; she was more like General Zia in that she followed an essentially pro-American foreign policy. He was a man of more than average vanity; she reveals little about herself.

She is part Radcliffe and Oxford, with an extremely well-stocked mind, full of feminist literature, peace marches, the Oxford Union, and with a very liberated social life. She is also part feudal Sindh, a haughty aristocrat, the daughter and granddaughter of immensely wealthy landlords, whose inheritance gave her the right to rule. And she was also part of an accumulating myth: of a populist father, extraordinary, brilliant, and frightening, who was overthrown by a usurper and killed; of his two sons, who sought revenge, one of whom died mysteriously, while the other went underground and disappeared for years; and of the slip of a girl who, after a decade of imprisonment and struggle, routed her father's old enemies to become prime minister.

Rawalpindi is a chaotic mixture of pungent bazaar, Army headquarters, Victorian bungalows, and public parks. There was palpable excitement in my jeep as the crowds lining our route to the *jalsa* grew; then, suddenly, they mushroomed.

Endless waves of people—nearly all of them men, mostly young and mostly, to judge from their appearance, lower-middle class— enveloped the motorcade, pushing, shoving, setting off fireworks, and firing Kalashnikovs into the air. The sunroof of the silver truck opened, and Benazir appeared. Her head and chest were covered by layers of gauzy white veils, and she was illuminated by spotlights mounted on the top of the truck. She was an icon—beautiful, imperial, aloof—passing, almost dreamlike, through the dust and exhaust fumes.

The crowds grew frenzied at the sight of her. They pressed dangerously against her truck and against our jeeps, fighting to touch them and to catch a glimpse of anybody traveling in the magical convoy of Benazir. Car horns tooted, loudspeakers blared, and volley after volley of automatic gunfire pierced the air. I looked out from the jeep as best I could, past the hands, shoulders, and arms pressing against it, and it seemed that we were being showered from every window of every house and shop by rose petals and flowers. Thousands of them fell into our vehicles. It took us three hours to travel four miles.

When we finally reached our destination, Liaquat Bagh, a public park, the scene was tumultuous. After being held hostage in her truck for nearly ten minutes by the mob, Benazir was extricated by about fifty security guards. She looked rather irritated as she climbed some wooden steps and strode across a platform, where I had joined the assembled VIPs. Then, almost immediately, she was transformed. Tens of thousands of people filled the park, and others spilled into the surrounding streets and lanes; still others crowded on rooftops, and some hung from nearby trees. She waved and grinned as the crowds roared their approval—cheering, clapping, and stomping their feet. The din became deafening: more automatic weapons were fired into the air, more fireworks filled the sky. A campaign song of the Pakistan People's Party, or PPP, blared from loudspeakers in a half-disco, half-tribal beat:

Listen, all you holy warriors!
Look at Benazir, the nation joins her!
Long live Bhutto! Long live Benazir!

"She was right, thank God!" one of her aides confided with relief. Benazir's gamble on this public appearance had proved the pundits wrong. Her obvious popularity would harden her resolve to demand new elections, whatever the cost. She had been seeking a new poll since 1990, when, after being dismissed as prime minister, she went down to a crushing defeat at the polls, which swept Nawaz Sharif to power and which she charged had been rigged. Her campaign to oust Sharif's government had taken various forms, including a "long march" the previous year, which he had ruthlessly suppressed; now she was threatening to stage another, bringing hundreds of thousands of supporters into the streets and laying siege to Islamabad until new elections were called, and in the process risking a return to martial law. (It was this threat which would be a key factor in forcing a reluctant Army to intervene and schedule the new polls.)

"We came to power not with silver spoons in our mouths but from the jails!" Benazir now shouted to the crowd, with a forceful jab of her hand. "Do you want elections?"

"Yes! Yes!" the onlookers thundered back. "Benazir! Benazir!"

"Everyone should be equal before the law, so why did the same court that had ruled that the dismissal of our government was justified rule differently now? The final verdict should be in the people's court! Will you join me in our campaign to march on Islamabad?"

"Yes! Yes!" thousands of voices roared.

For thirty minutes, Benazir played the crowd like a maestro— fiery, impassioned, her eyes blazing and her slender hands slicing the air. From time to time, she adjusted a white veil to keep it modestly covering her head.

As I looked down from the platform and out into the crowd, I realized that there were no women, as far as I could tell. Then I spotted them, behind the platform, in an enclosure roofed with dark-green sheeting hung from poles. Most were exceedingly well dressed, each wearing a silk *shalwar kameez*. Their hair was painstakingly coiffed, and none of them had covered their heads. On their fringes, milling about and straining to glimpse Benazir, was a group of perhaps sixty women dressed in black burkas. They had come to the Bagh from the Rawalpindi slums.

"What is the price of meat today?" Benazir demanded of the crowd. "What is the price of flour?"

The women on the fringes craned forward. Their heavy burkas contrasted sharply with Benazir's embroidered silk *shalwar*; their gnarled fingers with her soft, manicured ones. You could tell that they wanted to like this populist aristocrat, and that they did.

The political game is in Benazir Bhutto's blood. And if it is a paradox for the daughter of a patrician family to be preaching mass politics, then she fails to grasp it. It is just one of the anomalies of her life. She is an Eastern fatalist by birth, a Western liberal by conviction, and a people-power revolutionary—who had carefully modeled herself on Evita Perón and Corazon Aquino—through sheer necessity. She is an expensively educated product of the West who has ruled a male-dominated Islamic society of the East. She is a democrat who appeals to feudal loyalties.

Most people who know her describe her with stock phrases: "She's her father's daughter," or "She lost her youth in jail," or "She's the bravest person I've ever met," but they are used only after considerable thought. For Benazir is not an easy woman to talk to or to know. She doesn't like discussing emotions—you have to read between the lines. Invariably, she steered a conversation into politics and foreign affairs, gliding over what appeared to be a troubled relationship with her mother; the fact that her marriage, to Asif Ali Zardari, was arranged; and any talk of her enigmatic brother Mir Murtaza, who disappeared in 1979, after his father's execution, and formed the terrorist organization, Al-Zulfikar, which was dedicated to overthrowing General Zia's regime. Murtaza now lived in Damascus, and was Zulfikar Ali Bhutto's only surviving son.

A shadow crosses Benazir's face when she is asked about her father's well-documented acts of repression—the tortures and imprisonments—and the charges of a rigged election in 1977, which was his final bid to retain power. She remembers only one side of him: the genius without flaws; the populist reformer and spellbinding orator, who restored national pride after the humiliating defeat by the Indian Army in 1971; the man who returned Pakistan to—and gave it its longest period of—civilian rule. She has firmly shaped her memories, as she has compartmentalized her life, and I had been warned by her friends that her demand for loyalty to her father's legacy was absolute. She simply would not tolerate any criticism of him.

To reach Bilawal House, Benazir's Karachi residence, named after her first child and only son, you pass No. 70 Clifton, her father's handsome villa, where everything began. When Benazir was growing up in the house, Bhutto had served as foreign minister, administrator during a period of martial law, president, and then prime minister until he was overthrown by Zia ul-Haq. Bhutto's promotion of Zia, over several other generals, was a move that he later described as "the biggest mistake of my life."

Her home consists of two buildings—one her residence, the other a headquarters of the PPP. Enclosed by a high concrete wall, it sits in the middle of a desolate marsh of salt flats and sand, not far from the sea. For years, it was surrounded by an abandoned building site approved by General Zia in an attempt to intrude upon her privacy.

Disorderly lines of men stood outside Benazir's gate when I arrived. Some carried petitions, others wanted jobs, still others hoped to be put on the PPP's election ticket. There was not a woman in sight.

One of Benazir's aides accompanied me as I walked across a well-manicured lawn toward her residence. We passed a carport in which bicycles, scooters, and toys were lined up in neat rows. Sitting in a hallway just inside the entrance door, Benazir was waiting for us. "You're late," she said, standing up to receive us. Then she gave a dazzling smile. It was a characteristic welcome: a hint of steel embossed with charm.

She wore a fitted violet *shalwar kameez* with an embroidered bodice and sandals. Her *dupatta*, or long scarf, had slipped slightly off her head, revealing a cascade of auburn-tinted hair. Around her neck was a gold *tawiz*, or charm, meant to protect her from evil spirits with a verse from the Koran.

This was intended as a courtesy call—I had not seen her since her 1988 campaign—and I had been told that her advisers were sharply divided over whether she should agree to my request for a series of interviews during the coming weeks. But she had clearly already made up her mind. "Let us begin," she said abruptly, discouraging all small talk—something she always seems to consider totally irrelevant.

The condition of our first meeting was that no personal questions be asked, and she was exceedingly guarded about herself yet full of opinions on everything from the political crisis in her country to Clinton's election campaign.

"No, this is not my most serious political crisis," she said, and, "No, I was not born to rule."

Her quicksilver temperament and fierce intelligence were never more evident than now, as she hectored her way through the interview. She sat perched on the edge of a rattan chair, ever at the ready, sometimes examining her short, pink-polished nails.

One of her former ministers, a distinguished-looking man nearly twice her age, came into the hallway and whispered something to her. She was obviously not pleased by the interruption, or perhaps by the news. She snapped instructions to him in a blend of Sindhi, English, and Urdu. She then stood up with finality, whereupon he went out. I discovered that this is what she always does when she wants someone to leave.

She called for tea and coffee—she drank Diet 7UP—and eyed me across a large coffee table, the surface of which was bare except for a box of Kleenex, her purse, and two books: *Islam and the Economic Challenge*, by M. U. Chopra, and Shaista Suhrawardy Ikramullah's colorful essays on Moghul women, *Behind the Veil*. Almost at once, she was interrupted by a telephone call, and I studied my options as quickly as I could. Our political conversation had not gone well, so I decided to disregard the condition. Clearly, I could not understand her politics until I had a measure of her personal life.

She had spent an eighth of it in prison or under house arrest: she was about to turn forty and had first been arrested at the age of twenty-four, after returning home from Oxford, where she had studied politics, economics, and international affairs. Street protests against her father had begun earlier that year, and within days of her return, he was arrested, and she set aside her plans to enter the foreign service and devoted herself exclusively to his defense. Within two years, Zulfi Bhutto was dead.

The remaining family members scattered across the globe. Her brothers, Mir Murtaza and Shah Nawaz, went into hiding in Afghanistan. Her sister, Sanam, the only apolitical member of the family, lived in London exile. And Begum Nusrat, the long-suffering family matriarch who had spent four years in and out of prison or under house arrest, went into exile in France.

When Benazir had concluded her telephone call, I asked her what her starkest memory from those years was.

"What an unusual question," she replied, and her entire look changed. She became pensive and reflective, and then she said, "The martyrdom of my father, and my own feeling of helplessness. I knew that morning that he was going to be killed, but there was nothing—nothing—I could do. That's my starkest image, the one that comes back to haunt me, over and over again."

She paused and seemed to be studying the room. After a few moments she went on. "Equally stark was finding my brother Shah Nawaz dead on the floor." (The youngest of the Bhutto children and Benazir's favorite brother, Shah Nawaz died, apparently of poisoning, in July of 1985, in his apartment in Cannes, after having spent a number of years on the fringe of the guerrilla world in Libya, Syria, and Afghanistan, as the "military commander" of Al-Zulfikar.)

"I had never seen a dead body before," Benazir went on. "He looked as if he were sleeping. But he was so immobile, like a marble statue." She stopped and said nothing more about him.

Then she continued. "My life had been so different before my father was overthrown. I had been exceedingly protected by my parents, and had done only fashionable things. Then, suddenly, I was thrust onto a stage, where life became stranger than fiction. My life became so bizarre. In a sense, it was larger than life.

"So much has happened. After I won the election, I was of the naïve view that an electoral victory would end the hardship, the trials. But this wasn't true. During the time I was prime minister, I lived under the shadow of a strong military, a hostile president, an entire constituency that Zia had built: extreme right-wingers, religious bigots, and politicians bred during that era of military dictatorship. They had one thing in common: they were dead set against allowing me to rule.

"Then, when my government was dismissed, there were the same death threats, the knocks on the door, the torture of my party workers—although it was not on the same magnitude as during my father's time. I remember when my husband was arrested"—Asif Ali Zardari was detained on politically suspect charges of murder, kidnapping, and extortion in October of 1990, after her government fell—"it brought back all the images of my father and his arrest. When my father was arrested, we never changed his room. We kept his bedroom slippers as they were, his reading glasses, his writing pen. Everything was kept as it had been, waiting for him to return. He never did.

"When my husband was arrested, I would look at *his* glasses, *his* writing pen, *his* papers, and wonder if *he'd* ever come back. It was an enormous joy when he was finally released this February, so I'm not saying that there have not been moments of great triumph and great happiness: my swearing in as prime minister, the first such woman in the Islamic world; the birth of my children; my relationship with my husband. But there have been far more moments when I have found myself embroiled in a life larger than my own, on a much larger canvas. In a sense, my life has not been my own."

Pakistan is not an easy country for anyone, let alone a woman, to rule. Fourteen thousand people are born each day; more than a thousand of those will die within a year. Angry students cling to a vision of an Islamist utopia, and equally angry mullahs chant prayers from the country's countless mosques. For this is the *Islamic* Republic of Pakistan—the world's only nation created on the basis of Islam. A half-century later, the idea of a Muslim homeland has yet to work. Shiite Muslims assassinate Sunnis on Karachi's streets; Sunni Muslims massacre Shiites inside mosques. No one in this disparate land seems to bond in the name of Islam. It is perhaps because of this often antagonistic religious diversity that no leader since independence—neither Benazir nor her father nor the Army generals—has defined precisely what Pakistan is meant to be: A Muslim nation? Or a theocratic Islamic state?

As a result, Pakistan, more than any other country I've known—and especially its dynastic families, like the Bhuttos—has embraced the legacy of the empire. The country's power structure, as a consequence, has changed little since the British left. It is still dominated not only by the military but also by the tribal chiefs and the feudal landed aristocracy, none of whom are by nature democratic, and all of whom find a woman leader unnatural at best. Only the Islamic clerics have joined the triumvirate since independence.

But it was the Army that was the final arbiter of affairs, and when I traveled through Pakistan in the summer of 1993 I found that it was effectively in control of Benazir's anarchic home province of Sindh. Truckloads of commandos, backed by armored personnel carriers, riot equipment, and jeeps, had fanned out through the province the previous year to restore order across a vast desert plain from which heroin—approximately 30 percent of the West's supply—was exported, where dacoits were indigenous, and where murder was commonplace.

It was from the town of Larkana, on this plain, that Benazir's political inheritance sprang. She was born in June of 1953, into one of Sindh's wealthiest and most influential feudal families, the oldest of four children of Zulfi Bhutto and his second wife, Nusrat Ispahani, an Iranian beauty and debutante, who was considered by the conservative Bhutto family to be far ahead of her time. (Bhutto's first wife, a cousin whom he married in an arranged match when he was twelve, continued to live on the family compound.)

Benazir spent much of her childhood on the sprawling estate—it covers at least ten thousand acres—in the midst of the desert, where families live in walled compounds, ringed by rifle sights; where landlords are often brutal and peasants are serfs; where women are in purdah and men enjoy their whiskey and pheasant shoots.

Her father was one of the first sons of a Sindhi feudal lord to be educated abroad: he was sent to Berkeley and Oxford, and returned home a highly sought-after barrister and a brilliant raconteur. He soon attracted the attention of the military ruler General Mohammed Ayub Khan, and in 1958 the general offered him a ministerial position in his martial law regime. Bhutto was only thirty, and he never looked back.

He moved his family to Karachi, and there Benazir, Mir Murtaza, Sanam, and Shah Nawaz grew up under the watchful eye of an English governess, who taught them table manners, netball, and cricket, and who recited nursery rhymes. Their father, ever indulgent, bought their clothes from Saks Fifth Avenue—the measurements of all the Bhutto offspring were on file there—and although he pampered them all, more or less, it was clearly Benazir whom he was molding and tutoring to become his political heir. When she was six, he began reading her tales of the exploits of Napoleon from his library—thousands of first-edition volumes, one of the largest private collections in the world. When she was eight and was studying under Irish nuns at Karachi's Convent of Jesus and Mary, he introduced her to Chou En-lai. And when she was ten and Bhutto was foreign minister, he woke her in the middle of the night to sit at his side as he received bulletins on the assassination of President John F. Kennedy.

In 1969, when she was sixteen, her father insisted, in spite of her own misgivings—and those of the college—that she enter Radcliffe. There, by her own account, she was initially lonely and shy, hated the cold weather, but relished the first anonymity of her life. Nonetheless, one of her classmates told me, during her first semester she cried most of the time. Things were decidedly better by her second term; she had abandoned her silk-lined *shalwar kameez* in favor of sweatshirts and jeans. She became addicted to peppermint-stick ice cream and rock concerts, memorized lengthy passages of Kate Millett's *Sexual Politics*, and marched against the war in Vietnam. "I felt very strongly about it," she told me. "I was an Asian, and Asian blood was being spilled."

The following year, blood was being spilled even closer to home, and 1971, Benazir's third year at Radcliffe, proved to be a turning point for her. After nearly a year of anarchy and revolt in East Pakistan, which the Pakistani Army had brutally suppressed and which left more than a million Bengalis dead, the Indian Army moved in, and the third Indo-Pakistani war in twenty-three years began. In December, East Pakistan, backed by a victorious India, became the independent nation of Bangladesh. Benazir Bhutto had become a fiery, defensive Pakistani nationalist.

If professors criticized the Pakistani Army's genocide, she would lecture the lecturer in a vehement, angry voice. When, that December, her father summoned her to join him at the United Nations—where he was fighting a futile battle to forestall Pakistan's dismemberment—he tutored her in the importance of deceit, having her interrupt his meetings in the Pierre Hotel with the Americans or the Soviets or the Chinese to announce imaginary phone calls from one or another of the delegations not in the room, in order to keep his adversaries guessing about his next moves. "One of the fundamental lessons of diplomacy is to create doubt: never lay all your cards on the table," he told her.

"I follow[ed] his instructions but not his lesson. I always lay my cards on the table," she wrote in her autobiography—the closest she was able to come to criticizing her father in it. Some Western ambassadors who have dealt with her find her assertion difficult to accept.

During these marathon negotiations, Benazir met the senior George Bush, who was then the U.S. ambassador to the United Nations, and spent many acrimonious hours in the Pierre suite.

"Ah, you're at Radcliffe," he said when they were introduced. "My son is up at Harvard, too. Call me if you ever need anything." And he handed her his card. Eighteen years later, they met again, this time at the White House, and she requested sixty F-16s.

The Indo-Pakistani treaty ending the war and relinquishing East Pakistan was negotiated in the vice-regal splendor of the palaces of the Raj, in the British summer capital of Simla, which had become the capital of the Indian state of Himachal Pradesh. Benazir was part of her father's ninety-two-member entourage, which was otherwise exclusively male, and she continued to absorb the fine art of foreign affairs. "Everyone will be looking for signs of how the meetings are progressing, so be extra careful," her father cautioned her. "You must not smile and give the impression you are enjoying yourself while our soldiers are still in Indian prisoner-of-war camps. You must not look grim, either, which people can interpret as a sign of pessimism . . . Don't look sad and don't look happy." It was a lesson she would never forget: appearance would often take precedence over reality.

In Simla, Benazir met Indira Gandhi—who had also been groomed by her famous father as his dynastic heir. The Congress Party elders had prudently acquiesced—as those in the PPP would later do with Benazir—assuming that Mrs. Gandhi would be malleable and that they could run her as a figurehead. Both women ran the elders instead. When Benazir met Indira, she was unnerved but intrigued by her. She describes the Indian leader in her autobiography as a woman of "silk and steel" with "a cold aloofness" about her. "She kept staring at me," Benazir writes. "Was she seeing herself in me? . . . She was so small and frail. Where did her famed ruthlessness come from?" She points out that Indira's father was dead, and asks, "Was she lonely?"

As Benazir's Radcliffe graduation neared, she pleaded with her father to allow her to stay in the United States to do her master's degree, but he was adamant that she go to Oxford instead. He had already enrolled her there, at birth.

The years there proved to be the happiest of her life. Classmates have described her, variously, as resembling a maharani, beautiful, monarchical, and very rich, and as a jet-setting princess, given to driving a yellow sports car—which was littered with parking tickets—at considerable speed, and being squired around by handsome young men in velvet jackets, who competed for her attentions at Lady Margaret Hall.

It was at the Oxford Union that she gained her formidable debating skills, under the tutelage of invited guests who ranged from Germaine Greer and Arthur Scargill to Harold Macmillan and Edward Heath. She became the Union's president, the first in many years to paint the president's office (powder blue) and change its decor: an antique Bukhara carpet—a gift from her father—covered the floor, and a print of ancient Rome, which had been in his room at Christ Church in 1950, hung on the wall.

While Benazir was at Oxford, she was invited to tea by Margaret Thatcher, who was then the Opposition leader in the House of Commons, and was returning her father's hospitality. Despite their age difference, the two women had much in common and became fast friends. They were brought even closer together when they were both prime ministers, and they consulted frequently on their scrambler telephones, sometimes planning common strategy, sometimes charting the political downfall of a common foe.

I asked Benazir one morning, as we sipped coffee in her Karachi sitting room, what the basis of her friendship with Lady Thatcher was.

"Oh, I'm very fond of her," she said, perking up immediately. "Of course, she did many things that I can't defend: her cuts in health and education, for example. But privatization, in the Thatcher sense, was innovative. I admire it enormously. And she has political conviction; she's not an opportunist, and she doesn't test the wind. She goes where she wants to go. I admire her single-mindedness. It's far better to have firm convictions than to study the Gallup polls. And she's got tremendous courage. I remember the Falklands War. There were many who felt she was foolhardy. The Falklands were far away, small, unknown. But she fought for them, as some women wouldn't have had the courage to do. And with Bosnia, again, I admired the way she spoke out; that's leadership. I can't bear smoke-filled rooms and weaselly politics."

The two women had met over scones and tea sandwiches at the Dorchester Hotel one afternoon, when the power struggle between the president and the prime minister was assuming a threatening form. Benazir briefed Lady Thatcher and implored her, "What *should* I do?"

"Side with neither of them," Lady Thatcher advised. "They will use you and dump you. Let them fight it out and bleed each other."

And that is exactly what they did.

Benazir underwent profound changes between 1977, when her father was overthrown, and 1986. These were the years of imprisonment, London exile, and house arrest. She and her mother, sometimes together but most often separately, were shunted across the country and detained in some of its most hideous jails. There were also further, extended periods of house arrest, at No. 70 Clifton or at the Larkana estate, where prison rules still applied.

Her worst period of imprisonment came in 1981, when she was held for five months, from March until August, in solitary confinement in the Sukkur jail—a sprawling brick complex, medieval in design, in the Sindh desert, where temperatures often reached 120 degrees.

One evening over dinner at a fashionable Karachi restaurant on the Arabian Sea, two of Benazir's friends and aides, who had been imprisoned in Sukkur at the same time as she, told me about prison life. Like Benazir, they had been charged with no crime and had been offered no promise of release. Along with some fifteen thousand other political prisoners, they were being held "preventively." Shammin N. D. Khan, a rotund woman of cheerful disposition and hennaed hair, was in her late middle years and was a former member of the National Assembly, who had joined the PPP at its inception in 1967. As a consequence, she spent more than six years in Zia ul-

Haq's jails. Muneera Shakir was younger, perhaps forty, with black hair, oval eyes, and a slightly shy smile. She had been pregnant when she was imprisoned and was denied any medical care. On the day she was released, she gave birth, and within hours the baby died.

"Of course, we never *saw* Benazir during that time," Shammin recalled. "She was kept totally isolated, locked in a wing of the prison that had been emptied of all other inmates before she arrived. We were held in a crumbling barracks at the other end of the grounds or, sometimes, in tiny cells with no windows—no ventilation—and it was unearthly hot. We were all being held under what is called 'rigorous imprisonment': that meant we were being punished, and we had to work."

Some two hundred women political prisoners in Sukkur, all from the PPP, scrubbed the prison's floors and disinfected their cells; killed mosquitoes, flies, and rats; worked in the kitchen; did the laundry; or stitched and repaired their jailers' uniforms. Muneera often spent five or six hours a day washing a hundred or so uniforms by hand, beating them against rocks, then ironing them on a cracked concrete floor. Benazir, by contrast, had absolutely nothing to do.

Benazir's health deteriorated badly during her prison years; the medical facilities in Sukkur were nonexistent. According to Amnesty International, lashing and torture were not uncommon in General Zia's jails, nor was rape. Most of the victims were from the PPP.

Once a month, the women were permitted visitors, but only family members. And most of their family members were in prison themselves. From time to time, small groups of women were taken into the prison courtyard and, under guard, were ordered to do gardening; but nothing grew. They would glance across the prison grounds, toward the dun-colored isolation wing just beyond an open sewer, where Benazir was being held. Her cell was separated from the rest of the compound by four sets of padlocked gates, and consisted of four walls of open bars. She was confined, to all intents and purposes, in a giant metal cage. There was no furniture except a rope cot, and no toilet or running water; she bathed, when she could, from plastic buckets, under the watchful eyes of her female guards. There was only one light—a bare ceiling bulb—and it was extinguished every evening at seven o'clock. From time to time, one or another of her guards would leave a bottle of poison in her cell. If General Zia had a purpose in mind in subjecting her to all this, it was apparently to break her and to humiliate the Bhutto family.

Some days later, as I sat with Benazir in her drawing room, munching chips and sipping cranberry juice, the conversation turned to the past, and I asked her about her Sukkur imprisonment.

"Even now, though so many years have passed, I shudder when I think of it," she replied. "It was like being buried alive in a grave. You live, yet you don't live. The days turn into months. You grow older, but there's no measure—nothing is a landmark. I'll never forget how hot the desert was. There seemed to be a constant dust storm swirling inside my cell. I was always sticky from sweat, and often coated with grit. My skin cracked open from the dryness, and the sweat felt like acid as it cut into my skin. My entire body changed: I couldn't eat, yet I always felt bloated—my stomach seemed to expand. I discovered later that I'd become anorexic, and as though that were not enough, my teeth began to rot and my hair fell out."

Her voice was flat, perhaps too controlled, as she talked; only her flashing eyes betrayed the emotion that she must have felt. "Sounds become so important in solitary confinement," she went on. "Like the sounds of dead bats falling on the roof of my cell. What did I do all that time? It's strange, when you're released you can't remember how you passed the time. I used to ask my father in his death cell how he survived in prison, and he said that he'd pick a day from his life and go through the entire day, minute by minute. And that's what I did. It forced me to keep my memory intact. I also kept a diary at the beginning, I exercised, and I read the one newspaper that I was permitted each day as slowly as I could, doling it out, word by word." It was from a paper she saw while she was imprisoned that she learned that her brother Mir Murtaza was alleged to have masterminded the hijacking, in March of 1981, of a Pakistan International Airlines plane, securing the release of fifty-five political prisoners at the cost of one passenger's life.

I asked Benazir what her most difficult moment in prison had been.

She didn't answer immediately. Then she said, "The day that a jail official told me"—falsely—"that I was to be tried inside the jail, by a special military tribunal, and sentenced to death. I was stunned—I couldn't believe that they'd do it, though one side of me said that they would. A few hours later, someone left a bottle of poison inside my cell."

She fell silent, as if she were considering whether or not to go on. Then she said, "You have tremendous mood swings in prison. Sometimes I would think to myself, My father is dead, my brother is dead, my mother has cancer, and I'm rotting away in this cell. I have suffered and made sacrifices—and for what?"

She looked away, and then turned back toward me, and I asked what had sustained her during those years.

She responded without hesitation. "Anger," she said.

December 1, 1988, was a beautiful late-autumn day. There was a slight chill in the air that afternoon as guests arrived at the jarringly ornate presidential palace in Islamabad for Benazir's swearing in as prime minister—only the second, after her father, to be popularly elected in the history of Pakistan. Prior to the elections the previous month, she had never run for office; nor had she ever held a salaried job. On one side of the center aisle in the lavish audience hall were her friends and aides: young, elegantly dressed women in brocade and silk, whose *dupattas* hung from their shoulders, rather more Paris chic than Islamic pure; young men in double-breasted blazers and houndstooth suits who were full of witticisms, bantering in Oxonian English—the language they always spoke. On the other side of the aisle were the generals, straight-backed and unsmiling, and vaguely

Kiplingesque, some with their mustaches waxed into curls, and all carrying swagger sticks. Here and there—sitting together in protective pockets, it seemed—were groups of anonymous bureaucrats, wearing the traditional formal dress, the *kurta shalwar*, and groups of mullahs in large turbans and long, flowing robes. In the front row, Nusrat Bhutto, who as co-chairman of the party had worked exhaustively on the running of the PPP's campaign, dabbed at her eyes; across the aisle, Lieutenant General Hamid Gul, the chief of ISI, looked on disapprovingly.

Such a mixture, and such an occasion, would have been unthinkable only a few months earlier, but following the August crash of General Zia's plane, General Mirza Aslam Beg, the new Chief of the Army Staff, had pledged to hold free and fair elections. And he did.

Just after three o'clock, the lofty gold-mosaic doors leading from a foyer into the audience room were opened, and Benazir, escorted by presidential guards resplendent in gold turbans and starched white uniforms and carrying golden swords, walked the length of a red carpet, accompanied by the dour, domeheaded President Ghulam Ishaq Khan. She told me later that her first reaction as she glanced around the room at the generals, at the president, and at the mullahs and bureaucrats was "Can I trust them?" All of them, in one way or another, were products of the eleven years that Zia ul-Haq had ruled.

As Benazir and President Ishaq Khan continued down the aisle, she glanced at him. He had been her father's Secretary of Defense and was reliably believed to have warned General Zia that Bhutto was about to remove him, thereby provoking the general, if he had any lingering doubts, to stage his 1977 coup. She passed General Gul, the key Zia lieutenant, and committed Islamist, who had assumed formidable authority during the jihad as the dispenser of CIA arms; he and his predecessor (who died aboard Zia's plane) had also orchestrated the politicalization of the ISI as it had never been politicized before. More recently, he had used the agency's considerable power and funds to cobble together a rightist and religious electoral alliance to oppose the PPP; he and the ISI had also created Benazir's chief rival, Nawaz Sharif, a leader of the Muslim League. A pale and plump industrialist in his forties, who was from Lahore, Sharif had been plucked from obscurity by Zia to become one of his key protégés. He was now the chief minister of Punjab, and Benazir knew that without the support of Pakistan's most populous and powerful province she would not be able to rule. Would Sharif permit it, she wondered? Would General Gul?

When she reached the dais, a mufti began chanting prayers, the generals stood at attention, and Benazir, dressed in shimmering emerald green silk and a white *dupatta*—the colors of Islam and of Pakistan—took the oath of office, administered by the president. She placed her hand on a copy of the constitution, which her father's government had promulgated in 1973, but which had been rewritten by Zia ul-Haq to award sweeping powers to the president, including the power to dismiss the prime minister.

I had asked Benazir during the last days of her 1988 campaign what it was like to be the first Pakistani woman to run for prime minister.

"I've never thought of myself as a woman," she said. "I am, of course, but I'm more a person who was caught up in dictatorship. Circumstances pulled me into political life—my father's murder, my mother's illness." (Begum Nusrat was successfully treated for lung cancer.) "I never sought leadership of the People's Party for myself. But fate has such turns and shifts. When I was a child, there were many attempts on my father's life. Politics *scared* me. I remember the hushed voices when we would tiptoe into the drawing room, where the grown-ups were talking about demonstrations and guns. 'Don't speak in front of the children,' someone would say when they noticed us. This is a life I never wanted for myself."

When the swearing in was completed, a rather austere reception began in a nearby banquet hall, and over sweetmeats and milky tea, Benazir greeted her guests. For a fleeting moment, she looked slightly bemused, apparently noticing that more of the dignitaries had clustered around General Beg than around her. Groups of them came and went by turns: first, the Army generals, to whom she had already committed herself to effectively cede control of the country's nuclear-weapons program, of its high-risk policy in Afghanistan, and of its support to the anti-Indian insurgency in Kashmir. (Her authority over the military proved so marginal that when she requested the ISI files on her brother Mir Murtaza the agency refused to send them to her.) The generals were followed by the mullahs, who had already begun to shriek with despair at the evils that would befall a nation with a woman at its head. "They'd been saying the most audacious things," Benazir told me. "They issued *fatwas* that I must be stopped, and they circulated pamphlets saying that the Holy Prophet was weeping tears of blood: 'Oh, why, why, a woman elected prime minister?' Some of them even rushed off to Saudi Arabia to seek advice. Clergymen from Yemen to Egypt pulled out their holy books. I must say, my election did trigger a great debate in the Islamic world." During the campaign, the mullahs, assisted by Sharif and General Gul, had also air-dropped thousands of leaflets featuring doctored photographs of Benazir dancing in a Paris nightclub, and her mother, in a sequinned Western evening gown, waltzing at the White House with President Gerald Ford. "Anti-Islamic" was scrawled across the leaflets in thick lettering.

Standing slightly aloof in the mirrored, wood-paneled hall, as Benazir continued to receive her guests, was Robert B. Oakley, the ambassador of the United States, who had played a not insubstantial role in her swearing in. For thirteen days following the election, in which the PPP had amassed the largest number of electoral votes, President Ishaq Khan had nervously consulted with his generals and bureaucrats, and with Nawaz Sharif, while Benazir, just as nervously, had paced the floor of the drawing room of her dentist's bungalow, near the presidential palace, as she waited to be invited to form a government. On the fourteenth day, Ambassador Oakley called on the president and made it clear that the United States believed that Benazir should be sworn in.

Now the president and the prime minister stood together in the banquet hall, scrutinizing each other warily. The president wiped samosa from his lips and muttered a few words of congratulations. Then he abruptly turned to leave. "It's prayer time," he said.

"May I join you for prayers in the mosque?" Benazir asked.

"It's for men only," the president replied, and he began shuffling off. Then he turned around and added, "But you can watch."

No two images of Benazir look quite alike, and one senses that as prime minister she was never quite certain how to project herself: Should she be the avenging feudal daughter of Sindh? The urbane internationalist? The demure Muslim mother and wife? Or the impetuous aristocrat who, with arrogant ease, could plunge into the maelstrom of political maneuvering and intrigue?

She had little time to decide which persona fitted her best, for after twenty turbulent months in office she was dismissed. Confronted by a deadly combination of political, military, and religious foes, she did well, according to many Pakistanis, to last as long as she did; it was longer than many had expected she would. For although she cut a glamorous and popular figure abroad, at home she never really seemed to get a grip on either the country or the government. Pakistanis grew weary of her supporters' chants of "eleven years of tyranny" to explain away the nation's ills. Disillusionment followed, and Benazir's inexperience showed. In its nearly two years of existence, her government passed virtually no legislation.

She presided over a sliding economy, a deteriorating security situation, a growing communal threat, a confrontation between democracy and the Army, and dangerous diplomatic drift. She was harassed by an energetic opposition, led from the Punjab by Nawaz Sharif; she was destabilized by violence in her home province of Sindh; and she was faced with the growing hostility of both the Army and the Muslim clerics. Above and beyond this, she laid her administration open to the charge of corruption. Among the worst offenders, according to the president and the generals, were her flamboyant, controversial husband and her father-in-law.

There was a familiar ring to the president's charges against her to justify the dismissal of her government: corruption, nepotism, mismanagement, and loss of the people's confidence. Three times in the previous five years, Pakistani prime ministers had been dismissed on those grounds—real or imagined—by the president or the Army, or a combination of both. But Benazir had to live up to higher expectations than the others did.

"People were expecting a liberal, Western-educated woman with forward-looking programs," I was told by Dr. Hamida Khuhro, who is a formidable woman herself—an Oxford-educated friend of the Bhutto family but a political opponent in the feudal Larkana constituency. "When Benazir came to power, she could have set the trend, but the first thing she did was to shroud herself in a chador, the most obstructionist, outward manifestation of Islam, and begin praying incessantly at saints' tombs, the most superstitious part of Islam. She's vastly superstitious, and it shows. She could have been a reformer, but she wasn't; she did nothing for women, which she could have done. And with her education and her background, she simply has no excuse." (Benazir later told me, "There are some who would have liked me to solely champion women's causes. As a political leader, I can't.")

A Western ambassador said, "Benazir's a dreamer, a great conceptualist. She says all the right things, but she has no follow-through. She wasn't able to focus, to move things forward, or to control situations. Maybe she'll pick better people next time. It's her streak of loyalty that kills her; she always goes back to what people have done in the past—how they served her father, how much time they spent in jail—rather than considering what they could do in the future. She therefore failed to tap an enormous pool of brilliant young intellectuals and technocrats who could have turned this country around. Instead, she relied on the feudal landlords, who catered to her illusion that it was her birthright to rule. She's one of the most bewildering women I've ever met: one moment, she is utter charm; the next moment, she's so antagonistic that she comes perilously close to impertinence. But she's not a sulker; she's a battler and a sur-

vivor, and that's not all bad. Basically, she's driven: she's a PPP politician with the name Bhutto, and she never stops. She'll do anything
to get elected, and she simply cannot accept that anyone can do this
country any good except her. She's a wonderful campaigner; she
gives wonderful speeches. But the basic question we always come
back to is: Can she rule?"

A top presidential adviser, and one of Pakistan's ranking bureaucrats, remarked to me one morning that he was perplexed by
Benazir. "I told her from the beginning that she simply must try to
get on with the president. Here is a man, Ghulam Ishaq Khan, who
has been around forever; in him she could have found a friend, a
philosopher, a guide. He was seventy-three, for God's sake, and she
was only thirty-five. But she thought she knew better; I think she
was very badly advised. She should have tried to understand him,
but she was arrogant and impetuous, and acted, on occasion, slightly
like a Moghul empress. But that being said, in spite of everything—
she's been out in the cold now for quite some time—she remains the
only political leader in this country heading a political party with
roots nationwide. She is, in every sense of the term, the only national leader we have, and the only one who has genuine support in
the West." He paused for a moment, and then he said, "Her main
weakness is her husband. It's a pity. I wish she had married someone
else."

Asif Ali Zardari, a party-loving sportsman with a colorful past, was
an extremely charming forty-year-old businessman, with a handsome, rugged face, set off by jet-black hair and a thick, black
handlebar mustache. His main preoccupations before he married
Benazir were polo by day and discotheques by night. His one concession to her political vulnerability, after their engagement was announced, was to dismantle the disco in his Karachi living room.

Their marriage was an odd alliance and astonished many of
Benazir's friends—even those already accustomed to unpredictability

on her part—not only because she was marrying Zardari but because she had agreed to a marriage that was arranged.

She had been present during most of the negotiations between the two families (which took place in London in July 1987, over five nerve-racking days), as had he. "I avoided him as much as possible," Benazir said of the man whom she had met only once before, at a dinner party, but really couldn't remember very well. She maintains—not altogether convincingly—that it was not an "absolutely" arranged match, since she had been given the power of veto after Asif was chosen by her aunt.

Over the five days, the Bhuttos and the Zardaris came and went from a Bhutto family flat. But unlike conventional arranged marriages in Pakistan, before which investigations are made into family finances and status, the London talks were dominated by the question of whether Asif could cope with a wife as powerful and politically dominant as Benazir.

On the evening of the fifth day, she decided that he could, she told me one morning, adding, "Fate presented itself in the form of a bee."

Twelve of us were wedged—somewhat precariously, I thought—in one of Asif's Pajeros, as he drove us along a precipitous mountain road on our way to an old hill station of the Raj for a family outing. Benazir had invited me along the night before, explaining that it would be quite simple and casual, and it clearly was: Benazir and Asif, three children—Bilawal, who was four; Bakhtawar, three; and Asifa, four months—two nannies, three security guards, Benazir's political assistant and constant companion, Naheed Khan, and me, together with baby carriages, picnic baskets, baby bottles, baskets of cherries, boxes of diapers, and two mobile telephones. In front of us and behind us were two more Pajeros, one Mercedes, and two security cars. "My husband likes to travel in an entourage," Benazir said.

"What about the bee?" I asked now.

She explained that on the fourth day of the negotiations she had gone, with a niece, to Windsor Park—while Asif had gone to a polo match—and a bee had stung her hand. By the evening, when the Zardaris arrived at the flat, Benazir's hand was swollen and she was in considerable pain. Asif had insisted on taking her to a hospital and had arranged for a doctor and a car. Her most revealing comment was, "For once, I was not the one in charge."

She nonetheless continued to show a notable lack of enthusiasm for arranged marriages generally, and when the subject of her own came up she discussed it almost as one removed. So one morning over coffee, a few days earlier, I had asked her mother, Nusrat, why Benazir had agreed to such a marriage. (Despite the fact that Asif had been chosen by Zulfi Bhutto's sister, his widow—who had been rather desperately urging Benazir to marry for years—had been an ardent supporter of the match.)

An elegant woman with large eyes, a spirited disposition, and an easy smile, Begum Nusrat Bhutto was then in her mid-sixties, yet it was easy to imagine her as the striking, raven-haired beauty that she was when she married Zulfi Bhutto in Karachi in 1951. Theirs was not an arranged marriage but, rather, a love match, which was almost unheard of then. And all their children eventually followed their example and married for love—except Benazir.

"Things were very different in the fifties," Begum Nusrat explained. "Islamic fundamentalism wasn't strong, and I was always a free bird. Zulfi was also not yet in politics—he was still studying at Oxford—so we could do as we chose. But with Benazir it was a very different situation. She was already in politics, meeting loads of men; she couldn't afford a scandal. What if she fell in love? What if it was with the wrong man? Her life—her political life—would be ruined. She had resisted even the idea of marriage for years. I remember one day when we quarreled, and she said, 'Mummy, if you ask me one more time I won't marry at all.' But finally she relented, and agreed to an arranged match."

Ironically, the marriage, a liaison of convenience that was meant to silence gossip and, perhaps as important, to provide heirs to carry on the Bhutto legacy, had proved to be one of Benazir's greatest liabilities. Zardari was no Dennis Thatcher. "Her husband is her jugular," a Western ambassador told me. "He is generally perceived to be corrupt, and is known as Mr. Ten Percent, but she seems to be absolutely infatuated with him, and during her time in office she never bothered to rein him in." (During the government of Nawaz Sharif, Zardari was jailed for nearly two and a half years, either on or awaiting trial on politically suspect charges of murder, conspiracy, and extortion. He was now released on bail, after being acquitted in nine cases. He was still fighting a tenth.)

As we continued up the mountain road, we passed a number of shrines to saints, and I noticed that Benazir discreetly and slowly moved her head from right to left—a gesture of homage to the dead.

When we reached our destination, a sprawling bungalow with open verandas and sweeping lawns that was the summer residence of the governor of the North-West Frontier Province, Benazir busied herself with preparations for lunch, the nannies busied themselves with the children, and Asif and I sat together on the lawn.

There were recurring reports of growing tension between him and Begum Nusrat—with whom Benazir's own relationship was becoming increasingly strained—and I had been told by a number of party members of disputes between the two, over party matters, over his business dealings, and over his perceived influence on Benazir, so I asked him if it was true that, as his critics charged, he was trying to hijack the PPP.

"That's utter nonsense," he replied. "Even though I'm a member of the National Assembly"—and at one point he was a minister as well—"I don't think I'll ever become a politician, although I must admit I am becoming a formidable player in this political game."

"What's the difference?" I asked.

"For a politician, the game is a 100 percent profession, not a part-time job; it consumes you totally. And I'm not ready to make that commitment. At least, not yet. Now I still get my one hour of riding time each day, spend time with the kids, look after my little business. And if people like Jatoi, Mumtaz, and Pirzada"—all top lieutenants of Zulfi Bhutto—"were not able to hijack the party after Bhutto's death, how possibly can I?"

"You've been compared to Hillary Clinton," I said.

"I love it!" He roared with laughter. "Unfortunately, I don't think the comparison fits."

After lunch and naps and walks in the woods, Benazir and I sat in the garden, where her children were collecting ladybugs and picking flowers for her, and I asked if she worried about their safety, considering the number of threats on her life.

"Of course I do," she replied. "When I was prime minister, there was an attempt to kidnap my son, Bilawal—to kidnap him, can you believe it, from the *prime minister's house!*"

She paused and looked down into the valley, beyond the lawn, then turned back toward me. "It's really not been easy," she said. "But I lived in fear for my father's life the entire time I was growing up, and I'm determined that I'm not going to lead that life again, nor am I going to permit my children to have that kind of fear. I've adopted a philosophical view, and I don't dwell on threats. I feel that the time of death is written; in that sense, I'm a fatalist. But now that I have three children I do worry; they're so small. What would happen to them if something happened to my husband and me? Who would take care of them? But I try not to dwell on it. God saved me before. That's why I'm religious. Throughout my life, there's been no one to protect me—except my God."

One of the more enduring mysteries surrounding the Bhutto family was that of Benazir's brother Mir Murtaza, who had vanished from Pakistan more than a decade earlier, intent upon avenging his father's death. He had claimed responsibility for a number of attempts on Zia's life, including one that involved firing a heat-seeking missile at the presidential aircraft; the missile was deflected by a nearby kebab stand. A tall, handsome, and charismatic man, who was now thirty-nine, he had followed Benazir first to Harvard and then to

Oxford, which he left early in his second year, after his father's arrest. Since that time, he had moved from Afghanistan—where he shared offices with the PLO in Kabul—to Libya and Syria, and had been charged with masterminding not only the PIA hijacking but also a number of bombings and the assassination of a prominent politician who had been riding in a car with the judge who had signed Zulfi Bhutto's death warrant in 1979. From time to time over the years, Benazir and Mir Murtaza had met—in Paris or Damascus—and many people within the PPP wondered why during her prime ministership she had granted amnesty to others but never to him.

"He's a potential problem for her," a Western diplomat told me. "This is a male-dominated society, and he's the son; his return could badly split the party, if he challenged her as his father's legitimate political heir."

And one party member, who had met Mir Murtaza in Damascus a month or so earlier, told me that Murtaza was considering doing precisely that. "He's increasingly concerned about Asif's growing role within the party, and about the reports of his financial irregularities. Basically, Murtaza and Asif loathe each other," the party member said.

When I asked Asif what his relationship with his brother-in-law was, he remained quiet for a moment and then replied without answering. "Murtaza's had a very difficult life," he said. "He was very young when he left. It was the age of revolution; people were into armed struggle, and how do you fight martial-law tyranny? The man who killed your father? In our culture, which is very tribal and traditional, the fact is that Zia killed his father, and any son would have been expected—would have been forced—to fight back."

By the mid-1990s, Afghan refugees had assumed a commanding role in the North-West Frontier Province's lucrative smuggling trade. They had cornered part of the arms market and entered the heroin trade: some independently, others with Pathan tribesmen whose opium-to-heroin refining labs flourished in the remote border areas of the frontier—areas that, like Balochistan, were ruled by tribal law and were even further beyond the government's writ. Pakistani narcotics agents had been astonished earlier in the year when, on raiding a heroin laboratory in the jagged ridges of the Khyber Pass, they found that the refiners had affixed "missing" CIA antiaircraft weapons atop their tiny shacks. Over 50 percent of the heroin available in the United States originated in these border lands of Pakistan and Afghanistan.

And—not far from the Peshawar airfield from which Francis Gary Powers embarked on his ill-fated reconnaissance mission over the Soviet Union more than thirty years earlier—inside the scores of Afghan refugee camps, a new race of Palestinians was being bred. This would hardly have been of comfort to Zia ul-Haq, who in 1970 had commanded a Pakistani brigade in Jordan charged with protecting King Hussein's throne and who was a key protagonist in the bloody events known as "Black September," which forced thousands of Palestinians—including Yasir Arafat and the leadership of the PLO—to flee Jordan for Lebanon.

I had returned to Peshawar to meet Major General Nasirullah Babar, who had been Benazir's chief of staff, in the hope that he could tell me about her relationship with the Army, both during her prime ministership and now, and whether he thought the generals would permit her to come to power again. Another key question, as she began her new election campaign, was how she—or whoever came to power in October—would repair Pakistan's badly tarnished relations with the United States.

As I wandered through Peshawar's narrow, muddy lanes, dodging huge, brightly painted trucks and eyeing, and being suspiciously eyed by, men wearing floppy turbans—many of whom carried AK-47s on their shoulders or hips—I realized that in Peshawar, more than in any other place in Pakistan, you could actually see many of the irritants dividing Washington and Islamabad. Peshawar is a statement on the legacy of the jihad.

It seemed to me that, in a sense, everything dividing Pakistan and the United States—other than Pakistan's nuclear weapons program—had sprung from this: Pakistan's bitter sense of betrayal after it had served Washington's interests as a frontline state; the strain on its social and economic structure caused by the influx of thousands of mujahideen and millions of Afghan refugees; the new drug and Kalashnikov culture, bred from the profligate leakage of arms from the CIA's pipeline; and Washington's threat—despite a reprieve in the summer of 1993, after two successive chiefs of the ISI were dismissed—to declare Pakistan a terrorist state. Particularly worrisome to the United States was Pakistan's expanding role in arming and training insurgents to fight in Kashmir, but another factor of growing concern—which was shared by Benazir—was the presence in Peshawar now of nearly three thousand Afghan Arabs, the veterans of the jihad. They were all exceedingly well trained and exceedingly well armed, and many of them were followers of Sheikh Omar Abdel-Rahman, the Egyptian cleric who had been sentenced to life imprisonment for his role in the first World Trade Center bombing and in a related conspiracy to bomb other New York landmarks. They were also followers of Osama bin Laden.

Bin Laden had worked closely with Saudi intelligence in funding the jihad before coming to Peshawar in 1984 as a mujahid himself. Here he had befriended Gulbadin Hekmatyar and Sheikh Omar, and had fought in Afghanistan with the forces of the Wahhabi warlord, Professor Abdurrab Rasul Sayyaf. But he counted the Palestinian cleric Sheikh Abdullah Azzam (who in earlier years had been his professor of Shariah law) as one of his closest friends. And it was from Azzam's service office, in Peshawar's tony neighborhood of University Road, that bin Laden first forged ties with the leaders and foot soldiers of militant Islam. Of the thousands who passed through Peshawar during the jihad, many trained in bin Laden's largest military camp, which he artfully called Ma'asadat al-Ansar, or the "Lion's Den." Today, those who stayed on spoke glowingly of him.

After the Soviets withdrew from Afghanistan, in 1989, bin Laden left Peshawar and returned home to his native Jidda, and to his place in his family's business empire. There he incorporated his Afghan training camps and the various Islamic charities he controlled into the umbrella organization al-Qaeda—or "the Base"—which raised funds and recruited and trained fighters for new jihads. (A decade later, fighters supported by al-Qaeda would form part of a collection of militant Islamist groups—including five in Pakistan—that received bin Laden's patronage on four continents.)

Before calling on General Babar, therefore, I stopped at the rambling stucco bungalow just down the road, which was the residence of Gulbadin Hekmatyar, who was, by now, the prime minister of Afghanistan, and with whom bin Laden and the Arabs in Peshawar were closely aligned.

I was greeted warmly, if somewhat warily, by one of Hekmatyar's deputies, Nawab Salim, a roly-poly man with a small beard and Levantine looks. He was dressed in a long white robe and a white crocheted prayer cap, and he left his sandals at the door before entering the sitting room. He wore orange polish on his toes.

After a brief exchange of amenities—Salim had studied agriculture at a university in Virginia and was eager to hear what was happening there—I asked him if in his view the Afghan Arabs posed a threat to Pakistan, as many Pakistanis believed.

"None whatsoever," he replied. "They are all law-abiding citizens, with proper papers"—papers that they had received from the ISI. "But they're being persecuted by the United States: hundreds of them are being picked up; their houses have been raided, their offices have been raided, their hostels and hotels. This place is swarming with CIA agents, FBI agents, intelligence agents from Egypt and Algeria, who have been permitted to interrogate these poor chaps in jail. That's a flagrant violation of their human rights!" He calmed down after a moment and adjusted his prayer cap, then ensconced himself more comfortably in his armchair.

All those arrested were soon released, and when I asked a Western diplomat if any had been expelled he told me that "somewhat less than twenty" had left Pakistan. A Pakistani general later expressed his concern to me. "The Afghan Arabs could cause one hell of a problem for us," he said. "But what can we do, send in the Army and clean them out? And what would the implications of that be? There'd be a monumental uproar within Pakistan from the religious right, from the ISI. These guys have powerful supporters here, including Gulbadin. So what do we do? Risk a war between the Pakistani Army and the mujahideen?" He paused for a moment, and then he said, "These guys are *your* creation. And you have created one hell of a mess!"

Benazir, too, faulted the United States for having played a major role in the creation of the Afghan Arabs and in the rise in Pakistan of militant Islam. "Look at your great jihad," she had said, with an exaggerated sweep of her hand, as we chatted one morning about the war in Afghanistan. "The U.S. government armed these groups, trained them, gave them organizational skills; huge, huge amounts of money were spent, and both the money and the Islamic zeal spilled over here. Then the Americans retreated to Washington, and look at the mess they left." It was one of her most biting criticisms of the United States. She went on to say that she was particularly concerned over growing Islamist influence in the North-West Frontier, and that "breaking the stranglehold of the Islamic clerics" would be one of her major election planks.

Now, therefore, I asked Salim if the mujahideen (whether Afghan or Arab) still in Pakistan would support Qazi Hussain Ahmad, the erudite leader of Pakistan's largest fundamentalist party, the Jamaat-e-Islami, in the elections against Benazir. (Qazi Hussain, who was visiting Osama bin Laden in the Sudan at the time, was considered by Western intelligence sources to be a key Pakistani link—along with the ISI—between the mujahideen and radical Islamist groups in Kashmir, Bosnia, and the Middle East.)

Salim replied matter-of-factly, "If we want, it is our right."

"What do you think of Benazir?" I asked.

"Her father was a great man. He was the one who brought Gulbadin and a number of others to Pakistan in 1973; he armed and trained them in anticipation of 1979. Bhutto foresaw the Communist threat."

"And Benazir?"

"She's a woman," he said.

"Hmm, you've been to *that* house," General Babar said after greeting me with a firm handshake and a broad smile when I arrived at his. He did little to disguise his concern, muttering that the United States bore full responsibility for "setting these chaps loose." That having been established, he led me through an interior courtyard and into a beautifully appointed room of dark wood and antique carpets, whose walls were lined with books.

A thoughtful and well-spoken man who still possessed a general's bearing and stride, though he had retired from the military several years before, Babar, who was in his mid-sixties, had been a close confidant and aide to Benazir's father and had served as governor of the North-West Frontier Province during Bhutto's prime ministership. He had then, in turn, served Benazir, not just as her chief of staff but as her primary conduit to the military establishment. (Later that year, he would become her powerful Minister of the Interior, and the key protagonist involved in shaping Pakistan's allegiance to the Taliban.)

I began by asking General Babar how cooperative the generals and the president had been during Benazir's rule.

"It was a battle from day one," he replied. "Let me give you an example. Immediately after she was sworn in, we went to the president's chambers, and he told her—rather nonchalantly, I thought—that a Russian aircraft had been hijacked and was heading toward Pakistan. She was totally bewildered. *She had just been sworn in!* She looked toward me, and I said, loud enough for the old man to hear, 'We'll block all the airfields,' and that is precisely what we did. The president was testing her, and he never stopped. Neither did the Chief of the Army Staff. His resistance lasted until the end."

One of Benazir's former ministers had told me that her most troublesome problems were posed by the ISI, which continued to

run domestic surveillance operations; counsel her political oppo-
nents, including Nawaz Sharif; and conduct an aggressive policy in
Afghanistan, to the increasing annoyance of her government and the
United States. I asked General Babar if this was true.

"Absolutely," he replied. "We had no control over these people.
They were like a government unto themselves. The ISI, the Army,
and the president had been running the show for so long that they
simply didn't want to give it up. They got so carried away with the
jihad that, unwittingly or not, they got involved with all these fundamentalist movements across the Islamic world. They thought that
once they got Afghanistan they'd go across to the Soviet Central
Asian republics and into Kashmir. And I must tell you that these
holy warriors are still continuing to do just that."

After a brief pause, he said, "I must be absolutely frank. She had
very limited contact with the Army the entire time we ruled. They,
of course, generally briefed us on military matters, but what General
Beg did was to limit her exposure to the corps commanders and the
general-officer corps. I kept telling her she had to go around more,
expose herself, visit the cantonments. But with all the problems we
had—with Nawaz practically declaring Punjab an independent state,
with the president sitting forever on the files, with Beg, in keeping
with his character, playing a duplicitous, dual role—with all these
pinpricks, we were never able to force the point."

A servant in starched livery and white gloves entered the drawing
room with kebabs, coffee, and cakes. As we ate and drank, I asked
General Babar if the generals would permit Benazir to come to
power again.

"It's a very different Army now," he replied. "General Abdul
Waheed"—who had become Chief of the Army Staff earlier that
year—"appears to have none of the political ambition of General
Beg. He impresses me as a strictly professional soldier, and he's certainly not an Islamist, as General Beg was. However, I have been led
to understand that at the moment, with this political mess between
the president and the prime minister, most of the corps commanders

are fed up with the politicians all around. Yet that being said, they know that this is 1993, and that a coup would be totally unacceptable to the United States."

How much Benazir knew about her country's nuclear-weapons program, which had been launched by her avowedly pro-nuclear father, was a matter of dispute. Some U.S. intelligence analysts suspected that her scientists and her generals did not trust her, and she was therefore "not in the loop"; others suspected that she knew about the program but had chosen to distance herself from it. I had learned earlier that she had been briefed extensively on it—not by her Army establishment but by the American ambassador to Pakistan and the director of the CIA.

So I asked General Babar now how well informed she was in the spring of 1990, during her prime ministership, when Pakistan moved from being able to fabricate a nuclear weapon to actually making one.

He thought for a moment before he replied, and although he didn't answer my question directly, he said, "We had a very limited nuclear club, six or seven people, including the prime minister and myself. Zia went on record in the mid-1980s saying that we were only a screw away from the bomb: only the assembling was left. Then beginning in 1989 and through April of 1990, with all the problems we had with India over the Punjab and especially over Kashmir"—where the anti-Indian insurgency had begun—"the president and General Beg panicked, and we crossed the threshold. It was presumed that, as chief executive, she knew, and that was one of the reasons that our government was sent scuttling by the Americans."

By the spring of 1990, not only had Pakistan joined the nuclear club but it had also quickly exploited the unrest in Kashmir: the ISI was operating at least thirty military training camps on Pakistan's side of the border for Kashmiri militants. And by May of that year, a senior Pakistani general told me that the country's nuclear weapons arsenal had been placed on alert—and Indian and Pakistani forces were "eyeball to eyeball" along the frontier—when Robert Gates, a long-time CIA official who was then serving as the deputy national security adviser, rushed to New Delhi and Islamabad, after the first Bush Administration became convinced that the world was on the edge of a nuclear exchange between India and Pakistan.

Benazir had enjoyed enormous popularity in Washington until June of the previous year. Then, according to a senior State Department official, attitudes began to change. As he explained, "When she stood on the floor of the United States Congress, promising, to thunderous applause, that Pakistan neither possessed nor intended to assemble a nuclear bomb—the very day after she had received a detailed briefing on the weapons program from the director of the CIA—her worth was diminished in the eyes of the United States."

In October of 1990, two months after Benazir's government was dismissed and a year and a half after the Soviets completed their withdrawal from Afghanistan, the United States suspended all military and most economic assistance to Pakistan when President Bush no longer certified that Islamabad did not possess a nuclear device.

By the late summer of 1993, foreign diplomats had already begun to predict that when the October elections were held they would essentially be a personality contest—the third in five years—between Benazir and Nawaz: she, a spirited, tempestuous, modern feudalist from Sindh; he, a shy, sometimes awkward, traditional industrialist from Punjab. She was more sophisticated and secularist; he was more conventional and fundamentalist. Her most notable achievements when she ruled were in foreign policy and human rights; his were in economic reform and in dismantling the socialist economy that her father had built.

Other than her People's Party and his faction of the Muslim League, the only parties of any serious consequence in the polls were the fundamentalist Jamaat-e-Islami and the ethnic Mohajir National Movement, or MQM, a Karachi-based party of descendants of Muslim migrants from India, whose members had fought pitched battles over the years with the native residents of Sindh.

One morning, as I sat in Benazir's office discussing the elections with Begum Nusrat, I asked her if she ever had any contact with her son, Mir Murtaza.

"Of course," she replied. "I just saw him in Europe a few weeks ago. He's such a lovely boy—really a man now—but being abroad all these years, he's lost so much of his life. He's *so* like his father: the way he looks, the way he walks, the way he talks." Then she said, "I'm now negotiating with the authorities to bring him back."

I was so startled that I could think of nothing to say, and she went on. "He wants to enter politics here, and people are now negotiating, on my behalf, with the Army and the president, but he must be given amnesty, and his return must be announced two weeks in advance. I don't want him to come back in secret, through the back door. He must be received properly by the people of Pakistan. He is, after all, Zulfi Bhutto's son."

"But what will this mean for Benazir?" I asked. "Murtaza has been quite critical of a number of things she's done. Won't it split the party if he enters politics?"

"Nonsense," she said, casually running her fingers through her hair. "There are many families in Pakistan where four or five members are politicians. Benazir will be here, and Murtaza will be here. Murtaza is really interested only in his own province of Sindh, not in being the prime minister of Pakistan."

"But Sindh is the family power base," I said. "It's the bedrock of Benazir's entire support. If she's challenged for power by her brother there, how can she continue to be her father's political heir, as he had chosen her to be?"

Begum Nusrat did not respond immediately, and her eyes turned to ice. It was clear that she was angry and bitter even before she spoke. "He didn't choose Benazir—*I* did," she said, and her voice began to rise. "*I* was to have been my husband's political heir. But because I was ill, *I* told the party that I would like Benazir to stand in my stead. They couldn't make her chairman, because I already was, so they coined the phrase 'co-chairman,' which we *both* still are."

A few weeks after our conversation, Murtaza's wife, Ghanwa, who is Lebanese-born, arrived in Karachi to file his election papers as an independent candidate for seats in both the Provincial Assembly and the National Assembly in twenty-three constituencies in Sindh; in almost all cases, he would stand against the PPP—even in the Karachi slum area of Lyari, where he would challenge Benazir's husband, Asif. Ghanwa, who was met at the airport by Begum Nusrat, immediately moved into No. 70 Clifton, where Zulfi Bhutto's widow had set up a campaign headquarters for her son. Ghanwa was accompanied by Zulfikar Ali Bhutto, the family patriarch's three-year-old grandson.

The morning before I left Pakistan, I went to Benazir's parliamentary chambers in Islamabad to say good-bye. She ordered tea and coffee, and we talked about her election plans.

"I shall miss our interviews," she said, to my surprise. "Have you gotten everything you need?"

I told her I was still curious about one thing. "You titled your autobiography in its British edition *Daughter of the East*, and in its American edition *Daughter of Destiny*. Which are you?"

"What a difficult question," she said. "I don't know."

She became reflective, tilting her face as she rested her chin on her hand. Then she went on. "I'm partly a child of destiny. Fate put me where I am now, against my own inner wishes, but I chose to stay on, when I could always have opted out. Of course, I did have a sense of duty to my father and the causes he espoused, and now I have a duty to those people who believe in me and to myself. A daughter of the East or a daughter of destiny?" She repeated the titles. "Did I have a choice?" She paused, as if she were considering her next words carefully, and then she said, very deliberately, "I am a daughter of the East. I was born into it; conditioned by it; thrust into a political system which is Eastern—a political system in which I have to win or lose. And, more than that, as a daughter of the East I want other women, born into this tradition, this environment, where they're forced to submit to those societal pressures and those fates which have been written for them, to see how I fight—as a politician, as a woman, as a mother—and how I survive. I want to show them that they can rise above these pressures, too, and that they can demand to make their own choices, and not have others—fathers, husbands, or brothers—make their choices for them."

Benazir Bhutto was returned to power in October of 1993 and she ruled for three years, until her ouster in November of 1996—again, on charges of gross mismanagement and corruption. But this time, as opposed to her first term, she no longer faced a hostile army or president. This time, she had only herself to blame. Three months later, in February of 1997, she went down to a devastating defeat at the polls when Nawaz Sharif returned to power with a landslide, virtually two-thirds majority, and turned his attention toward consolidating control. Rarely had the Bhutto legacy seemed so tarnished. The Zia legacy continued apace.

What appeared to be a promising start to Benazir's second term was deflected almost immediately by an extraordinary family feud, when in November Mir Murtaza returned home. In quick succession, he laid claim to his father's legacy; she agreed to his arrest (based on charges of insurgency, which he already faced). Begum Nusrat, perhaps not surprisingly, sided with her son, as she had done during his election campaign—in which he won a seat in the Sindh Provincial Assembly—when she went to the hustings on his behalf, holding his son aloft and proclaiming the male line of her family to be her husband's rightful heirs. Even by the standards of Pakistani politics, the drama was unique; and the chattering classes chattered, endlessly. Then in September of 1996, Mir Murtaza was killed in

Karachi in a gun battle with police. Around midnight on the evening in November that Benazir's government fell, some twenty arrests were made and charges later brought for conspiracy to murder Mir Murtaza. Among those indicted were a former director of the Intelligence Bureau and Karachi's former chief of police. The man indicted for ordering Mir Murtaza's death was Benazir's husband, Asif.

As the years passed during Benazir's second term, even some of her closest advisers and ministers began to slip away, the men and women who had stood by her for so long in prison, under house arrest, and then in exile abroad. Her rule became increasingly flawed, and she was seen, more often than not, as incapable of coming to grips with the enormity of the problems Pakistan faced: the deteriorating economy, now nearly bankrupt; endemic sectarian violence, especially in Karachi, her hometown, which by the end of her rule had become a city as fearsome as the years of protracted civil war had made Beirut. Many of her friends also told me that she had returned to power changed: there was a new vindictiveness, based in large part, they said, on her obsession with having been removed from power in the past. There was also an impertinence, bordering on arrogance, that only she could rule, and a turning away from the liberal politics she had long embraced. But, most of all, she and Asif and their entourage were seen as hopelessly corrupt. Pakistanis increasingly began to describe her government as a commercial enterprise: she, the chairman of the board; he, the managing director, whose own drive for power—and, even more prominently, for wealth—had become even more encompassing than was hers.

Yet friends of Benazir's were, and continue to be, divided on how much she knew when, in January of 1998, *The New York Times*, following a three-month investigation, published excerpts from a devastating set of documents that were at the heart of a widening corruption inquiry against Benazir and Asif—an inquiry launched at the behest of Nawaz Sharif. According to investigators, the government had traced more than $100 million in kickbacks and favors awarded to Asif to foreign bank accounts and properties controlled by Benazir's family. And this, the investigators said, was only a minuscule part of what was involved: they had found evidence that Benazir's family and associates had generated more than $1.5 billion in illicit profits through kickbacks in virtually every sphere of government activity. Benazir's friends—many of whom had quarreled with her over the years about her husband's business activities— were, nonetheless, stunned by the enormity of them.

In April of 1999, the Lahore high court sentenced Benazir to five years imprisonment for corruption, disqualified her from holding federal office, and fined her—along with her husband—$8.6 million. She was in London at the time, and never returned home. Asif, who was by then a senator and had been in a Karachi prison since November of 1996 for his alleged role in Mir Murtaza's death, received the same sentence as his wife. They both denied the charges and appealed to the Supreme Court, which in April of 2001 set aside their conviction and ordered a retrial, based in large part on the discovery of a bizarre set of tapes that strongly suggested collusion between one of the senior judges of the Lahore court and members of Nawaz Sharif's government.

Few people were as taken aback as General Pervez Musharraf. Within days of the court ruling, his government announced that it was accelerating its investigation in nine other corruption cases against Benazir and Asif. Two months later, in June of 2001 (and then again in July of 2002), Benazir was sentenced in absentia to three years in prison after she failed to appear in court to answer new charges of corruption—charges brought against her this time by the government of her former Director-General of Military Operations.

As of mid-July 2002, Benazir Bhutto remained in exile, continuing to divide her time between London and the Persian Gulf sheikhdom of Dubai, where her three children are in school. Asif, by that time, had been transferred to Attock Fort, a Moghul prison fortress perched high on a hill on the road between Peshawar and Islamabad. When I drove by it shortly before Washington's newest war in Afghanistan began, only a lone guard stood on its roof surrounded by parapets, which in turn were flanked by prickly acanthus shrubs; just beyond was the confluence of the Indus and Kabul Rivers: the former translucent and clear, the latter muddy and brown. Bus after bus overtook us, careening dangerously along the road. I learned later that the buses were en route to a religious rally in Islamabad, which was being held to recruit volunteer soldiers for the Taliban. Afghanistan, or so it seemed to me, was moving ever farther south.

CHAPTER 6

DÉJÀ VU

THE TIMING hardly seemed fortuitous. On May 1, 2002, only twenty-four hours after the controversial and flawed referendum that extended Pervez Musharraf's presidency for an additional five years—with the tacit approval of Washington—Pakistani officials acknowledged that a small number of U.S. ground forces had been given reluctant permission to operate inside Pakistan. But almost from the beginning, things began to go awry, nearly as awry, in fact, as the general's dubious referendum had been—a referendum in which voters had the choice of voting "yes" or "no," in which no opposition candidate was permitted to stand, and in which organized rallies by political parties, except for one on the last day of the campaign, were banned. Most Pakistanis stayed away from the polls—according to the Minister of Information, Nisar Memon, as many as 75 percent of them. (The opposition, which had urged a boycott, claimed that as few as 5 to 10 percent of eligible voters had cast a vote; the government, for its part—after chastising Memon—claimed a turnout of more than 50 percent, which no one outside it found to be remotely credible.)

Indeed, the largest voter turnout appeared to be in government offices (where supervisors were seen dutifully shepherding their employees to the ballot box), in prisons, and in hospitals. Election officials were so alarmed by the embarrassingly low turnout that, by the end of the day, dozens of them were discovered by the press stamping thousands of ballots with a resounding "yes." One woman proudly told journalists that she had voted for Musharraf sixty times. It appeared increasingly that the general was intent on prolonging military rule in Pakistan indefinitely.

By so doing, he had further widened the chasm between the country's democratic politicians and his Army-backed regime, at the very time when he most needed a political consensus to rally the nation behind America's war on terrorism and, as part of that, to deal firmly with Pakistan's militant Islamists. He was thus clearly irritated, a Pakistani official said to me, by one of the referendum's stranger twists: the forging of a tactical alliance (if only a temporary one) between his two greatest nemeses—Benazir and Nawaz.

The referendum, in a sense, was a journey backward in time to 1984 and a similar contest held by Zia ul-Haq, who had spurred the rise of the forces of jihad, and on whom Pervez Musharraf increasingly appeared to be fashioning himself. For as Zia had done before him, Musharraf had not only moved to enhance and consolidate the singularity of his rule, but, two months after his referendum, he unveiled a plan—which even General Zia had never dared to do—to rewrite the country's constitution, in advance of the October parliamentary polls, in a way which would insure that the Army would be Pakistan's ultimate political authority. A National Security Council that he proposed would, in effect, supersede any popularly elected civilian government. His proposals were greeted by a clamour of protest, which further isolated him.

If Musharraf had hoped to bolster his legitimacy, he had, in fact, badly diminished it. And he did so at precisely the time that instability in Pakistan was already on the rise. Terrorist attacks had increased palpably in the months since October when Musharraf had turned against the Taliban and, guardedly, toward Washington. Few foresaw when that occurred that his new alliance with the United States on Afghanistan would lead directly to a showdown with India over Kashmir.

In December 2001, pro-Pakistani militants attacked the Indian parliament, leading to an ultimatum from New Delhi on December 31 that twenty alleged terrorists be turned over to India at once, and that terrorist infiltration into Kashmir cease immediately. It did not. And in May 2002, Islamic militants launched one of the deadliest attacks in the disputed state in recent years, an attack on a bus and then on the family quarters of an Indian Army base that killed thirty-four people, the majority women and children. Indian officials were quick to blame the Lashkar-e-Taiba and the Jaish-e-Mohammed—both Pakistani-based, both on the State Department's list of foreign terrorist organizations—for the two attacks. By January 2002, a million Indian and Pakistani troops were poised along their frontier—the highest state of mobilization between the two nuclear-armed nations in thirty years.

In quick succession, sectarian violence in Karachi claimed scores of lives; in late January, a *Wall Street Journal* reporter, Daniel Pearl, was kidnapped and brutally killed; five more foreigners (including two Americans) died in a grenade attack in March on a church in the heavily guarded diplomatic enclave of Islamabad; and in early May, a suicide car bomb in Karachi incinerated a Pakistani Navy bus, killing another sixteen people, nearly all of them French, and Frenchmen who were working on a submarine project for the Pakistani military establishment.

No country was more critical, or pivotal, to U.S. military objectives than Pakistan. But, at what cost to it?

And now, with Musharraf's prestige further diminished by his proposed constitutional amendments and his empty victory at the polls, many in Washington had begun to question how reliable an ally he would be—despite intense pressure from the United States—in launching large-scale attacks against concentrations of al-Qaeda fighters in the tribal areas of Pakistan. If the general agreed (and he was resisting tenaciously), it would mark a major widening of Washington's nine-month-old counteroffensive against terrorism.

The U.S. objective was to pursue and ferret out members of al-Qaeda—and perhaps even Osama bin Laden himself—who were believed to be regrouping in the craggy mountains and rolling hills on both sides of the Pakistani-Afghan frontier. One Pakistani official conceded to me that some five thousand or more al-Qaeda fighters and members of the Taliban were believed to have slipped across the border into Pakistan—most of them through the tribal areas of the North-West Frontier and, even more conspicuously, through Balochistan. But diplomatic and strategic constraints had kept al-Qaeda's vanguard beyond the reach of U.S. troops, something that had led to growing frustration and irritation in Washington. Musharraf would permit the Americans access, but on his terms.

The former Army commando had made it abundantly clear as early as March 20, when Major General Franklin L. Hagenbeck, the commander of U.S. forces in Afghanistan, in an interview with *The New York Times*, first publicly broached the idea of "hot pursuit"—in other words, chasing al-Qaeda fighters into Pakistan—that this was not an idea that was attractive to him. He feared that such a move would further inflame the Pathan elders who held sway in the border tribal lands—and whose natural affinity was as much with the Taliban and bin Laden as it was with Pakistan—and Islamic militants across the country who, for a number of years, had shared terrorist training camps with al-Qaeda in Afghanistan and had set up support centers for bin Laden's fighters across Pakistan.

The general was thus highly embarrassed when the tribal elders told the press—two weeks before his government even acknowledged that U.S. ground forces might become involved militarily in Pakistan at all—that some forty U.S. commandos were already there (as perhaps bin Laden was) in the remote fastness of Waziristan. They were operating from a command center in Miram Shah, just over the pass from Khost, a key Afghan base for U.S. military operations in the war. A dusty little border town buffeted by rolling hills,

Miram Shah, were it anywhere else, probably wouldn't warrant much attention at all, but it was a gateway to the tribal lands: areas that the Pakistani Army itself had not entered for years, that is, not until America's war on terrorism began.

Officially, Musharraf and his government continued to insist that the Americans were not even here—only a few "communications experts," the general said. His disclaimers transported those of us who had covered the earlier Afghan war back twenty years to the doctrine of "plausible deniability," the doctrine fashioned by Zia ul-Haq and the CIA during the jihad. One of the major differences this time, however, was that the tribal leaders now had cellular telephones. Each day we waited for their reports on what was *really* happening in the mountains above Miram Shah.

One tribesman spotted, with "absolute certainty," he said, "a squad of seven Americans" scouring the mountain trails. When Pakistani officials heard about this, he went on, they forced him to sign a statement that the Americans were, in fact, across the border in Afghanistan. "How can you see that far?" he asked, protesting as he signed that the GIs were most certainly inside Pakistan. Then we began to hear other tales. In the tiny storefront shops that lined the lanes of Miram Shah's bazaar, entrepreneurial tribesmen were offering a complete fashion transformation to bin Laden's new generation of mujahideen. For only $100 their beards were shaved, they received a new set of clothes, and they were sent on their way with false identity papers, which allowed them to slip through the checkpoints on the roads to major cities and towns. If any difficulty presented itself, they, perhaps, had to pay an additional $25 or so to the Pakistani border militiamen manning the posts.

And so the men in the shadows, using a portfolio of disguises and pseudonyms, appeared to move with ease, traveling between the Pakistani tribal lands and southern Afghanistan—sometimes protected by the Pathan tribes, sometimes by the drug barons— in a circle of a few hundred square miles, crossing through the same mountains passes and over the same little-known tribal trails through which the mujahideen's convoys passed during the jihad years.

Some twenty thousand Pakistanis—including thousands of tribes-men from Balochistan and the most remote reaches of the North-West Frontier—had been enlisted by the ISI in support of the jihad. (By 2002, their numbers had burgeoned: as many as 500,000, in-cluding some 100,000 fighters, were involved in the jihad industry.) Some were known to the sixty or so officers from the CIA and the Special Forces who were overseeing the war, but most of them were not; little accountability was provided by the ISI. But there was little doubt that the tribesmen flourished on the CIA's last battleground of the Cold War.

The agency used them as guides, scouts, drivers, and trackers, and for logistical support. Some secured the precipitous mountain passes on the Afghan frontier for weapons transport; others crossed the border to collect intelligence; still others, under the cover of the CIA, smuggled arms and drugs. Nearly everyone in the tribal lands was in one way or another affected by the jihad. Yet they were and still are fiercely independent Pathans and Baloch who do not take kindly to outside military forces, especially American. As a result, as they had done in the mid-1990s when they had assisted two of America's most wanted men, who were also two of their own— Ramzi Ahmed Yousef and Mir Aimal Kansi, both from Balochistan, both of whom came of age on the jihad's battlefields—slip across the Toba Kakar mountains out of Pakistan, they were now employing their American-honed skills to assist al-Qaeda fighters to traverse the same steep mountains and rocky valleys through which, twenty years before, the CIA had sculpted trails during the jihad.

The tribal areas were off-limits to foreign journalists now, and one morning as I sifted through old files, I was struck by the fact that, in a sense, I was visiting the present in the past. The major dif-ference of any consequence, at least for me, was that now it was the Americans; then, it had been the Soviets.

I had scrawled "hot pursuit" in my notebook nearly half a dozen times one late-October afternoon in 1984 as I sat with the commander of the Kurram Militia, an elite border force, on the sprawling lawn of the old military cantonment of Parachinar. A picturesque border town in the Kurram valley, it was Pakistan's last line of defense—a few hours north of Miram Shah and seventy-five miles from Kabul. Beyond it lie only the Safed Koh mountains and desolate stretches of no-man's-land. The tranquility was abruptly shattered that afternoon by the roar and sonic booms of Soviet MIG-17 fighter-bombers scrambling overhead. Now, according to our tribal sources chattering on their cellular phones, it was being shattered by American helicopter gunships. The Soviets, with little success, had been attempting to seal the 1,400-mile-long, exceedingly porous Pakistani-Afghan frontier, as the Americans and the Pakistanis, with equally limited success, were attempting, on the other side, to seal the border now.

Then, just outside Parachinar, in the Kurram valley's dried-up riverbeds, I had watched the mujahideen load some twenty camels with ammunition and artillery shells. They were making one of their last forays across the jagged mountain peaks before the snows began. No one doubted that their raids against Soviet garrison towns would lead to yet more reprisals against an increasingly vulnerable Pakistan—as no one doubted that the American raids would do so now.

By the last days of April 2002, an odd assortment of peasants and students and tribal chiefs—along with the mullahs of Miram Shah—were furious with the United States. Two to three hundred Pakistani troops, assisted by a dozen or so Americans, had raided a madrasah there, and it was not just a madrasah but one that belonged to the powerful Mullah Jalaluddin Haqqani, an ISI protégé and the kingmaker of Khost, who had been closely allied with the CIA during the jihad and, after it, with Osama bin Laden and the Taliban. Shops closed in fear or protest as Pakistani helicopters hovered overhead. But well before the sprawling complex was turned upside down, the al-Qaeda fighters who had been there had left. It appeared that they had been alerted in advance. After the Americans and the Pakistanis withdrew, the students and the mullahs and the tribal chiefs gathered in Miram Shah's tiny square, where they sat on rope charpoys and sipped sweet, milky tea. The mullahs announced to everyone assembled that, from that day, they should kill Americans on sight.

The question of permitting U.S. forces a high-profile presence here had been hotly debated for months by Musharraf's army-backed government. But by the end of March, the generals in Islamabad appeared to have scant choice, after U.S. communications intercepts led to the arrest in Pakistan of al-Qaeda's top recruiter and chief of operations, the elusive Abu Zubaydah. A Saudi-born Palestinian who, according to American intelligence sources, had assumed the number-three post in bin Laden's command, his capture netted the highest-ranking al-Qaeda operative in U.S. custody. And he was apprehended not in the Afghan border tribal lands, nor in a cave, but in an upper-class villa in Faisalabad, in the heart of the Punjab, hundreds of miles away. Before the evening was over, some fifty al-Qaeda fugitives—including twenty-five foreigners—had been swooped up in this prosperous mill town, and in the Punjabi capital of Lahore—confirming Washington's worst fears that al-Qaeda was regrouping not only in the tribal lands but also in the major urban centers of Pakistan. The arrests nonplussed bin Laden's former backers in the ISI. Pervez Musharraf was mortified.

The ensuing friction between Islamabad and Washington was not the only irritant dividing the two. In fact, from the very beginning of Pakistan's involvement in Washington's newest Afghan war, strains in the relationship between the two capitals had begun to occur: not only over the length of the U.S. bombing of Afghanistan and the composition of a broad-based government there, but also over whether, and to what extent, U.S. forces would be permitted to operate inside Pakistan. Indeed, the strains had become palpable enough that by the spring the question being increasingly asked of the new Pakistani-American relationship was: How long will it last?

For since Musharraf—at the strong urging of Colin Powell, the U.S. Secretary of State—made a forceful address to the nation on

January 12 in which he condemned Islamic extremism, banned five extremist groups, and ordered some two thousand arrests, the Pakistani general had steadily backed down. Of those arrested, some 75 percent had been released. And of the banned groups, the Lashkar-e-Taiba, the largest and strongest, was now reborn as Jamaat-ad-Dawa, and the magazine *Soldiers of Mohammed* (published by the group of the same name, the Jaish-e-Mohammed) was selling briskly as *Al-Islah*, meaning "reform." Indeed, within hours of Musharraf's address, those of us on the mailing lists of the groups he had banned received e-mails from them, informing us that they were going underground to regroup and that we would be receiving their new e-mail addresses and Web sites. By the spring, we had. Islamic militancy in Pakistan was very much alive.

For the extremist groups, which since the days of Zia ul-Haq had formed part of the fabric of Pakistan's political cloth, continued to have powerful support within Musharraf's Army establishment, most significantly within the ISI—which had created them. The intelligence agency, for its part, continued to thrive and, by the time of Musharraf's referendum, it remained—despite contrary pledges to the United States—what it had been for so many years: a kingdom within the state. As a result, the agreement to allow American forces, if for the moment only on a small scale, to pursue bin Laden's fighters inside Pakistan seemed a trade-off—as long as Pakistan's equally militant fighters were left untouched.

There was a sense of déjà vu by May of 2002. For not only was the United States back in Pakistan, and, even more self-consciously, in Afghanistan, but the mujahideen armies, the warlords, and tribal chiefs whom Washington had sponsored twenty years ago, to such disastrous effect, had largely been returned to power in Afghanistan—by the United States.

Burhanuddin Rabbani, the Tajik leader of the Northern Alliance, which controlled the interim government in Kabul, was already vying for power there with the government's interim leader, Hamid Karzai, a Pashtun aristocrat. Abdurrab Rasul Sayyaf, the Wahhabi warlord with whom Osama bin Laden had fought, was a spoiler or a kingmaker, depending upon whom you spoke to. And the "Butcher of Mazar-e-Sharif," as he is most widely known, Abdul Rashid Dostum, a noted chameleon, now held sway over his fiefdom again, as the warlord Ismail Khan presided over Herat, which he won back from the Taliban with the assistance of American bombs. The only notable exception appeared to be Gulbadin Hekmatyar—the favorite of the ISI and of Zia ul-Haq during the years of the jihad, who, as a consequence, had received roughly 50 percent of the CIA's arms. Now the agency appeared to have had second thoughts, for in the early days of May, the CIA, using a missile fired from an unmanned surveillance drone, attempted—and failed—to assassinate him. The aborted undertaking came after Hekmatyar vowed (as he had done in 1992 with lethal effect) to unseat the central government.

Few heroes had emerged from the jihad and, of those who did, two of the most prominent were now dead. Ahmed Shah Massoud was assassinated by two alleged "journalists"—both Tunisian-born, both followers of Osama bin Laden. The legendary commander, who had captured Kabul in 1992 to the abiding fury of the ISI, bin Laden, and Hekmatyar, had only reluctantly agreed to an interview with the unknown men. Within fifteen minutes, Massoud lay in a pool of blood, never regaining consciousness. It was September 9, 2001.

The following month, on October 26, Abdul Haq, the irascible commander of Kabul, with whom all of us who covered the jihad had spent endless hours, over endless cups of tea, was also dead. Seen by some U.S. officials as the potential leader of an anti-Taliban uprising in the southern Pashtun belt, he was captured within a week of secretly returning to Afghanistan and summarily executed by the Taliban who, according to American intelligence sources, had perhaps been assisted by the ISI.

And not far from the area where Abdul Haq died, in the hundreds of mud-walled villages and towns, tiny places lining the steep and rocky valleys that run east through the mountain range, thousands of al-Qaeda members who fought in the jihad—and the generation that followed them—continued to come and go between Pakistan and Afghanistan. They were Egyptians and Saudis and Yemenis, Pakistanis and Palestinians, Africans and Asians who came of age on the battlefields of Afghanistan. And that is one of the most startling ironies of today's militant Islamist movement, not just in Pakistan but across the Muslim world: the vast majority of its leaders were funded, armed, and trained—with the same enthusiasm with which they were now being pursued—by the United States.

They had now begun returning home, for this is where it all began, here in the tribal areas of Pakistan. And twenty years after that, the Afghan Arabs—and the Pakistanis who trained and fought with them—were streaming back. Osama bin Laden himself had been spotted a number of times, or so it was claimed, by Afghan intelligence sources and Pakistani tribal chiefs. He was, at once, in North Waziristan, in the Tirah valley, and then in Balochistan. He was seen near the village of Maidan, north of Miram Shah, or so it was said, with Ayman al-Zawahiri, an Egyptian surgeon, who is bin Laden's chief ideologue and designated heir. Al-Zawahiri himself was later reportedly seen with Jalaluddin Haqqani, the Afghan warlord whose madrasah was raided in Miram Shah, after all of its occupants had fled—some on horseback, leaving trails of dust in the air. Indeed, after nine months of a sustained, largely American military campaign, only Abu Zubaydah had been captured; and only Mohammed Atef, a former Egyptian policeman who had been al-Qaeda's military chief, had been killed. Otherwise, the ranking leadership of al-Qaeda remained intact and at large.

Meanwhile, in the coffeehouses of Miram Shah, Parachinar, and Thal, the tribal leaders gossiped about the mysterious strangers who came and went, perhaps even bin Laden himself. He knew every ridge and mountain pass, every CIA trail. For this was the area where Osama bin Laden had spent more than a decade of his life.

Sixteen years have passed since Osama bin Laden led a group of a few dozen men—Saudi Arabians, Egyptians, Algerians, and Pakistanis, whom he had recruited and trained—out of a cluster of caves concealed in the steep mountains that encircled Jadji, a village in Afghanistan's Paktia Province not far from Miram Shah and just across the Pakistani frontier. A tall, imposing figure, his face framed by a full black beard, he had come to the jihad in 1984 from his native Saudi Arabia, only recently out of university. Nevertheless, he had already shown impressive skill in fund-raising for the war, and in civil engineering and management. Now on that spring evening in 1986, he had taken up a Kalashnikov for the first time to lead the jihad's first Arab unit, which he had formed in the caves surrounding Jadji only a few months earlier.

Thousands of mujahideen were dug into the mountains and the mile-deep valleys of Paktia, especially in and around the Soviet-supported provincial capital of Khost (the same area from which U.S. forces would be operating by the fall of 2001). But bin Laden's was the only exclusively Arab camp. And now, for the first time—fighting under the nom de guerre Abu Abdullah—he was about to directly encounter the Soviets. The Battle of Jadji, as it became known, raged for more than a week, and although bin Laden's unit achieved no significant victories, it stood its ground. As word of the battle spread through the mountains and the ravines, especially among the thousands of Afghan Arabs from around the world who had streamed into Afghanistan to fight in the war, it became part of the jihad's mythology.

This is how Osama bin Laden began to invent himself and also to build up a following of his own. In the years to come, he would take up, on his own terms, the political mantle of militant Islam. Since then, against the odds, he has reportedly managed—so far, at least—to survive U.S. cruise-missile attacks, an unrelenting high-tech air campaign, and a succession of political crises, conspiracies, and attempts on his life. In August 1998, the mysterious Saudi multimillionaire was declared Washington's most-wanted fugitive after he was accused of being the mastermind of the bombings of two United States embassies, in Nairobi and Dar es Salaam. It was not long after the embassy attacks that U.S. cruise missiles struck targets in

Afghanistan believed to be bin Laden training camps, killing a number of people—including officers of the ISI—but not bin Laden, who was then forty-three years old.

And now, as he had done so many times over the years, he had returned, or so Afghan intelligence officials said, to the tribal areas of the Pakistani-Afghan frontier.

Today, nearly four years after one of the costliest and most complicated international criminal investigations in U.S. history—and one of the most devastating bombing campaigns in recent memory—the U.S. government appeared divided on how to deal with him. Every strategy of the Clinton and Bush Administrations had backfired, from covert operations, to what was euphemistically called "bringing bin Laden to justice," to our bombing campaign after the World Trade Center towers were felled, to our earlier missile attacks, whose clear objective was to kill bin Laden and his key aides. Some American officials I spoke to conceded that they could only hope reports that bin Laden is seriously ill—reports he has denied—prove to be true.

It was déjà vu all over again.

After the bombings of our African embassies, U.S. Special Forces were dispatched to the border areas of Pakistan, as they've been dispatched now. And on both occasions—in 1999 and 2002—perhaps as bedeviling as anything else was bin Laden's silence, and elusiveness. Now, he appeared only from time to time, via videotapes broadcast by Al-Jazeera, a satellite news channel headquartered in the Emirate of Qatar, that has often served as an outlet for him; one of the most recent tapes, which aired in April 2002, was sent to the station by express mail from Islamabad. Then, six months after the bombings in Nairobi and Dar es Salaam, in February 1999, bin Laden had "disappeared" somewhere in the mountains of Afghanistan. The United States, at the time, had pressed Pakistan to establish a snatch team to cross the border and capture him. Washington's pleas, for all practical purposes, were ignored.

So bin Laden continued to come and go, moving between a villa in the Taliban's capital of Kandahar and a farm on the outskirts of the eastern city of Jalalabad. He had already established a network of two dozen or more military training camps in the rocky valleys and mountains of Afghanistan. And by the time, in 1999, that U.S. Special Forces first arrived, thousands of Afghan Arabs had also returned to Kandahar and Khost, to Kabul, to the mountains of Tora Bora and Jalalabad—as they had returned to Peshawar and to Pakistan—to support bin Laden's operations there.

Some were instructors in his training camps; others, management experts and economists, ran his businesses. Still others served as liaisons between and among the two dozen or so bin Laden–supported militant Islamist groups.

By September 11, 2001, some five thousand or more Islamic extremists from as many as forty countries around the world had trained in bin Laden's camps. Some then went off in search of new jihads in Bosnia, Tajikistan, or Kashmir. Others trained and went home—to Pakistan, Saudi Arabia, and Egypt; to Algeria and the Philippines; to the West Bank and Gaza Strip—where many became engaged in open warfare with secular governments. Still others were dispatched to perhaps as many as fifty countries where they joined "sleeper cells" and waited for their turn to strike. And strike they did.

Whether it was bin Laden's plans, or his money or training, or, at the very least, his inspiration, U.S. officials assert that over the last four years not only was bin Laden behind the African embassy bombings (in which 224 people died), but also an October 2000 attack in Yemen against the destroyer the USS *Cole*, in which seventeen American sailors lost their lives. And finally, the most devastating attack of all, on September 11, 2001, when nineteen young men—fifteen from bin Laden's native Saudi Arabia—became human missiles as they crashed four hijacked commercial planes into the World Trade Center towers, the Pentagon, and a Pennsylvania field. Nearly three thousand people, most of them Americans, were killed that day.

In October, the United States struck back with the most formidable military might it had deployed since the Vietnam War. By the end of the year, the Taliban had been overthrown and the complex of caves in the White Mountains of Tora Bora, where Osama bin Laden had sought his final refuge of the air war, had been pulverized. Rising to nearly thirteen thousand feet in the mountains southeast of Jalalabad, Tora Bora's countless miles of tunnels, fortified bunkers, and base camps, which were dug deeply into the steep rock walls, all formed part of what had earlier been a CIA-financed, fortress complex built for the mujahideen during the jihad years. My mind wandered back to when I had first heard of it: Thirteen years before, when a mujahideen fighter in Peshawar had explained to me that Tora Bora, in Pashtu, meant "Black Widow." "No good will come of those caves," he had told me then.

In May 2002, when British Royal Marines began scouring the Paktia caves, they found truckloads of antiaircraft and antitank weapons—thirty truckloads of ammunition in only one day. But they did not find Osama bin Laden, whom U.S. intelligence officials had conceded the month before had almost certainly slipped away. He had most likely been secreted out of the cave complex in the early days of December, when the U.S. bombing of Tora Bora was the most intense. Captured al-Qaeda fighters, interviewed separately, told U.S. interrogators that they recalled an address that bin Laden gave to, among others, members of his elite, international "055 Brigade" inside Tora Bora on or about December 3. Then the al-Qaeda leader disappeared, perhaps into Pakistan—less than twenty miles away.

As for the Taliban's leader, Mullah Mohammed Omar, the one-eyed visionary who spoke with the Prophet Muhammad in a dream, he, too, escaped, fleeing American soldiers on a motorbike. And despite the reputed austerity in which he lived, as it had been described to me in Peshawar by Maulana Sami ul-Haq, it was discovered that inside his compound in Kandahar, Mullah Omar lived a most indulgent life, replete with pink-tiled bathrooms, imported faucets, an elaborate fountain, and an ornate mosque. There was even a small indoor stable with ceiling fans for cows.

As his adopted country fell to the United States, Osama bin Laden remained almost a phantom, more myth than man. His face was everywhere and nowhere.

When it appeared, it was most likely on the Arabic-language network Al-Jazeera: in October, on the day that the U.S. bombing of Afghanistan was launched; in December, after the Tora Bora campaign, when he appeared in ill health—ashen and gaunt, his left arm motionless by his side, and his Kalashnikov propped up behind him on the right. Pakistani and American intelligence officials spent hours poring over the tape and scrutinizing bin Laden's every move, for the leader of al-Qaeda is left-handed. Then, in April 2002, bin Laden appeared on Al-Jazeera again and, to the consternation of U.S. officials, he looked perfectly fit. The tape was undated, but officials at the station told me that it could have been produced in the middle days of March, since its narrator referred at one point to an upcoming Arab League summit, the latest of which took place on March 27 and 28.

Bin Laden's demeanor was consistent on all the tapes. He was, at once, calm and relaxed; then, by turns, swaggering and boastful; instinctively cunning and a formidable foe. He taunted the United States and he praised the September 11 suicide hijackers, framed most often in the camera's eye by barren rock and a solitary Kalashnikov. But his most unguarded, and chilling, moment came in a videotape, time-stamped November 9, 2001, in a Kandahar guesthouse and released the following month by the Pentagon. How it was obtained by the United States and how it was filmed remain matters of considerable dispute.

Wearing a camouflage flak jacket over his *shalwar kameez*, a white turban, and a gold ring, bin Laden strode into the guesthouse followed by Ayman al-Zawahiri. A Kalashnikov hung from his shoulder, possibly the same Kalashnikov which he has often claimed to have captured from a Soviet general, whom he had killed during the jihad. His guest of honor that evening, according to U.S. intelligence sources, was a militant Saudi cleric, disabled from the waist down, who had been smuggled into Afghanistan by a member of the Saudi Arabian religious police. Sheikh Ali Saeed al-Ghamdi, a former assistant professor of Islamic theology at a seminary in Mecca, had arrived from the mountainous province of Asir, in the kingdom's southwest—the same province from which the majority of the fifteen Saudi hijackers had also come.*

As the evening progressed, the men laughed and talked, ate and drank in the small white room, in which flowered throw pillows were piled on a couch. Then bin Laden began to talk and, with evident pleasure, described the September 11 attacks to the sheikh, using his hands to narrate. "We calculated in advance the number of casualties from the enemy," he said. "We calculated that the floors that would be hit would be three or four . . . I was the most optimistic of them all . . . I was thinking that the fire from the gas in the plane would melt the iron structure of the building and collapse the area where the plane hit and all the floors above it only. This is all that we had hoped for." He then went on to say that the men who carried out the attacks—nine of whom he named—knew in advance that they were on a "martyrdom operation," but that they did not know the details until just before they boarded the planes.

Bin Laden's voice was gentle as he spoke, as was the movement of his hands. He adjusted his turban, stroked his beard.

Sheikh al-Ghamdi praised bin Laden and smiled obsequiously. Then bin Laden pointedly asked the sheikh how the attacks had been received by a number of radical clerics in Saudi Arabia—which on the videotape emerged as a crucial link to al-Qaeda. The men

---

*Although Saudi diplomats in Washington confirmed that the visitor was Sheikh al-Ghamdi, a Saudi official in London later told the British press that the man was, in fact, Khaled al-Harbi, a veteran of the jihad who had also fought in Bosnia and Chechnya, and had lost his legs in combat.

talked of a soccer metaphor and dreams, of poems and prayers. The evening was devastatingly ordinary.

As bin Laden smiled benignly into the camera lens, the Kandahar guesthouse was surrounded by scores of guards—Egyptians, Algerians, Jordanians, and Saudi Arabians—veterans of the jihad who were now denounced by the kings and presidents of half the Arab world.

In the weeks that followed, there were more unconfirmed spottings of bin Laden; and more unconfirmed reports of his death. Pervez Musharraf caused an uproar in Pakistan—and in Washington—when he told CNN in a January interview that bin Laden might have died of kidney failure in the Afghan caves after becoming separated from his dialysis machine. Some days later, CBS News reported that bin Laden had, in fact, received dialysis in a military hospital in Rawalpindi, Pakistan. His last known treatment, according to that report, had occurred the night before the September 11 terrorist attacks. The Pakistani military spokesman, of course, quickly denied the CBS report.

These developments, however, have obscured the larger questions facing the U.S. government: how to respond to an enemy who is a man and not a state; who has no structured organization, no headquarters, and no fixed address; and whose followers live in different countries and feel a loyalty not so much to that man as to the ideology of militant Islam. According to several intelligence officials, the Clinton and Bush Administrations' answer, to a large extent, had been to do precisely what Osama bin Laden himself had been doing over the years—sculpting a figure larger than life and, as a consequence, ignoring dozens of other leaders and groups spread across the globe. In the process, they had also obscured the driving force behind radical Islam's assault—an assault that has arisen largely in reaction to the corruption and oppression of Islamic governments themselves.

"Is Osama bin Laden the exclusive font of terrorist evil?" one former State Department official said to me. "No," he went on. "This is an informal brotherhood we are seeing now, whose members can draw on each other for support. Al-Qaeda is not a terrorist organization in the traditional sense. It's more a clearinghouse from which other groups elicit funds, training, and logistical support. It's a chameleon, an amoeba, which constantly changes shape according to the whims of its leadership, and that leadership is Osama bin Laden. It's highly personalized. Bin Laden is a facilitator—a practitioner of the most ancient way of doing things in the Middle East. If you were to kill him tomorrow, all of the networks would still be there." He went on to say that he believed that the equally serious threat bin Laden posed to the interests of the United States—above and beyond future attacks against U.S. facilities or on U.S. soil—lies in his ability to further destabilize friendly Muslim governments, such as those in Pakistan, Saudi Arabia, and Egypt, whose support is geopolitically crucial to us.

Other U.S. officials agree, and warn that bin Laden's financial backing has reached from Egypt to Algeria, from Yemen to Somalia, from Saudi Arabia to the Philippines—and, to most lethal effect, to Pakistan and Afghanistan. He has supported Islamic fighters not only there but also in Chechnya, Kosovo, Bosnia, Tajikistan, and Kashmir. And the groups that enjoy his patronage are everything that al-Qaeda is not: they are well structured; many have long histories and specific (and often legitimate) complaints and concerns. They are not controlled by bin Laden; they have, however, been embraced by him.

It had sometimes been said—at least until September 11, 2001—that al-Qaeda was essentially an Egyptian organization with a Saudi head. For when the movement was forged in Peshawar, during the last days of the jihad, bin Laden's closest partners were Egypt's al-Jihad, which in 1981 had played a major part in the assassination of the Egyptian president Anwar Sadat, and the Gama'a al-Islamiya, the country's largest militant Islamist group, which had led an insurrection in the 1990s against Hosni Mubarak, who succeeded Sadat. By the time al-Qaeda was born, Ayman al-Zawahiri, now the group's chief ideologue, was the military head of al-Jihad. He had first met bin Laden in Peshawar in 1985, and over the years became his chief mentor and confidant. Because of him, more than anyone else, al-Qaeda's ranks are full of Egyptians. Al-Zawahiri quickly installed his own faithful deputy, Mohammed Atef, at bin Laden's side. Atef became al-Qaeda's military chief. The relationship was further joined when Atef's daughter—in a lavish Afghan ceremony—married one of bin Laden's sons in January 2001.

Moving between Afghanistan and Peshawar, al-Zawahiri and Atef were instrumental in cobbling together an alliance in February 1998 under the banner of the World Islamic Front for Jihad against Jews and Crusaders—which included not only the Gama'a al-Islamiya and al-Jihad, but two of Pakistan's militant Islamist groups, the Jamiat-ul-Ulema-e-Pakistan (or JUP) and the Harakat ul-Mujahideen, both of which, along with the JUI, were heavily funded by the ISI. (Indeed, in the last days of December 2001, a spokesman for the Afghan Ministry of Defense said that intelligence sources had reported that bin Laden was in Pakistan under the protection of the JUI's leader, Maulana Fazlur Rahman—the same religious leader who had set up thousands of madrasahs across Pakistan during the jihad.)

Six months before the bombing of our African embassies, the World Islamic Front issued a three-page call to arms to kill Americans around the world, under the signature of all the leaders of its component parts. Yet in November 1998, three months after the embassy bombings, when the Justice Department handed down a 238-count indictment, al-Zawahiri, Mir Hamzah of the JUP, and Fazlur Rehman Khalil of the Harakat were not even charged. In fact, the indictment concentrated almost exclusively on Osama bin Laden, charging him with conspiracy to kill Americans and accusing him of involvement (without detailing his specific role) in much more than the embassy attacks. It charged that, as the leader of a terrorist conspiracy for nearly ten years, bin Laden had attempted to procure the components of nuclear and chemical weapons. According to the indictment, bin Laden also had a logistical and training role in the 1993 killing in Somalia of eighteen American servicemen, one of whose bodies was seen on television being dragged through the streets by a mob. (In an interview broadcast on CNN in May 1997, bin Laden himself boasted that his followers had played a role in those deaths.)

Yet the indictment did not provide persuasive evidence that bin Laden personally planned or directed the bombings of our embassies in Africa, and, by 2002, the government had still not produced such evidence. Ambassador Robert B. Oakley, who led the State Department's Counter-Terrorism Office, called bin Laden's boast of involvement in the Somali deaths "preposterous." And when President Clinton said that bin Laden was responsible for a 1995 assassination attempt in Addis Ababa against Hosni Mubarak, the Egyptian president, one member of the Gama'a al-Islamiya to whom I spoke was outraged: the group had labored for more than a year to plan and execute the attempt, he said. Given bin Laden's genius for self-promotion, one worried U.S. official told me that the administration's attempts to concentrate solely on him, and in effect to grant immunity to the two dozen or so militant Islamist groups that al-Qaeda trained and financed, only helped him. In fact, the real bin Laden is more interesting, and perhaps more dangerous, than the fantasies that have surrounded him.

Osama bin Mohammed bin Awad bin Laden was born in 1955, the seventeenth of some twenty surviving sons of one of Saudi Arabia's wealthiest and most preeminent families. (His father, Mohammed, sired more than fifty children, with a total of eleven wives—mainly Egyptians and Saudi Arabians—in part to consolidate strategic alliances through extended families.) Osama's mother, the patriarch's fourth and final official wife, was, by contrast, from Syria. Osama was her only son, and their relationship continues to be close.

The elder bin Laden had immigrated to the kingdom in the

1920s from the Hadhramaut, a poor and deeply conservative area in Yemen, and had built a construction company into a financial empire, based in large part on his friendship with King Abdul Aziz, the founder of Saudi Arabia. One of Osama's most vivid childhood memories, he has told friends, is of his father's early success in expanding the sacred Islamic shrines of Mecca and Medina. The young Osama lived a privileged and pampered life. As was customary in the kingdom's prominent families, tutors and nannies, bearers and butlers formed a large part of it.

And if it is a paradox for the son of a patrician family to be preaching terror and mass Islamist politics, then Osama bin Laden fails to grasp it. It is just one of the anomalies of his life. He is an Eastern fatalist by birth, a Western-educated management expert and high-tech engineer, who has carefully modeled himself on the legendary twelfth-century military hero Salah al-Din. He is an introverted loner who relishes visibility. He is a man of more than average vanity, who reveals little about himself. It is actually quite hard to say who Osama bin Laden really is.

He is part puritanical Wahhabi, reared in the severe traditions of Wahhabi Islam, yet at one time he may have led a very liberated social life. He is part feudal Saudi, an aristocrat who from time to time would retreat with his austere father to the desert and live in a tent. And he is part of a Saudi generation that came of age during the rise of OPEC, with the extraordinary wealth that accompanied it: that same generation whose religious fervor or political zeal, complemented by government airline tickets, led thousands to a distant Muslim land to combat the Soviet occupation of Afghanistan.

Bin Laden had shown no interest in politics before then. According to family members, he was bookish and withdrawn, spending much of his time alone. But after a trip to Pakistan in early 1980, he returned to Jidda transformed. Over the next four years, before he moved to Peshawar permanently, he traveled throughout Saudi Arabia and the Persian Gulf raising millions of dollars for the jihad. Some of the funding came directly from the Saudi government, some from official mosques, and some from the kingdom's financial and business elite—including members of his family.

Milt Bearden, the CIA's station chief in Pakistan, who ran the agency's side of the war in Afghanistan from 1986 to 1989, told me that bin Laden and other fund-raisers, largely from Saudi Arabia and the Gulf, contributed as much as $20 to $25 million a month to underwrite the war—a total of $200 million to $300 million a year.

And, after Jadji, there were other battles for bin Laden, too. Most notably, the badly organized, bloody siege of Jalalabad, a pivotal military operation planned and directed by the ISI in March 1989, after the Soviets had withdrawn, in which the single largest number of Afghan Arabs fought together—under the direction of Pakistani Army officers—during the jihad. There was also the battle of Ali Khel—in which bin Laden led a Saudi contingent in an operation planned by the CIA—an operation in Paktia Province, not far from Jadji and the area struck by U.S. cruise missiles in 1998 and by "bunker busters" and "daisy cutters" in the autumn and winter of 2001.

During (and also after) the jihad, bin Laden met frequently with Hassan al-Turabi, an erudite Islamist who would later effectively control the rigid Islamic government in the Sudan. He dined regularly with General Zia ul-Haq and the inner circle most responsible for conduiting the CIA arms. He cultivated generals from the ISI, as he befriended some of the most anti-Western of the Afghan resistance leaders fighting the jihad.

It remains unclear whether it was during those years or after 1996 (when bin Laden returned to Afghanistan) that he first met Sultan Bashiruddin Mahmood, one of Pakistan's leading nuclear scientists. A radical Islamist with exceedingly unorthodox views, Mahmood—along with a fellow nuclear scientist, Chaudry Abdul Majid, and five members of a Mahmood-founded purported charity—was arrested in late October 2001 at the urging of Washington and interrogated about his links to bin Laden and the Taliban. Since his retirement in the late 1990s, he had been coming and going from Afghanistan regularly, as an ostensible philanthropist and the founder and chairman

of Ummah Tameer-e-Nau—or Islamic Reconstruction—which
U.S. officials suspected was a bin Laden front. Mahmood told American interrogators that he had met bin Laden only twice. What had
they discussed? the investigators asked. "Flour mills," Mahmood
said.

So alarmed were officials in the Bush Administration by the possibility that bin Laden might have obtained nuclear technology from
Mahmood that CIA Director George J. Tenet was hastily dispatched
to Islamabad to discuss the matter with Musharraf personally. But
four months of investigation failed to produce any significant results
other than the fact, one Pakistani official told me, that Mahmood
failed "six or seven" lie detector tests. By January 2002, all of the
men had been released, although Mahmood was placed under a
loose house arrest, and he remained on the U.S. list of designated
terrorists.

For years, U.S. officials had been attempting to trace bin Laden's
efforts to procure fissionable material that could be converted into a
bomb. One such incident had been documented in a trial, in February 2001, in New York of four men who were convicted of having
played roles in the bombings of the U.S. embassies in Africa. One
government witness, Jamal Ahmed al-Fadl, a Sudanese who had previously been one of bin Laden's close aides, testified that, as early as
1993, he had attempted to buy one cylinder of South African uranium for al-Qaeda for $1.5 million. And by 1993, Sultan Bashirud-
din Mahmood, a thirty-eight-year veteran of Pakistan's nuclear
program, had emerged as the country's most public and most prominent proponent of "Islamic science." His theories, even to many Islamists, seemed exceptionally odd. He argued that the energy of
spirits, or jinn in the Koran, could be harnessed to solve the world's
energy crisis, and in 1998 he published "Cosmology and Human
Destiny," in which he wrote that sunspots had determined the
course of world events, including World War II and revolutions
against colonial powers. The fact that a man with such ideas had
risen to such prominence in the Pakistani Atomic Energy Commission was worrisome enough. But for U.S. officials, his conversations

with Osama bin Laden about "flour mills" were even more trouble-some.

By the time bin Laden returned to Saudi Arabia, in 1989, to assume his place in his late father's construction empire, the Bin Laden Group, the family's business interests had spread to three continents. (Before the September 11 attacks, fifteen of bin Laden's siblings were living in Europe, and four of his half brothers, along with seventeen nieces and nephews, in the United States.) And there were other areas in which bin Laden found his native Saudi Arabia changed: with the collapse of the oil boom the kingdom faced growing economic and social problems and, according to the State Department's annual human-rights reports, the Saudi royal family was also becoming increasingly repressive and corrupt. Bin Laden began to criticize the kingdom's feudal regime openly and to support its opposition groups. His half brothers and some of his royal friends—including Prince Salman bin Abdul-Aziz, the governor of Riyadh, and Prince Turki bin Faisal, the chief of Saudi intelligence, with whom bin Laden had worked during the jihad—attempted to restrain him, and for a time he devoted himself to personal matters: expanding his holdings (which were based, in large part, on more than sixty companies, many of them in the West) and producing heirs. He now has four wives, carefully chosen for their political connections or their pedigrees, and some dozen children.

Bin Laden's quietude, however, did not last long. By the time he returned to Jidda he had already become somewhat of a hero for his role in the jihad. And now, as opposed to those earlier years, when he was standoffish, shy and soft-spoken, many said, he moved with calm assurance through the world of militants and mullahs, equally at home with Islamic scholars, the Afghan guerrilla leaders with whom he had fought, and generals abroad, including Sudan's president, Omar al-Bashir, and Pakistan's heirs to Zia ul-Haq. It was also during that time that bin Laden increasingly came under the sway of two of Saudi Arabia's most militant clerics, Sheikhs Safar Hawali and

Salman Awdah—whose views are considered revolutionary by the Saudi regime, and whose *fatwas* bin Laden began to propagate. In 1991, the royal family expelled him from the kingdom for his political activities, and his family publicly renounced him. He sought refuge in the Sudan.

After that, bin Laden's political evolution accelerated. His departure from his homeland coincided with the arrival there of thousands of U.S. troops for the Persian Gulf War. When the Saudi regime permitted them not only to occupy its soil but to remain after the victory, bin Laden's antipathy to both the regime and the United States was inflamed.

In his eyes, the United States had become to Saudi Arabia what the Soviet Union had been to Afghanistan: an infidel occupation force propping up a corrupt, repressive, and un-Islamic government. When Saddam Hussein invaded Kuwait and the Saudi dynasty welcomed U.S. troops onto its soil, near Islam's holiest shrines—of Mecca and Medina—the House of Saud, for bin Laden, lost its remaining legitimacy.

During five years of exile in the Sudan, from 1991 until the spring of 1996, bin Laden divided his time between Khartoum and London (where he owned large and opulent estates). He placed his wealth— a personal fortune estimated at more than $250 million, largely in foreign bank accounts—at the disposal of militant Islamic groups around the world. Whether he retained access to his family's fortune, which is estimated to be worth some $5 billion, is a matter of dispute. For although the family—whose American condos and designer clothes Osama disdained—has publicly renounced the activities of its prodigal son, there are many who believe that it remains a source of financial support. Bin Laden's relationship with some family members, including one of his brothers-in-law, a Saudi financier named Mohammed Jamal Khalifa, continues to be close. And in the spring of 2002, authorities in Switzerland, at the request of France, opened an investigation into the financial activities of one of bin

Laden's half brothers—Yeslam Binladin (who spells his name differently, in part, to distance himself from Osama)—for possible money-laundering; and another half brother, Ghalib Mohammed Binladin, is being investigated for his connections to the Bahamas-registered Al-Taqwa Bank, which, according to U.S. Treasury officials, provided financial support to Osama before and after the September 11 attacks. Both the brothers and officials of the bank have strongly denied any links to bin Laden, or any financial impropriety.

Mohammed Jamal Khalifa, for his part, was a prime conduit for funding militant Islamic groups in the Philippines, Filipino officials assert. According to U.S. investigators, there is evidence that during the mid-1990s, when he was the head of the Islamic Relief Organization—a quasi-government Saudi charity—in the Philippines, Khalifa was "directly linked" to several of the men convicted for their role in the first World Trade Center bombing in New York, including its mastermind, Ramzi Ahmed Yousef, and, also, Wali Khan Amin Shah. Not only were the two veterans of the jihad involved in the Trade Center bombing, but they were later convicted in a Manhattan court of planning to blow up American jumbo jets—as many as twelve of them over the Pacific in what would have been a spectacular two-day spree. At their trial in 1996, it was revealed that another defendant, Abdul Hakim Murad (from Balochistan like Yousef and Shah), had been tasked with carrying out a kamikaze-style plane crash into the headquarters of the CIA—and that was seven years ago. Murad, like at least six of the hijackers in the September 11 attacks, had received flight training in the United States. His videotaped confession in 1995 was noted four years later in a U.S. intelligence report that suggested that al-Qaeda might hijack a U.S. plane with the intention of crashing it into a government building, like the Pentagon.

Not only did Murad confess but Wali Khan Amin Shah, who described himself as one of bin Laden's key operational aides, agreed during the trial to cooperate with federal authorities. U.S. investigators, who continue to suspect that wealthy businessmen in Saudi Arabia and the Gulf helped finance some of Yousef's activities, were hopeful that Shah would be able to provide a link between Ramzi Yousef, Osama bin Laden, and the first World Trade Center bomb.

In the years preceding his arrest in Pakistan and extradition to the United States, in February 1995, Yousef had largely divided his time among the Philippines, Afghanistan, and Peshawar—where he most often lived at the House of Martyrs (Bayt Ashuhada), a bin Laden–financed guesthouse. During that time, the paths of the two men must have crossed, since bin Laden, too, frequently traveled to all three places from his headquarters in Khartoum.

While bin Laden was based in the Sudan, the Saudi regime warned him more than once that it would countenance no actions directed against the Saudi throne. He ignored the warnings. In the early 1990s—during the first Bush Administration, and presumably with the knowledge of the United States—the Saudis secretly dispatched hit teams to Khartoum with a contract on bin Laden's life.

Then inexplicably, in November 1996, or so bin Laden claimed, the Saudi royal family invited him to return home. His assets and properties, which the government had seized, would be returned to him, he said in an interview with *Al-Quds al-Arabi*, in exchange for his swearing an oath of allegiance to King Fahd. Bin Laden refused. Saudi officials would neither confirm nor deny that the offer was made; indeed, over the years they had consistently refused to comment on anything about bin Laden—a testament, perhaps, to their continuing bewilderment about how to cope with him.

The effort to contain the rise of militant Islam in Saudi Arabia—the repository of the world's largest oil reserves—requires extraordinary delicacy, both on America's part and on the part of the Saudi regime. Over the years, the regime's actions have been confused, contradictory, and frequently inexplicable.

The Saudis had, of course, been obsessed with driving the Soviets out of Afghanistan, and Washington's financial commitment to that war had been exceeded only by theirs. At the time the jihad was getting under way, there was no significant Islamist opposition movement in Saudi Arabia, and it apparently never occurred to the Saudi rulers, who feared the Soviets as much as Washington did, that the volunteers it sent might be converted by the jihad's ideology. But as September 11 showed, the next generation of the children of the jihad clearly were.

Thousands of Saudis fought in the jihad. Largely funded and supported by their government, they came from good families, some immensely wealthy ones. They trained and they bonded; they raised money and they fought. In the months following the September 11 attacks, some commentators expressed the view that the role of the Saudis and the other Afghan Arabs who fought in the jihad had been overstated. But this is not the point: the point is not what *they* did for the jihad but, far more important, what the jihad did for them.

I asked a diplomat who had served in Peshawar during the war years what, in his view, made the Saudis different from the other Islamists who came to fight.

"Their government sent them," he replied. "It was the patriotic thing to do. But when these guys got there, they met others and began to network; they found a whole new world out there. And despite their wealth, they were underemployed, frustrated, an accident waiting to happen—and it did. Also, unlike the others who went to Afghanistan as members of Islamic groups—Gama'a, al-Jihad, Hamas, and the like—there *were* no organized Saudi groups. That's what makes these guys very different: *they* set up the networks when they came home."

Other U.S. officials agree and warn that despite the Saudi government's efforts to blame the usual regional suspects—Iran, Iraq, and Sudan—for the unrest in the kingdom, the Islamist discontent in Saudi Arabia is real, and the movement is basically homegrown. Perhaps as a result of this, and of an ill-advised attempt to buy protection for the throne, the kingdom's princes and foundations and wealthy businessmen, who include a number of bin Laden's friends, have long been the primary financiers of many of the world's militant Islamist groups.

In September and October 2001, the Bush Administration—to the abiding discomfort of the House of Saud—publicly named ten of the movement's members and financiers. The most prominent was Yasin al-Qadi, an immensely wealthy investor and businessman, who moved with ease in the elite of Saudi society. But in running the Muwafaq Foundation—along with trustees from some of the kingdom's other most prominent families—he had transferred millions of dollars from Saudi businessmen to bin Laden over the years, the U.S. Treasury Department charged, and it placed him on a list of forty-five individuals (along with organizations) whose assets should be seized. Curiously, the charity itself was not placed on the list, ostensibly because, according to Treasury officials, the U.S. government was unable to locate it.

Then in February of the following year, a French intelligence report published by *The Washington Post* highlighted the role of another of Muwafaq's prominent trustees, Khalid bin Mahfouz, in funneling millions of dollars to bin Laden–controlled charities. He did so as the director of the National Commercial Bank, one of Saudi Arabia's largest banks and the banker to the royal family. Prior to becoming the director of that bank—which his family controls—bin Mahfouz had served as director of BCCI, the Pakistani bank that had collapsed in the early 1990s following discoveries that it, too, among other things, had funneled money to the mujahideen for the CIA during the jihad and, after that, held accounts for Osama bin Laden. (In 1995, bin Mahfouz paid $225 million, including a $37 million fine, in a settlement with U.S. prosecutors to avoid possible charges in the United States for his role in the BCCI scandal.)

Yet in April 1999, when bin Mahfouz was placed under house arrest after Saudi officials, at the insistence of Washington, audited the National Commercial Bank, U.S. officials were never permitted to question him. Nor were they ever permitted to interrogate one of bin Laden's key financial aides—Sidi Tayyib, a man of considerable influence, whom Saudi intelligence officials had detained that same year at the strong urging of Washington. But following their own investigation, the Saudis bluntly told their CIA counterparts that there was no basis for treating Tayyib "like a criminal." Tayyib, who is married to one of bin Laden's nieces, probably knows as much as anyone else about bin Laden's intricate financial empire.

The Saudis' vacillation over the years and their attempts to appease bin Laden—which are based, in large part, not only on their fear of him but also on their fear of further mythologizing him—is worrisome.

And the strains in the U.S.-Saudi relationship, as a consequence, have become even more pronounced since the American war against bin Laden began—a war that has affected U.S. policy throughout the Islamic world: not only in Pakistan and the Middle East but, as pronounced as anywhere else, in the kingdom of Saudi Arabia itself. Although the House of Saud has continued to permit American troops to billet in the country, it has prohibited them from conducting air strikes against Iraq. It has also moved slowly in scrutinizing its Islamic charities and in instructing its banks to seize the assets, if any assets are found, of those groups or men on the Bush Administration's al-Qaeda financing lists—as it had moved slowly, in earlier years, in refusing to permit U.S. officials to question any Saudis with alleged ties to Osama bin Laden. Even before the United States was denied access to either Sidi Tayyib or Khalid bin Mahfouz, the royal family, in a barely disguised attempt not to further antagonize bin Laden and his followers, had not allowed the FBI to interrogate any of the suspects allegedly involved in the 1995 and 1996 bombings of American military installations in Riyadh and Dhahran—bombings that were clearly aimed at the Saudi dynasty as well as at the United States.

As bin Laden's international image and stature increased—along with his support, both financial and ideological, among some of the kingdom's elite and the elites of other states in the Persian Gulf—any Saudi hopes of quietly resolving its bin Laden problem by force became less tenable. And each time the U.S. administration raised the stakes and further enhanced bin Laden's prominence, more and more disaffected Saudis flocked to join the kingdom's militant Islamist underground, of which bin Laden—as September 11 showed—remained a central part.

Thus, when the U.S. government charged bin Laden with conspiracy in regard to the bombings of our military installations in Saudi Arabia, the Saudi Minister of the Interior quickly announced that the kingdom had no information to substantiate accounts that bin Laden had ever engaged in any terrorist activities on its soil. And when President Clinton and Boris Yeltsin—who had discerned bin Laden's hand in Russia's own problems with Islamist militants in Chechnya—came together in a rare show of force at the United Nations in the autumn of 1999 to impose sanctions against the Taliban, the rulers of Saudi Arabia assiduously distanced themselves from both men.

For twenty years, Osama bin Laden had refashioned himself with extraordinary dexterity and skill, yet he never lost sight of his ultimate goal: the overthrow of the dynastic House of Saud. Likewise, Ayman al-Zawahiri and Mohammed Atef, and all of the other al-Qaeda leaders from Egypt's Gama'a and al-Jihad, remained intent on toppling Hosni Mubarak's Army-backed government. In their eyes, at least at the time that al-Qaeda was born, the United States government—along with the other issues and causes they would later espouse—was of merely secondary concern. Indeed, of bin Laden's inner circle, only Abu Zubaydah, the Saudi-born Palestinian who had been arrested in Pakistan in March 2002, had been imbued with the Palestinian struggle against Israel. When the newest Palestinian Intifada erupted in September 2000 in the West Bank and Gaza Strip, it was Abu Zubaydah who convinced bin Laden to embrace it. And although the Palestinian cause had never been of more than passing interest to the al-Qaeda leader before, he now claimed it as his own, masterfully. For this was the key issue that captivated the Arab street and, partly as a result, the United States—Israel's most stolid ally and by now one of bin Laden's most formidable foes—had become the object of uniform, militant Islamic rage. The confluence of developments served bin Laden well.

So alarmed was the House of Saud, not only by bin Laden's rising profile in the kingdom itself but, ever fearful of the Islamist challenge to its throne, that it was now even more intent on a transformation of its own—to turn what had been an often complex battle of wills between the Saudi royal family and its errant son into a far simpler conflict, one that would pit bin Laden and his followers against the United States.

In the early months of 1999, when Nawaz Sharif was prime minister of Pakistan and General Pervez Musharraf was entering his fifth month as Chief of the Army Staff, Washington had pressed Islamabad to set up a special commando unit—to be trained by the CIA—that would be able to infiltrate Afghanistan, find bin Laden, and capture or eliminate him. Although unenthusiastic, Musharraf agreed to establish such a group, and it was trained. But in the end, it never crossed over into Afghanistan. One U.S. intelligence official said that the project had been scuttled by the ISI, which by then was sharing a number of military training camps with al-Qaeda in the mountains of Afghanistan.

When I asked Musharraf about this late the following year, he thought for a moment and then replied, without answering, "Your government must deal with the Taliban direct. I've engaged with them endlessly about bin Laden, and I've told them that they must deal with him. But it's such a touchy issue. Nevertheless, I've made it clear that it was in their interest to finally resolve it." He then went on to say, "I think a middle way can be found on this whole issue of extraditing him [which was then being demanded by the United States]. He could be sent to a third country—as long as that country is not Pakistan."

I learned later from a member of one of Pakistan's militant Islamist groups that bin Laden was, in fact, visiting Peshawar at the very time that the general and I spoke.

The United States had not been the first country to have pressured Pakistan. In June 1998, Prince Turki, the Saudi chief of intelligence and once bin Laden's friend, had sought the help of

Islamabad to intervene with the Taliban and have bin Laden turned over to him. Musharraf, at the time, had not yet been elevated to the Army's top post, but one of his fellow officers told me that he had opposed the Saudi move. And Saudi Arabia was a country that the general knew well, for as Zia ul-Haq, in 1970, had commanded a Pakistani brigade in Jordan charged with protecting King Hussein's throne, Musharraf had served in 1984 with a Pakistani military contingent in Saudi Arabia, protecting the Saudi throne.

And, even before Prince Turki's plea was rebuffed, officials in Cairo were furious with the Pakistani government. In 1995, President Hosni Mubarak of Egypt had told me about a meeting he had had in Bonn in April 1993 with Prime Minister Nawaz Sharif. "It was a tough meeting," he said. "And I couldn't believe my ears: this man was the leader of Pakistan and he told me, quite frankly, 'We cannot control Peshawar. We cannot prevent these people from running loose.' I asked him then if he wanted me to send the Egyptian Armed Forces to Peshawar to clean up the mess."

Mubarak had demanded that all of the Egyptian jihadis—including Ayman al-Zawahiri—be extradited; Sharif demurred. Nevertheless, on Sharif's return to Pakistan, he reluctantly instructed the even more reluctant ISI to "look into Peshawar." I asked a Western diplomat based there what had happened then.

"It was absolute chaos," he replied. "This town has become one huge storefront since the jihad: there are storefront presses, storefront arms dealers, storefront drug traffickers, storefront mosques. The government started to review all of the NGOs"—nongovernmental organizations—"and all the expatriate workers here. But when they got to the thirty-five or so marginal organizations of the Arabs, they couldn't find the offices, the buildings, the people! Earlier that year, they actually conducted raids, and they were only able to find some two hundred Arabs, even though they had issued identity cards to more than five hundred the previous month. They set a deadline when all of the Arabs without proper papers had to leave. I think we're on our sixth or seventh deadline now, and somewhat fewer than twenty have actually left."

He turned more serious, and then he went on. "It's an immense problem for Pakistan. The government doesn't want to deport these people and send them back to trial or to their execution. And where can you expel them to from Pakistan? They're clearly not going to take them to the Afghan border and set them loose."

By October 1999, when Pervez Musharraf overthrew Nawaz Sharif, the lawlessness in Peshawar had become palpably worse, but the general, as his predecessors before him had done, seemed unable or unwilling to rein the Islamic militants in.

Now, in the aftermath of the September 11 attacks, he had gambled heavily in his attempt to restore his country's badly bruised relationship with the United States, confronting a growing array of critics, including skeptics in his own military constituency, who remember that Washington had walked away from Pakistan before, after the first U.S.-Afghan war.

By May of 2002, when officials of Musharraf's government conceded that a limited number of American troops would be permitted to operate from Pakistani soil, popular anger against the United States had turned to rage as a result of the civilian casualties suffered in Afghanistan due to the intense U.S. bombing there, and of the Bush Administration's stalwart support of Israel in its deadly standoff with the Palestinians. And the anger grew in the Army, too, as a consequence of both, and of the military sanctions still in place on Pakistan, the sanctions that had been imposed shortly after the end of the jihad.

CHAPTER 7

KASHMIR

THE ROAD TO MUZAFFARABAD, the capital of what Pakistan calls "Azad (or Free) Kashmir"—the part of the state that it controls—climbs steeply from 2,500 feet above sea level to 19,200 feet, dropping into plains and valleys, then lurching toward glaciers and snow-capped mountain peaks. In the spring of 2001, the Jhelum River, its waters churning and brown, attested to torrential rainstorms and the likelihood of floods. Wisps of blue smoke spoke of hidden villages beyond. As the Pakistani Army jeep in which I was traveling circumvented a landslide, then sloshed through Muzaffarabad's muddy streets, small children ran to the roadside to salute it—children whose parents were almost certainly younger than the independent nations of India and Pakistan; and younger than the 450-mile Line of Control, which we were about to follow and which separates them. Manned by forty-three military observers and twenty-two civilian officials from the UN, this cease-fire line, drawn through the valleys and mountain rock in 1949 (then revised slightly by the 1972 Simla Accord, following the last Indo-Pakistani war), is nearly as old as the United Nations itself. It is the second oldest

UN cease-fire line in the world. Three times, Pakistan and India had gone to war—twice over the prize of Kashmir, which is in a sense a forgotten artifact of the Partition of British India fifty-five years ago.

From behind us came the thudding sound of a military convoy of twelve olive green trucks carrying reinforcements to this most critical part of the 1,800-mile-long Indo-Pakistani front. That morning, though tensions were unusually high, the transfer had been routine, but seven months after that, in December, Indian leaders threatened a military strike into Pakistan after their parliament was attacked— an attack that they blamed on Pakistani-backed Islamic militants. And they also threatened to attack Pakistan in May of the following year, when militant Islamists struck again, killing, among others, twenty-two women and children at an Indian Army camp in Kashmir. As a result of the parliament assault, India began what would become a massive military buildup.

By January 2002, a million Indian and Pakistani troops faced each other across their frontier. In some cases, they were separated by only 1,600 feet, on either side of the Jhelum. By the end of May, the world's first war between two nuclear-armed powers seemed imminent, for the third time in twelve years: first in May of 1990 and then in the summer of 1999, following Pakistan's infiltration of Kargil. Once again, everything was held hostage by Kashmir.

And as world leaders, during the last weeks of May and early June, grew increasingly alarmed and sent envoys shuttling between New Delhi and Islamabad, the Pentagon warned that if the confrontation over Kashmir, now more than half-a-century old, escalated into a full-scale nuclear exchange, up to twelve million people could be killed immediately and as many as seven million injured.

For five months, since the attack on its parliament, India had been demanding that Pakistan immediately cease cross-border infiltration by Islamic militants into India's part of the state, and that it dismantle the 128 or so military training camps—which were not only in Azad Kashmir but also in the remote mountains of the North-West Frontier—that the ISI had set up over the years to train combatants, now largely to fight in Kashmir. More than a thousand eager young men passed through the camps each year, drawn mostly from the dozen or so private Islamist armies based in Pakistan—armies that grew out of the jihad in Afghanistan. Most of them were linked in one fashion or another, some directly, some not, to Osama bin Laden. The three most powerful and deadly of the groups were the Harakat ul-Mujahideen (or HUM), which had signed bin Laden's declaration of jihad in February of 1998; the Jaish-e-Mohammed, which was an offshoot of it; and the Lashkar-e-Taiba, or Army of the Pure, a largely Wahhabi group, reliably said to be funded by Saudi Arabia.

As we continued climbing the hairpin mountain road, I remembered something that a Pakistani professor had told me thirteen years before, shortly after Zia ul-Haq died. Then we had been discussing Zia's jihad, and the professor had said that theocracy was totally alien to Afghanistan; that Afghans fought because they had always opposed foreign domination, but that nationalism had always been their driving force. What Zia and the CIA and the ISI had done twenty years ago had been to transform an essentially nationalist struggle into a holy war. And that same combustible formula was now being applied, in the same way, by Musharraf and his ISI, and before him, by Nawaz and Benazir in the long-disputed, former princely state of Kashmir.

At the time of Partition, British India's 562 princely states had to choose between joining India or Pakistan and, with few exceptions, such as Kalat, most of them quickly did—except, that is, for Jammu and Kashmir. The state had a Muslim-majority populace and a politically naïve Hindu maharaja, Hari Singh, who procrastinated for two months, finding both options to be equally unpalatable. He really hoped for independence, as unrealistic as it seemed at the time, but he was jolted out of his complacency. No sooner had he begun consulting with his aides than the Muslim inhabitants of the Poonch-Mirpur region of Kashmir, which abutted Pakistan, revolted against his rule. The rebels set up their own Azad Kashmir government and sought assistance from Pakistan to "liberate" the rest of Kashmir. On

October 20, 1947, armed Pathan tribesmen, backed by Pakistani troops, poured across the border from northwestern Pakistan. The maharaja panicked and appealed to India. Jawaharlal Nehru airlifted in Indian troops, and the Pakistanis were driven back to what is now essentially the Line of Control, retaining about a third of the contested state, while Hari Singh, despite the fact that 77 percent of his subjects were then Muslims, ceded his principality to the government of India. According to the Instrument of Accession to India, which he signed, the state of Jammu and Kashmir was granted, exceptionally, a semiautonomous status (whereby it would control its own affairs, except for currency, defense, communications, and foreign affairs). Pakistan was furious. It simply did not accept that a Muslim-majority state would, of its own accord, accede to a Hindu-dominated India. The first of three Indo-Pakistani wars began.

Under the terms of United Nations resolutions, passed in 1948 and 1949, Pakistan was to withdraw its forces from the entire state—which it never did. India was to reduce its troops to a bare minimum—which, over the next fifty-three years, it rarely has. Once Pakistan and India did what they were charged to do, an internationally monitored plebiscite would take place, in which the Kashmiris would determine which nation they would join. That plebiscite was never held.

Pakistan blames India; India blames Pakistan because, it says, the Pakistani government never withdrew from Azad Kashmir. Islamabad charges that New Delhi, in defiance of the UN, has continued to occupy nearly two thirds of Kashmir. Things became even more contentious in 1972, when two of the world's most resolute foes signed the Simla Accord, which was interpreted by India as having delinked the Kashmir dispute from the UN, and transformed it into a bilateral matter between the two states. Pakistan has never publicly accepted that assertion.

Kashmir is a lush and awesomely beautiful place; strategically important and rich; a largely Muslim state with special privileges in the

Union of India. A mountainous never-never land sandwiched between Afghanistan, the former Soviet Union, China, and Tibet, Kashmir was a prize that both Hindus and Muslims were vying for long before the British left. Hand-carved wooden houseboats lilt gracefully on its lakes, which are accentuated by Moghul gardens and, beyond, apple orchards, verdant meadows, and saffron fields. Yet by the time I first visited Kashmir, in June of 1983, the glue that held it together was already beginning to crack.

In the summer capital of Srinagar, nestled in the Vale of Kashmir and set superbly on Dal Lake, Kashmiri Muslims had already begun to fear that their special status of autonomy was eroding; Islamic fundamentalists had begun to clamor for the holding of that long-delayed plebiscite, mandated so many years earlier. The late Sheikh Mohammed Abdullah, the legendary "Lion of Kashmir," an immensely popular politician who had been a leader of the movement for independence from Britain, had dominated the Kashmir political scene for fifty-two years. With his death the previous September, his son, Dr. Farooq Abdullah, who was known as the "Lion Cub," had dynastically assumed the political mantle of his father.

Late one afternoon, I skirted the corniche of Dal Lake, then drove through terraced gardens of roses and jasmine, and called on him. A medical doctor who had spent fifteen years in England and had a British wife, he was then the chief minister (the state's highest elected official), and he still is. Since the Vale of Kashmir was the most sensitive part of the state and the only area where Muslims were in the majority—the southern region of Jammu was 65 percent Hindu, and Buddhists comprised 70 percent of the population of the border area of Ladakh—I asked the chief minister if he personally favored a plebiscite. He deflected the controversial issue. He then went on to say that successive Indian governments had eroded Kashmir's autonomy and had stripped away many of the constitutional prerogatives that the state should enjoy. Still, he said, as we sat on the manicured lawn of his home, "I have no doubts that I'm part of India. But there must be safeguards for my people's rights."

When I asked him about the call for "self-determination" (and a plebiscite) already being advocated by his new political ally, Maulvi Mohammed Farooq, Kashmir's supreme Muslim religious leader— or mirwaiz—he leaned back in his chair and, with a sweep of his large hand, rolled his eyes. He then went on to say that this was a "political improbability." The mirwaiz, he explained, "speaks for himself."

Some sixteen miles away, on the placid banks of the sanctuary of Nagin Lake, Maulvi Mohammed Farooq, who was in his mid-thirties, challenged the chief minister's assertion that there was no longer a Kashmir dispute. "We have United Nations observers here, there is a cease-fire line," the mirwaiz said to me, and his voice began to rise. "There have been scores of resolutions before the United Nations, so how can they say that the issue is dead?" He thought for a moment, and then he smiled. "India miscalculated badly," he went on. "It thought that when Sheikh Abdullah died, the movement died, too. But I am telling India, it is very much alive."

Wearing dark glasses, a flowing *choga* robe, and a peaked, woolen cap, popularized by Mohammed Ali Jinnah, the mirwaiz was the head of the Jamia Islamia mosque, the largest and richest in the valley, where, as in the rest of Kashmir, Islam was heavily influenced by its mystical Sufi branch. His alliance with the chief minister was of considerable consequence. For he was believed to control as many as 200,000 votes in elections that were about to be held—elections in which Farooq Abdullah, as the new leader of the National Conference Party, would make his political debut. By entering an electoral alliance with him, the mirwaiz had, in fact, buried a forty-five-year-old feud that had erupted between his uncle—who subsequently became the president of Azad Kashmir—and the venerable "Lion of Kashmir." (Sheikh Abdullah's supporters had adopted the symbol of the lion in 1938 and had relegated to the mirwaiz's supporters the logo of a goat.)

"How would you vote in a plebiscite?" I asked the mirwaiz.

"Certainly not for India."

Yet with a 100,000-man, regular standing Army already guarding

Kashmir's strategic passes and mountain peaks, it was clear that India was not about to relinquish the state. For above and beyond its geopolitical importance, Kashmir had come to represent a mirror for Muslim aspirations within a largely Hindu India. Although it had a population of only 4.6 million Muslims at the time (the number had doubled by 2002, in a total population of 130 million throughout India), it was the country's only Muslim-majority state. Thus the whole concept of a secular, multiethnic India would be threatened by its loss.

Pakistan, for its part, had been created on the basis of Islam, sculpted from British India for one reason alone: to provide a homeland for the subcontinent's Muslims. "Kashmir must be liberated if Pakistan is to have its full meaning," Zulfikar Ali Bhutto had said in 1964. Thus, as India was reinforcing its security apparatus in the disputed state, Islamabad was channeling funds to Maulvi Mohammed Farooq. And Pakistan's powerful religious party, the Jamaat-e-Islami, which was inseparable from the jihad and which had provided General Zia with his only political constituency, had also built up a sizable following in Kashmir, with seemingly unlimited funds—reliably said to be coming not only from Pakistan but also from Libya and Saudi Arabia—as it campaigned for a plebiscite regarding union with Pakistan.

Neither Pakistan nor India could afford to lose Kashmir: it was central to both their identities.

As a consequence, both had categorically rejected independence for the state. Their adamancy was reinforced by the fact that with potential breakaway states and provinces from India's Assam to Pakistan's Balochistan and Sindh, neither could afford to set a precedent.

In 1987, four years after my first visit to Kashmir, Chief Minister Farooq Abdullah, whose pro-India National Conference had entered an electoral alliance with the Congress Party (which ruled the central government), retained power in state elections that were perhaps the most fraudulent in Kashmir's history. And two years after that, in 1989, largely in response to them, a grassroots insurgency in

Kashmir began. In May of the following year, Maulvi Mohammed Farooq, who was by then considered to be a moderate voice on Kashmir's increasingly turbulent political scene, was assassinated by unidentified gunmen in the garden of his home and succeeded by his son, seventeen-year-old Umar.

Each time I returned to the state over the coming years, I had asked the same question over and over again: if there were a plebiscite, how would you vote?

One afternoon, in the autumn of 1999, when Indian national elections were under way, I sat in the tiny square in the village of Shalimar. A mantle of snow capped the Himalayas, and there was a nip in the air. Women were bringing in the last of the harvest from terraced, patchwork fields. Beneath a massive sixteenth-century Chinar tree, which dominates the square, the talk, as usual, was of politics.

"How would you vote?" I persisted again.

There was only a temporary hesitation, and then one old man said that the people of Kashmir wanted to be independent. They always have.

As we neared Chakothi, a Pakistani town perched prominently on the Line of Control, in the spring of 2001, we stopped at one of a string of roadside diners, festooned with tinsel and Pakistani flags, for kebabs and cups of sweet, milky tea. These were the haunts of truck drivers, and a dozen or so of their brightly painted vehicles were lined up in a neat row. We chose an outdoor table under a leafy tree and were joined by the proprietor, a large man named Mustafa, who had a pleasant smile and betel-stained teeth. The fighting across the line had intensified in recent weeks, he told my interpreter (a retired Army major) and me. "They're eyeball to eyeball again," he said, "shouting, glaring, sometimes using the foulest language I've ever heard. Then there's a silence, and one or the other side, maybe out of boredom, lobs an artillery shell across."

Both sides were, predictably, blaming the other for provoking this round; both sides were on maximum military alert. And on both sides of the Line of Control, it was civilians who were suffering the most. In one village just down the road, several shells had fallen only two days ago, Mustafa said. The village, like others on the Indian side of the line, had been turned into a ghost town. Indeed, every village we passed through showed the scars of years of fighting in this little-known war. Farmers told us that it was too dangerous to work in the fields; schools had closed. Most children, in any case, had to travel miles in order to attend school—and Pakistan was a country with an illiteracy rate of 54 percent, one of the highest in Asia.

Yet by 2000, for the first time in its history when it was not at war, Pakistan's military spending alone was greater than all of its development spending combined. Twenty percent of its budget (and over 5 percent of its GDP) was spent on defense, a total of some $3 billion. The budget allocated only 8 percent to education. (India, at the same time, invested about 3 percent of its GDP, or about $13 billion, in its military establishment.)

Mustafa beckoned to a nearby table, and three young men came over and joined us and they talked of jihad. A wizened mullah joined us, and he talked of Islam.

"Would you be willing to fight in [Indian] Kashmir?" I asked one of the young men.

He stroked his beard, and then he grinned. "I already am," he said.

The conversation didn't progress much beyond that. He said his name was Ahmed, that he belonged to the HUM and was a "soldier of Allah" under the "direct command" of a retired Pakistani brigadier. He could not talk further without permission, he said, and he gave us a cell phone number in Muzaffarabad. Then he disappeared, leaving us with only a number that didn't work and a nom de guerre.

I wondered how many other young men had passed through this town and made their way to Pakistani Army checkpoints along the

Line of Control, where they were helped across—given rations, weapons and ammunition, and even air cover, if the need arose. For what had begun as an indigenous, secular movement for Kashmiri independence in 1989 had by the mid-1990s increasingly become an Islamist crusade to bring all of Kashmir under Pakistani control. By the spring of 2001, 40 percent of the militants fighting Indian troops in Kashmir were not Kashmiris: they were Pakistanis and Afghans.

When the insurgency first broke out, it was led by a Kashmiri group called the Jammu and Kashmir Liberation Front, which had championed an independent, multireligious state. Its leader was Yasin Malik who, after a number of years in Indian jails, renounced armed struggle and became an executive member of the All Party Hurriyat Conference, a coalition of twenty-three political parties and organizations—all based in Indian-controlled Kashmir—that has seen its fortunes rise and fall over recent years. One of its founding members was the now twenty-nine-year-old son of Maulvi Mohammed Farooq, the new mirwaiz, Maulvi Umar. With a spiritual following of several million Muslims, he could be a powerful voice on Kashmir's political scene. But the authorities in New Delhi have refused to speak to him, as they have refused to engage any other moderates who favor a plebiscite in the embattled state. And by so doing, they had permitted the Pakistani-based Islamic militants to become the Kashmiris' most prominent advocates. Indeed, of the dozen or more groups fighting on the battlefield, the only one of prominence that was really indigenous was the Hizbul Mujahideen, the oldest and largest of the groups. Its fighters are thought to number about a thousand or so, and they insist that although they are Muslims, they are not Islamists. Nevertheless, they are linked to the Jamaat-e-Islami, and their leadership is not in Srinagar or Jammu but across the border in Azad Kashmir.

We said our good-byes to Mustafa, and proceeded to the heavily fortified town of Chakothi, on Pakistan's front line. Except for its sandbags and sentry posts, little distinguished it from the other towns and villages we had passed through: it was poor and muddy; its buildings were weather scarred and bleak; men with long beards, wearing Jinnah caps, huddled together on charpoys, sipping tea; no women were to be seen.

When we reached the forward position, we were greeted warmly by a Major Khan, whose crisp fatigues were complemented by a dark beret and a swagger stick he carried under his arm. His brigadier (who was meant to brief us) had unexpectedly been summoned to Rawalpindi, he said, so he would show us around. We walked to a spindly bridge overhanging the Jhelum, and on the other side we could see the Indian fortifications; they were so close that we did not need binoculars. They were easily recognizable with the naked eye.

The major briefed us on troop concentrations here and there, but when I revisited my notes in the early days of June 2002, the figures no longer seemed as ominous as they had then. By now, 180,000 Pakistani troops and 250,000 Indians faced each other along the banks of the Jhelum.

As he walked us back to our jeep, I asked Major Khan how long he'd been here. "Two months," he replied. And then he added that his father, a career Army officer, had served here before him.

Retracing our steps down the mountain road just as the sun was beginning to set, we stopped for tea at one of the six UN field stations on this side of the line. A Scandinavian colonel, after prudently requesting anonymity, told me that at least once a day, for as many years as he could recall, either Pakistan or India had violated the cease-fire, and that the United Nations had neither the authority nor the mandate nor the men to do anything but report it. On at least three occasions over recent years, the United Nations had discreetly suggested that its observers go home. Each time, Pakistan had refused, for its greatest fear was that the Kashmir dispute would evaporate into history before it was resolved.

I asked the colonel how long a posting along a cease-fire line normally lasts.

"One year," he replied. "In principle, peacekeeping missions are temporary things. But the United Nations' temporary mission here has lasted for fifty-two years."

And so the observers, in their distinctive blue berets, continue to monitor and observe, to play cricket and chess—politely tolerated by India, and warmly embraced by Pakistan.

Meanwhile, on the other side of the Line of Control, some forty thousand lives had been lost, and the people of Kashmir were besieged by a bewildering number of armies that did not belong to them.

India, even before its most recent threat of war, maintained a security presence of five hundred thousand in Kashmir: its regular Army was supplemented by auxiliary forces from the Central Reserve Police, the Border Security Force, vigilantes, mercenaries, and an uncountable number of paramilitaries. Over the years, human rights groups had decried New Delhi's repressive policies. Disappearances and extrajudicial killings had become the norm. Armed men were around every corner.

Pakistan, for its part, had sent thousands of well-trained and well-armed Islamic militants across the Line of Control: some were Pakistanis, some Afghans, still others Afghan Arabs who fought and trained in Afghanistan. According to Indian estimates in early 2002, of the 2,400 militants active in the Kashmir valley alone, 1,400 were foreigners. And the militancy grew after Pervez Musharraf's humiliating withdrawal from Kargil. In the Hindu villages of Jammu, the foreign Islamists were targeting anyone whom they suspected of collaborating with India. And even before this occurred, nearly half of the Hindu population of the valley—a quarter of a million people, most of them Brahmans belonging to the Pandit caste—had been terrorized into flight. Vigilantes on both sides were killing other vigilantes with seeming impunity.

Over the years, as I came and went from Kashmir, nearly everyone I met offered a sad story or issued an appeal: Find my son. Let me work my land. Please, let it simply end. For it is the people of Kashmir, more than any others, who every day are torn between Indian repression and Pakistani Islamic militancy. All they ever wanted, according to the old man in the village of Shalimar, was to be independent. Yet now they were being occupied, in their view, by two different foreign armies, whose officers and men neither spoke their language nor understood their concerns.

On June 12, 2002, Secretary of Defense Donald H. Rumsfeld, the most recent in a stream of high-level emissaries shuttling between New Delhi and Islamabad in an effort to avert a conventional—if not a nuclear—war, said that he had "seen indications" that al-Qaeda fighters had by now arrived in Kashmir to join the Pakistani-backed Islamic militants already there. The statement was made in New Delhi and Indian leaders were quietly pleased, since this is what they had been saying for a number of weeks. Twenty-four hours later, however, in Islamabad, the secretary parsed his words following a meeting with Pervez Musharraf, saying publicly that he had no evidence that al-Qaeda combatants were, in fact, now operating there. A State Department official told me that there was "substantiated information," at the time Rumsfeld spoke, that some three hundred or more of bin Laden's fighters were active in Kashmir on both sides of the Line of Control, some on the battlefield, others in the sixty to seventy military training camps that peppered Azad Kashmir. They had arrived from the tribal areas of Pakistan just as the snows began to melt, after they had crossed the frontier, driven out of Afghanistan. Their presence, perhaps as much as anything else, was testament to the fact that Kashmir had become the inseparable subtext of the war in Afghanistan.

This was the message of the five men who, armed with assault rifles, explosives, and grenades, attacked the Indian parliament on December 13, an attack in which they and nine others died. And it was the message of three other men who, on May 14, with cold brutality entered the Indian Army camp in Jammu and methodically went from apartment to apartment killing thirty-four, most of them terrified women and children. And it was the message, on June 14, too, only a day after the American defense secretary left Pakistan, when a huge car bomb exploded outside the heavily guarded American consulate in Karachi, claiming at least another twelve lives—in an attack that was reminiscent of the 1998 bombings of U.S. embassies in Africa. And this was the second car-bomb attack in the lawless city in only a month, the first being the one that killed eleven French engineers working on a Pakistani submarine project.

All of the attacks were clearly aimed at the government of Musharraf, as much as at foreigners, India, or the United States. It was the general, after all, who had severed ties with the Taliban and aligned himself with Washington—to the fury of not only Pakistan's radical Islamists, its well-armed tribal chiefs, and its dizzying array of militant underground groups, but also, and most important, the hawks among the 10,000-man strong, octopodan ISI. The intelligence agency was not one that was easily tamed. Since the days of Zia ul-Haq, its activities had extended to every sphere of Pakistani life. It had assisted in running Musharraf's referendum campaign, as it had assisted in the years before in the ouster of Benazir and the coming to power of Nawaz. It had, of course, spawned the Taliban, as it had orchestrated the Kashmir jihad, emboldened by a legacy of twenty years of involvement with Pakistan's militant Islamists. And this was a prerogative that, even now, many in the ISI were reluctant to forfeit.

The agency's reasoning was simple enough, its former director, General Hamid Gul, explained to me. It needed a skilled and trained irregular force to battle and harass an Indian Army complement of 300,000 men posted in Kashmir—a military presence that was more than half the total strength of the entire Army of Pakistan. Thus the ISI funneled arms and men, and provided training and logistical support not only to Pakistan's dozen or so private Islamist armies but also to its other militant underground groups. What appears to have eluded the intelligence agency was that the "freedom fighters" of Kashmir were part and parcel of the armies that had trained and fought with al-Qaeda and the Taliban. Now they'd returned home to vent their rage against that very government that had sustained them, and also to engage in ever more deadly sectarian battles on Pakistan's streets.

General Musharraf's early fears, in the weeks following the September 11 attacks, of a violent backlash from the children of the jihad, and the generation that followed them, were being realized.

And of even greater concern to the general and his regime, according to one of Musharraf's aides, were growing indications that al-Qaeda had played a role in both of the Karachi car-bomb attacks, in the March grenade explosion in the church in Islamabad, and in the January kidnapping and murder of the *Wall Street Journal* reporter Daniel Pearl.* And there were indications, too, that three of Pakistan's most deadly Islamist groups—the Lashkar-e-Taiba, the Jaish-e-Mohammed, and the Lashkar-e-Jhangvi, a militant Sunni sectarian group—had agreed to pool resources, share expertise, and forge a loose alliance with bin Laden's men in order to launch joint operations against American targets. And they had done so at precisely the time that the U.S. military presence in Pakistan had grown to about a thousand men, a presence that was supplemented by ever-expanding contingents from the CIA and the FBI.

Intelligence officials informed Musharraf that they not only feared more terrorist attacks but expected them.

For on May 27, Musharraf had pledged that all cross-border infiltration into Kashmir would end, thus satisfying one of India's primary demands. The general had been told, more bluntly than ever before, that this was a pre-condition for American aid to Pakistan. Already furious with him for what they perceived to be his betrayal in Afghanistan—and now in Kashmir—the foot soldiers of militant Islam, whom Musharraf and his generals and his ISI had nurtured for so many years, now had every reason to seek to destabilize him.

---

*Two of those accused of being involved in the attack against the U.S. consulate, along with a member of the security forces, were later also accused of attempting to assassinate Musharraf in the spring, by detonating a car bomb in Karachi as his motorcade passed. U.S. officials were initially skeptical about this.

With Musharraf's pledge of a complete halt (at least for the moment—Indian officials say that the militants were told to be quiescent for four to six weeks) in the infiltration of men and arms, Prime Minister Atal Behari Vajpayee responded by ending a five-month-long ban on Pakistani commercial aircraft overflying India. He also agreed to withdraw naval vessels from Pakistan's coast, and he announced that he would be sending a new high commissioner to Islamabad. The threat of war between the two nuclear-armed rivals had receded, at least for now.

Who had won, and who had lost? American diplomacy had played a major part in brokering the beginning of a fragile process in a region of the world where its efforts had previously been confined to short-term crisis management. Deputy Secretary of State Richard L. Armitage and Secretary of Defense Rumsfeld—along with high-level officials from Britain, Russia, the European Union, and China—had worked relentlessly in their efforts to convince Musharraf to clamp down. In the column of gains and losses, this was a victory, if only a tiny one, for Vajpayee and India. New Delhi had finally succeeded, after more than a dozen years, in obtaining a pledge, now backed by the United States, that cross-border infiltration from Pakistan would end. Musharraf and his generals had also won the ultimate prize of a dialogue on Kashmir. After fifty-five years, the world, if it had not done so before, finally recognized that there was a Kashmir dispute—and one that had the potential of provoking a nuclear holocaust.

In a part of the world where face and honor are paramount, both the hawkish Muslim general—who only three years before had angrily derided his prime minister for capitulating to U.S. pressure by withdrawing from Kargil—and the man across his border who had risen to power as an equally hawkish Hindu nationalist, had agreed to a tentative compromise. But it clearly wasn't over, and the road ahead—a road which will include the monitoring of the Line of Control (possibly with U.S. technical surveillance); the stand-down of a million troops; elections in Kashmir in the fall; and, finally, a dialogue between India and Pakistan to address the root causes of the dispute—will be a long and dangerous one.

"My greatest concern is that whenever there's escalation, the other side responds tit for tat. They go on automatic pilot, and they don't have much control over what's happening," I was told in the middle days of June by retired General Anthony C. Zinni, the Bush Administration's peace envoy to the Middle East. The general had also played a major role in 1999 in averting yet another full-scale Indo-Pakistani war. "This is what makes it exceedingly dangerous, and it could all be repeated again in a couple of months. As soon as one side does something outside the box, the other side responds. There's also a lack of a quiet connection between the two; there's neither a hot line nor any other link. Both sides, as a result, are un-prepared on how to read each other. Therefore, the danger is if one side attacks with a conventional missile, for example, the other side is not sure what it means. There's also no understanding by either side of what the other's red lines are, and this is the most dangerous thing. We've played a role three times now [in 1990, 1999, and 2002] when there was a potential for war. But we always stepped in at the eleventh hour to avert a catastrophe. I really think this has got to change. We're the only country in the world that can bridge the two sides, that can open communication lines, and I think we must be-come engaged. India and Pakistan have got to move to a dialogue. They simply cannot keep ratcheting things up with no red lines."

He paused for a moment, and then he said, "India refuses to bring outside parties in, and I fault the Indians for this. And I fault the Pakistanis, too, for their incursions into Kashmir and for aiding these militant groups, many of which, as we all know, have links with al-Qaeda."

I asked General Zinni how concerned he was by the growing ev-idence that al-Qaeda was regrouping in Pakistan.

"I'm extremely concerned," he replied. "Al-Qaeda's desperate, and it will create havoc wherever it can in order to portray any cri-sis—whether it be Kashmir or the Middle East—as an issue of Islam versus the West. And this is one of the reasons why it's so important that we work with Musharraf: not so much because of what Musharraf is or is not, but because what would come after him would be a disaster. He's now engaged in an immensely delicate balancing act. He's trying to clean up the government; he's trying not to antagonize the extremists; and the economic problems he faces continue to be huge. He really wants to cooperate with the United States in the war against terror, but he's worried about his western front with Afghanistan; he's worried about India; he's worried about Central Asia."

In an October 2000 interview with *60 Minutes*, General Zinni had voiced his concern about the possibility that in a few years Pakistan's nuclear weapons could fall into the hands of the country's religious extremists. I asked him now if he still held that view.

"I don't think this is imminent," he said. "I think the government has firm control over them, and that there is enough responsible leadership in the Army to keep them out of the wrong hands. My concern [on the nuclear issue] would be if Musharraf fails for any reason: an economic failure or if the extremists find a cause to enhance their popularity, and a cause that would bring people into the streets."

"Such as?" I asked.

"Kashmir—or Afghanistan, if the government there doesn't hold and there's war and conflict again."

Philip Oldenburg, a South Asian expert at Columbia University, believes that "what India really wants is a statement of recognition of its existence. It's not just an end to cross-border terrorism but an end to Pakistan's game of undermining India's integrity from inside India itself. Now, with America's input, I suspect, this is no longer allowable. That being said, India's victory through coercive diplomacy will be dissipated unless it moves toward ensuring that Pakistan is reinforced as a democratic state. It's not in India's interest to continue to see Pakistan in a downward spiral. In the longest term, if India, seeing this as a victory, turns the tables and pushes into Pakistan to eradicate the terrorist training camps, it will be a defeat. It will also push Pakistan over the edge."

A number of Western diplomats had expressed their concern to me that Musharraf might not be able to survive a war. I asked Oldenburg if, in his view, Musharraf could survive a turbulent peace.

"On balance, yes, I think he can at least in the short term. I don't anticipate another Ayub movement, with troops in the streets," he replied, referring to the massive demonstrations that in 1969 had provoked the removal of another military ruler, General Mohammed Ayub Khan. "I just don't see a united opposition of the People's Party, the Muslim League, and the fundamentalist parties challenging Musharraf that way, unless, that is, the October parliamentary elections are blatantly and fraudulently rigged. As for the Army, I think Musharraf's capable of handling resistance there. He's promised his generals that he will set up a National Security Council, which will formalize the Army's role as a watchdog over political life.

"One of the more unsettling questions that I have is: How much control does Musharraf have over the militant groups? And my guess is that, directly, it's not that much. ISI assists the groups, absolutely, and in the case of Kashmir, it helped to launch a full-scale jihad. But once that was under way, it then got a flavor of inevitability, and I don't think that the ISI has that kind of direct control now. They do, of course, control the groups secondarily—through their control over supplies, sanctuaries, and training camps. By choking these things off, the groups will not be under control, but they will be on a leash. Can Musharraf then rein that leash in? I suspect so, to a certain extent."

But it was the other part of that equation which was of growing concern to officials in Washington. The road ahead for Pakistan and India toward a resolution of the Kashmir dispute was one that could be sabotaged any day, any place, by the armies of Osama bin Laden, Pakistan's militant Islamists, or even rogue elements within the ISI. For the spoilers of Kashmir would like nothing better than a war: a war that would destabilize Pakistan, provoke ever more lethal attacks inside India, and disrupt U.S. military operations against al-Qaeda.

"You are simply misinformed," Musharraf had remarked to me one morning, eighteen months earlier, as we sat in his drawing room at Army House. "There is simply no threat to Pakistan from these so-called fundamentalists. At most they comprise 10 percent of the population, these 'bearded ones,' and then we have another 10 percent of what I call 'liberal modernists.' These are the Pakistanis who are Westernized, overly Westernized in my view, and their ideas are as alien to our culture as those of the fundamentalists are. So you see, there's no cause for alarm. The two extreme poles balance each other out."

"But the liberal modernists don't have private armies," I ventured.

"All this talk of private armies is total nonsense," he said. "These men are freedom fighters, not terrorists!"

When I left the general, I went in search—as it happened the drive was only some ten minutes from his home—of one of the more infamous of the "bearded ones." The building was set just off one of Rawalpindi's broad boulevards, behind an iron gate, which my driver pounded on. A sentry box opened, and a man peered out. After presenting identification, the gate opened and I was led into a courtyard where a dozen or so men lounged about. All of them were bearded and heavily armed. I removed my shoes, as I was instructed to do, and covered my head with a scarf. After my bag and briefcase were searched, twice, I was ushered into a large room and presented to Fazlur Rehman Khalil. He was the founder and then the leader of the Harakat ul-Mujahideen (a group closely aligned with the ISI) until early 2001—when he was replaced by Farooq Kashmiri, the head of the group's operations in Kashmir, after it was decided that the HUM should appear to be more "indigenous." A corpulent man with a long beard, he looks somewhat like Santa Claus. His demeanor and manner were unnervingly calm.

He had been waiting for me in one of the HUM office suites, a ramshackle complex of files and computers and revolutionary tracts, where photographs of Osama bin Laden and the Great Mosque in Mecca shared equal space on the pealing walls. The HUM used to be called the Harakat ul-Ansar, until October 1997, when the State Department placed it on its list of terrorist organizations; it was the only Pakistani group on the list before the September 11 attacks.

"I am a mujahid," Khalil announced, before I could even ask. "And I have been a mujahid for nineteen years. It's an addiction, in a way, even worse than heroin." He pondered his observation, and then he smiled.

"Why did you sign bin Laden's *fatwa* calling for war against the West?" I asked.

"Because Osama bin Laden is the greatest mujahid who ever lived!"

He then went on to say that he'd known bin Laden since the days of the jihad, when they fought together with the forces of the Wahhabi warlord Abdurrab Rasul Sayyaf. Now he and bin Laden shared military training camps just across the border in Khost—where, by the end of 2001, the U.S. military would be operating. "I hate America," he said. "When you launched your cruise missiles in 1998, you hit one of my camps. I lost almost ten men."

"You know the Americans have called you a terrorist," I remarked.

"I feel very bad about this," he said.

He excused himself for midday prayers, and I quickly checked my notes. The HUM, according to the State Department, was active not only in Kashmir but also in Bosnia (and possibly Chechnya), Tajikistan, and India—one of whose commercial aircraft it had hijacked in December, 1999. After slitting the throat of a honeymooning businessman, the hijackers exchanged the flight's remaining passengers for three imprisoned Pakistani militants—including the man who later planned the kidnapping of Daniel Pearl—all of whom were linked to the ISI. It was also suspected by the State Department of having carried out or been linked to a series of kidnappings and murders of Westerners: tourists who had been trekking in Kashmir and on the streets of Karachi alone, two American diplomats in 1995, and, two years after that, four oil company workers, all Americans. According to Pakistani press reports, bin Laden was about to reinforce his security guard with men from the HUM.

When Khalil returned from prayers, I asked him if he supported Pakistan's nuclear weapons program.

He looked somewhat startled. "Of course, God has ordered it."

To my surprise, he called for tea, and then he asked what I thought about the "freedom struggle" in Kashmir.

I responded, as diplomatically as I could, that I did not believe that either side could win Kashmir militarily. I then asked him how long he had been involved in it.

"Forever," he replied.

I told Khalil that General Musharraf had told me that no more than 10 percent of Pakistanis supported the country's religious parties and its militant Islamist groups.

After a good deal of conversation with my interpreter, he instructed one of his aides to fetch an adding machine. "Well, the general is simply wrong," he stated emphatically. "And even if one gives him the benefit of the doubt, we are talking about 15.6 million people." He smiled.

Before leaving, I asked Khalil what would happen if Musharraf closed down groups such as his and abandoned Pakistan's longtime policy of jihad in Kashmir.

He thought for a moment, and then said simply, "He'd be the former leader of Pakistan."

As I was driven back to my hotel, in Islamabad, I puzzled over how the United States and Fazlur Rehman Khalil had fought together, on the same side, during the jihad in Afghanistan.

That evening I attended a dinner party given by a friend. Her bungalow was full of some of Pakistan's most prominent "liberal modernists."

"The religious right affects everything in this country," one writer remarked, "the economy, the law and order situation, the established rule of law, even our foreign policy. Musharraf is not one of them, but he's a hawk on Kashmir, and therefore he is highly dependent upon them. They, in turn, are emboldened by him. They have public meetings, and tens of thousands of people come at a time when political activity is banned. The religious right knows that it is too powerful for even the Army to take it on. Musharraf, perhaps, is allowing himself to be deceived, but he's got this agenda in Kashmir. And he's using the Islamists' fervor for the battle of Kashmir. Remember, he's a commando first and foremost. But now he's let the genie out of the bottle, and I suspect that in the coming years he's going to find that it's impossible to put it back in."

Even in this neighborhood of sprawling verandas and spacious lawns, sectarian violence was visiting as it never had before. There were five mosques within a few square blocks, and all of them preached different interpretations of Islam. A Shiite doctor, who lived just down the street, had been killed in Karachi a few days earlier, and a Sunni professor was assassinated as he prayed in Lahore.

When I returned to my hotel after dinner that night, a plain manila envelope with no return address was waiting for me at the desk. The handwriting on it was uncertain and cramped, and I didn't recognize it.

"Who brought this?" I asked the receptionist.

He shrugged his shoulders. "A man with a beard."

I looked at the package and then, gingerly, opened it.

Inside, emblazoned with orange lettering and a red Kalashnikov, was an Osama bin Laden T-shirt.

Where did the United States go wrong?

For bin Laden—along with many Pakistani Islamists—there were three signposts along the road: the jihad, which politicized him; the Persian Gulf War, which radicalized him; and the Palestinian intifada—combined with his sharp criticism of the repressive policies of the majority of Arab regimes—which gave him a cause that resonated on Arab streets. For the Pakistanis, there was also the battle for Kashmir, of course, a battle from which the United States had assiduously distanced itself, to the collective anger of both Pakistan's generals and its Islamic militants. For even though that battle was a battle that neither New Delhi nor Islamabad could win militarily, it was a battle that neither could lose politically.

A few weeks after the September 11 attacks, I participated in a debate in which an Afghan professor said, "Osama bin Laden has hijacked Afghanistan." And in a sense he had, but Afghanistan had also hijacked him. I am convinced that had there been no jihad, Osama bin Laden would almost certainly be back in Jidda parlaying a fortune of $80 million, which he inherited at thirteen, into an even greater sum than the $250 million he has today. Fazlur Rehman Khalil, I suspect, would probably be a bespectacled professor of theology. And Ayman al-Zawahiri, bin Laden's designated heir, with whom I had gone to school in Cairo twenty years earlier, would almost surely be in the posh suburb of Maadhi where he was born into a prosperous family, as Osama bin Laden was—and where he had been a promising surgeon before the jihad.

As I look back now and recall all of the Pakistani Islamists I've met over the years, they were as diversified as the movement itself. Some came from the madrasahs and were barely literate. Others were professors, generals, doctors, and economists.

How long will their war go on? Will they, too, bequeath it to their sons? For me, one of the most frightening things about the present movement is its anonymity. One of its foot soldiers could be the ordinary-looking, unbearded young man sitting next to you on a plane, in a restaurant or cinema—an unobtrusive man, leading an unobtrusive life, a man like Ahmed whom I had met in Azad Kashmir, and who had told me with a grin that he was a "solider of Allah." Or he could be a man like Mohammed Atta, who on September 11, 2001, crashed the first plane into the World Trade Center's north tower, before he had finished his Ph.D. Or he could be a man like Ahmed Omar Saeed Sheikh, who was sentenced to death in Pakistan in July, having been convicted of being the mastermind of the kidnapping and brutal murder of Daniel Pearl.* Saeed, a Pakistani born in London and a leader of the Jaish-e-Mohammed, had had a long association with the ISI both in Afghanistan and Kashmir. And U.S. investigators—who had sought his extradition to the United States—now believe that he also is the mysterious Mustafa Ahmad, who had wired more than $100,000 to Mohammed Atta in the months preceding the September 11 attacks. Before training in one of bin Laden's camps in Khost, Saeed had been a student at the London School of Economics studying statistics and math.

The members of al-Qaeda and its affiliate groups—whether they be in Pakistan, Egypt, or Saudi Arabia—are very different from the Palestinian suicide bomber who walks into a crowded mall with explosives strapped around his chest—a man, or even a woman now, largely from the refugee camps, who has no present, no future, no past. Conversely, the men—and the women—of al-Qaeda are, to a great extent, middle and upper-middle class; some come from families that are both prominent and prosperous. Most are university graduates, who were upwardly mobile before they set off, twenty years ago, to fight in America's first Afghan war.

And although the theater of operation against them is now, once again, in Afghanistan, the real battleground in the years to come will be Pakistan.

On June 10, three days before the American secretary of defense arrived in Pakistan, Maulana Sami ul-Haq, the militant Islamist and chancellor of the al-Haqqania madrasah, whom I had visited a year or so earlier, presided over a gathering of twenty-three political parties, a gathering that was conspicuous for the large number of maulanas and retired generals who attended it. Armed guards, some wearing black ski masks, mingled in the parking lot of Islamabad's

---

*Three other men were sentenced to life imprisonment. All of their lawyers, along with Saeed's, said they would appeal. A trial of other militants allegedly involved in the murder is also planned.

Holiday Inn, as the dignitaries came and went. The message of the meeting was simple enough: an immediate halt to Pakistan's cooperation with the United States in Afghanistan, and a warning to Musharraf against surrendering the cause of jihad in Kashmir.

A few months earlier, in the spring of 2002, Musharraf had hosted an elegant dinner party at Army House for forty or so guests. They were all CEOs or presidents of Pakistani and foreign banks. It was a gathering of Pakistan's financial elite. The conversation, as the evening progressed, was of predictable things: money matters; foreign investment, which was down dramatically; and the general's upcoming referendum campaign. Just as dessert was about to be served, one of the spouses remarked that the guests from Karachi were increasingly concerned about the security situation there.

Yes, Musharraf conceded, it was a problem and the government would have to work on it. Meanwhile, he told his assembled guests: "This is how I protect myself." And then, with a flourish of his large hand, the former commando reached into his breast pocket and pulled a silver-plated pistol out, and brandished it in the air. There was pin-drop silence in the room. None of the guests could recall anything like this ever happening in Pakistan before.

ACKNOWLEDGMENTS

THIS BOOK is the result of a journey of more than ten years, and in the process I became indebted to many friends. Some are named in these pages, and I thank them now. Any errors in fact or judgment are mine, not theirs. Equally important are the many Pakistanis whose voices, although not their identities, are part of this book. Their reluctance to be quoted is both prudent and understandable.

Some of the material in these pages first appeared in different form in *The New Yorker*. To my editors there, Pat Crow, Ann Goldstein, John Bennet, and Josselyn Simpson: I salute you all. I also owe a special debt to my intrepid fact-checking team at the magazine—Nandi Rodrigo, Anne Stringfield, and Gita Daneshjoo—who not only saved me from acute embarrassment but were also always there for me.

This book would not have been possible without the unflagging support of my editor at Farrar, Straus and Giroux, John A. Glusman, who from the beginning believed in it, and who was always patient to the end. I also owe special thanks to his assistant, Aodaoin

O'Floinn, who kept us sane through the pressure of deadlines; and to my agent, Heather Schroder of International Creative Management, for following things through. I am equally indebted to the Alicia Patterson Foundation, which provided me with a generous fellowship for writing and research.

And finally to my family, especially my mother, Barbara, my husband, Dean, and the memory of my late father, Clay: thank you, for your love and support.

Mary Anne Weaver
New York City
July 31, 2002

INDEX

A Note About the Author

Mary Anne Weaver, a writer and foreign correspondent for *The New Yorker*, is the author of *A Portrait of Egypt: A Journey Through the World of Militant Islam*. She was an Alicia Patterson Fellow for 2001. A specialist in South Asian and Middle Eastern affairs, she is a veteran foreign correspondent who has reported from some thirty countries over the last twenty years, based in New Delhi, Cairo, Athens, and Bangkok.

Married to the screenwriter and author Dean Brelis, she now divides her time between New York City and Santa Monica.